Sailing
True
North

Sailing
True
North

TEN ADMIRALS
and the
VOYAGE OF CHARACTER

———

Admiral James Stavridis,
USN (Ret.)

PENGUIN PRESS
New York
2019

PENGUIN PRESS

An imprint of Penguin Random House LLC
penguinrandomhouse.com

Photo credits
Page xxii: Ernst Wallis et al., *Illustrerad Verldshistoria* vol. I
(Stockholm: Central-Tryckeriet: 1875), plate 116 (Wikimedia)
26: Statue of Zheng He at Quanzhou Overseas Relations Museum,
photo by jonjanego (Flickr)
52: Portrait of Sir Francis Drake (circa 1540–96) (Bonhams)
74: Lemuel Francis Abbott, portrait of Rear Admiral Sir Horatio Nelson,
1799 (Wikimedia)
94, 118, 144, 168, 192, 224: United States Navy, the Naval History and
Heritage Command
256: United States Navy
262: Department of Defense photo by Claudette Roulo

LIBRARY OF CONGRESS CATALOGING-IN-PUBLICATION DATA
Names: Stavridis, James, author.
Title: Sailing true north : ten admirals and the voyage of character /
Admiral James Stavridis, USN (Ret.).
Description: New York : Penguin Press, [2019] | Includes bibliographical
references and index.
Identifiers: LCCN 2018053498 (print) | LCCN 2018056311 (ebook) |
ISBN 9780525559948 (ebook) | ISBN 9780525559931 (hardcover)
Subjects: LCSH: Admirals--Biography.
Classification: LCC V61 (ebook) | LCC V61 .S73 2019 (print) | DDC
359.0092/2--dc23
LC record available at https://lccn.loc.gov/2018053498

Printed in Canada
1 3 5 7 9 10 8 6 4 2

Set in Berling LT Std
Designed by Cassandra Garruzzo

To US Marine Corps
Shirley and Colonel George Stavridis,
my mother and father,
who shaped my character long before
I ever put to sea

———

Contents

Preface

When I wrote a book called *Sea Power: The History and Geopolitics of the World's Oceans*, I hoped to bring a mariner's eye to the vast world of the sea. While looking at each of the major global bodies of water, I tried to combine three things: the fascinating history of the various maritime regions; the current geopolitical challenges linked to them, both locally and globally; and my own four decades of seagoing experience. All of this was intended to make a coherent case for the importance of the oceans. It was a book about a long, complicated, and ultimately rewarding voyage around the oceans of the world. When people asked me how long it took to write *Sea Power*, I would truthfully say "about forty years." It was the culmination of my professional life, much of which was spent at sea.

In *Sailing True North: Ten Admirals and the Voyage of Character*, I have turned the lens of the work away from the physical universe of the oceans and into the realm of the biographical, personal, behavioral, and psychological characteristics of ten admirals whose careers stretch across 2,500 years of history. By using the "sea stories" of this colorful group of historical maritime leaders as a kind of canvas, I hope to illuminate for the reader the most essential qualities of character, demonstrate how they contribute to effective leadership, and make the case that by using this information, each of us can chart a course toward becoming the best we can possibly be within our own lives. In the end, a physical voyage at sea is a demanding undertaking, requiring intensity, energy, forehandedness, and intelligence, among many other qualities; but it is vastly easier than the inner voyage we all must sail every day of our lives. That voyage of character is the most important journey each of us ever makes.

I am also motivated by a growing sense in this postmodern era that we are witnessing the slow death of character, driven by a global popular culture that has turned increasingly away from classic values—honesty, commitment, resilience, accountability, moderation—to a world that moves at breakneck speed and refuses to slow down and consider what is right and just. Attention spans have spiraled resolutely downward. Take reading as an example: we were once ready to willingly read a multivolume work; many (including, according to many reports, our president) now balk at reading a single long book. Some readers avoid long journal pieces and demand briefer and briefer articles in slimmer and slimmer magazines. There is online impatience with long blog posts and we seem to have finally arrived at our current state: a Twitter world where many observers recently opined that they regretted the lengthening of a tweet from 140 characters to 280 because "reading the long tweets is taking up too much time." One abiding characteristic of most of the ten admirals in this book is that they were thoughtful, intellectually grounded individuals. Perhaps the long periods at sea that almost all of them experienced have something to do with that. Naturally, they manifested a wide variety of differing traits, and some were better and more admirable than others. I've selected them to help show the richness of the human character across both time and personality types. And above all, we learn from these admirals that the quality of finding sufficient time to think and reflect is a crucial part of building character. In our frenzied world today, we should learn from their collective example.

Alongside the cultural demands for short, ironic, value-neutral "thinking" comes the utter transparency of our times. As I will say again in this work, character is what you do when you think no one is looking—and in today's world, someone is *always* looking. We have lost the ability to hone our character in private, and our lives are on display seemingly from the moment we are born. Our intense self-obsession is reflected in the desire to constantly burnish our images on the endless social networks, something none of these admirals remotely encountered, and we are poorer for this characteristic. We overshare publicly and under-reflect privately on what our individual voyages mean. Do they add up to a journey that matters? Is the destination important? In the small hours of the morning, as we think about our lives, can we honestly say our voyage matters? Or do we drift endlessly on an uncaring sea? The answer to these questions is bound up inextricably in the heart of our character.

Finally, we are much diminished in our ability to learn and tell stories in order to advance our intellectual pursuits. In so many ways, the story of our lives is little more than a collection of the stories we have heard, inculcated, and then created and told about ourselves. Most of us want to be part of a society that is dependable, predictable, and stable—but this turbulent twenty-first century, both at home and abroad in an interconnected world—resembles that less and less. The stories we hear seem chaotic, disconnected, and thematically barren: school shootings of children by other children; wars without end in the Middle East; biological "advances" that presage a godlike power uncoupled from a humanistic, ethical perspective; leaders who routinely lie, cheat, and steal; followers who act out in spasms of anger, fulfilling Tocqueville's dire nineteenth-century prediction that the tragedy of democracy will be that in the end we elect the government we deserve. Self-talk matters deeply, and we must learn to tell ourselves, our peers, and above all our children the stories that inspire a better world.

In that regard, as I set out on this book, I wanted to tell a different set of stories from those that we see repeated again and again on cable news. I believe there is much to learn about character and what exists at the heart of every woman and man from hearing the stories of those who sailed before us. Because I am a sailor myself, I turned to ten illustrious, interesting, and highly varied naval leaders. Each of them led across decades and in different centuries and locales; their stories are different, and their characters were shaped in dramatically varied circumstances. Therefore, the lessons to be drawn—both about their leadership styles but more important about their character—are richly distributed. And not all are entirely heroic. But I offer their stories, which I believe, if taken in the aggregate, provide a more reassuring narrative than that unspooling before us on 24/7 news channels.

Let's begin with the difference between two terms that are often confused: leadership and character.

Leadership is broadly understood to be the ability to influence others, generally in order to accomplish a specific purpose. It is a tool, not a quality, and thus can be applied for both good and ill. We think of Franklin Delano Roosevelt as a good leader, and he was—Roosevelt had the ability to influence people to undertake huge, difficult tasks, from overcoming the Great Depression to winning the Second World War. But evil men can be very good leaders as well, using the tools of leadership to accomplish amoral and cruel purposes. Pol Pot, who conducted a horrific genocide in Cambodia as the leader of the Khmer Rouge in the late twentieth century, was a highly capable leader as well, in that he was able to marshal an enormous national effort to drive home a Communist ideology and ruthlessly massacre all dissidents and many innocents—killing perhaps three million people out of a population of eight million. Shocking? Horrific? Criminal? Absolutely. But Pol Pot's story is also a demonstration of strong leadership, albeit in the service of extreme evil. Leadership is all about the external effect and the ability to influence others.

Character, on the other hand, is about internal effect and the ability to influence oneself. John Wooden, the famous UCLA basketball coach and a fine leader, summed it up well: "Be more concerned with your character than your reputation, because your character is what you really are, while your reputation is merely what others think you are." It was from Coach Wooden that I first heard the idea that the true test of our character is what we do when no one is watching. Character is at its heart the ability to lead the inner self toward what is just and right. It proceeds from overcoming the strong amoral impulses—what Freud described as the id—and sailing toward the metaphorical light of moral choice. Character, unlike leadership, has both moral and ethical weight and can be more correctly described as either good or bad.

Sailors often have a unique opportunity to chart a course toward a good character. The sea is an unforgiving environment which daily poses hard challenges that depend on deep reserves of character to overcome. Sailing is hard and dangerous work, and the sea itself poses a constant threat, to say nothing of additional man-made dangers, from pirates to enemy aircraft to lurking submarines. It is also a contemplative world, where any sailor can walk out on a rolling deck at night and stare at the distant point where the sky meets the sea and recognize that we are merely the smallest part of a huge and diverse universe that stretches forever unto the mind of God, and which will last far beyond the age of human beings. This combination of attributes—the constant physical and moral challenge in daily life and the endless vision of eternity dangling before our eyes—creates a deepening of character in the best of sailors. And my thesis is that by learning about the lives of these ten admirals, each of us—sailor or not—can improve and deepen our own characters.

While clearly two different attributes, leadership and character often merge in a given individual, and certainly in the case of a number of senior maritime leaders like the admirals in this book. While it's not always the case, a man or woman of strong and positive character is often a highly effective leader. This is because most other people recognize and are attracted to a high level of moral strength. In many seagoing leaders in particular—where the oceans create such a distinctive backdrop—character becomes a vital part of the leadership skills they can deploy. It is therefore highly instructive to examine a handful of admirals, understand their individual "sea stories," and plumb the depths of their character—all with the idea of helping each of us navigate more effectively across the inner sea we all must sail.

In this volume we will begin our voyage more than 2,500 years ago with the admiral Themistocles, an ancient Greek facing an existential threat to his city-state, Athens; and conclude our long sail across history in the late twentieth century with a woman admiral, Grace Hopper, who helps bring the Navy into the cyber age. We will then look at resilience and briefly meet two living and recently retired admirals, Michelle Howard and Bill McRaven. All are different sailors, but the inner voyage of character that each sailed offers lessons we can study and apply. As with all ten of these admirals, the basic rocks and shoals of their voyages are roughly similar: the need for truth, justice, empathy, creativity, humility, humor, resilience, and balance, contrasted with avoiding arrogance, anger, pettiness, cruelty, desire, betrayal, jealousy, and hatred. We will see that none of these admirals was perfect—indeed, far from it in several cases. But we can sometimes learn as much from failures of character as we can from triumphs, and the nature of any human is not what they do when the choices are easy, and the metaphorical sun is shining, but rather what they do when the options are morally ambiguous, and the seas are rough. The test of character is taking the "hard right" over the "easy wrong," and some of these admirals fail that simple test on more than one occasion. We can learn from that failure as surely as we can from the much more common moral and ethical decisions most of these admirals make.

On a personal note, the concluding chapter of the book will draw from my own inner voyage over the years of my life, so much of it spent at sea. As an exercise, I went through my old logbooks recently and totaled up all the days I spent on the deep ocean, out of sight of land. The total is more than nine and a half years, day-for-day. Plenty of time spent out there in busy pursuits from gunnery to missile shoots, to simply standing the long watches steaming across the trackless oceans. But there was also a lot of time to read, reflect, and record internally my thoughts on what makes a life of character worth living. Leadership was an omnipresent demand for a young officer growing up in an ancient profession, rising from a very green ensign to, quite improbably, becoming a four-star admiral. Every day was an exercise in leading others. But the challenges I wrestled with most frequently were inside, as I sought to set my own compass to true north, seeking to live up to the standards I set for myself. I failed not infrequently. But voyage of character is long indeed, and in my case, still underway—although not often at sea these days, something I miss more than I like to admit.

Like the other admirals profiled in this work, I have on occasion succeeded and, on many occasions, failed. In the end, the measure of our lives is weighed on the scales of the choices we have made, and the ability to see oneself clearly is crucial on the voyage to character. In a sense, we each have three lives: a *public* one, defined clearly by the open statements we make from conversations at work to our posts on social media; a *private* one, the face that we share only with our very closest family and a few chosen friends; and a deeply *personal* one, known only to ourselves, where we struggle—often desperately—to make the right choices.

One should never forget that the scale by which you will measure your life is one you make yourself, forging it a bit at a time throughout the years of your life. Here in that truly personal zone, measured on the scale we construct ourselves, are the sea buoys of the channel that we should follow if our voyage is to end at the port of inner satisfaction. And as with any voyage at sea, there are dangers ahead—both obstacles imposed by the world and those we create ourselves. And we cannot simply avoid the hard choices by not embarking on the voyage. Oliver Wendell Holmes correctly said that "to reach a port we must sail, sometimes with the wind, and sometimes against it. But we must not drift or lie at anchor." My hope is that this slim book, with its small flotilla of sea stories, can provide some navigational advice, a few well-marked buoys, and even a sturdy lighthouse or two for all who are sailing on the sea of character. Let's get underway.

Sailing
True
North

CHAPTER I

The Power of Persuasion

Themistocles

———

BORN C. 524 B.C., ATHENS, GREECE

DIED C. 459 B.C., MAGNESIA, MODERN TURKEY

I first heard of Themistocles when I was an eight-year-old boy. My family had just moved to Athens, Greece, because my father, a major in the US Marine Corps at the time, had received orders to be the assistant naval attaché at the local US embassy. He had been chosen for this assignment for a simple reason: he was Greek American, and his first language was Greek. Although he was born in the United States, his was an all-Greek-speaking home and, until he went to elementary school as a five-year-old, he'd spoken only Greek. After combat tours in Korea and a stint earning a master's degree at Purdue, he was now, in the mid-1960s, being sent to the land of his forefathers. My mother, not of Greek stock, began taking lessons in the language. I just wanted to be sure my bicycle was in the shipment.

As part of preparing to move to Athens, my father began to talk to me about Greece. He began with mythology, fascinating me with stories of the gods of Olympus. Zeus, Poseidon, Athena,

Hephaestus, Ares, and many others started to populate my dreams. After we covered the gods, he shifted to Homer, and I learned the stories of the Trojan War, and about the wily Odysseus and his long voyage home to Ithaca. Even as a small child, I knew these were fables and stories, representing only some part of the truth. But after Homer, we began to talk about the *real* history of ancient Greece.

My father told me about the half-century nightmare of the Persian invasions of Greece between 499 and 449 B.C. A terrific natural storyteller, he laid out the saga of those years in bold, vivid strokes. I still cherish the recollection of his description of the Battle of Marathon in 490 B.C. and (of course) the heroic stand of the three hundred Spartans at the Battle of Thermopylae in 480 B.C. I loved the story of the monument there, which has carved upon it the words, "Go tell the Spartans / stranger passing by / that here, faithful to their laws / we lie." During those years in Greece, my father brought all those tales to life by taking the family to visit the sites of each of those famous battles.

Much as I enjoyed learning about the Spartans, my favorite of my father's stories—then and since—was that of Themistocles, the Athenian admiral who won the pivotal Battle of Salamis, also in 480 B.C. Numbers are always hazy in ancient historical battles, of course, but by most estimates the Greeks were outnumbered roughly five to one in the amount of heavy trireme warships with their triple banks of oars. After luring the Persians into the constrained waters of the Straits of Salamis off the coast of Athens, Themistocles led the free Greeks under his command to a smashing victory over the enslaved oarsmen of the Persian foe.

I asked my father again and again to tell me the story of Themistocles. At the time, I didn't appreciate the complexity of the ancient admiral's life and character—he simply loomed large as the winner of the most important naval battle fought by the ancient Greeks. And, though I often reenacted the battle with a set of toy ships on a hand-drawn map of the Bay of Salamis, the part of the story that most captivated my imagination was Themistocles's ability to inspire his men. I wondered what it was about him that allowed him so successfully to lead men into battle. My father tried to explain to me the complex mixture of charisma, inspiration, and rhetoric that Themistocles employed; although all of those words were well beyond my vocabulary at the time, I have since turned to them on many occasions.

In one such instance, I was searching for the right words for a huge dinner event as part of a patriotic celebration in New York City in November 2007. The title of the event was "A Salute to Freedom," and after quite a bit of thought, I ended up talking about our heroic US Navy SEALs by telling the story of Themistocles and his oration that had so deeply inspired the Greeks some 2,500 years before. And in the years since then, I have spoken many times about that battle and the character of Themistocles.

My father, who eventually retired as a full colonel of Marines and went on to lead a huge community college after earning a PhD in education, had passed away by the time of that 2007 speech; but I know he would have been very proud to hear his son, by now improbably a four-star admiral, retelling the story of Themistocles to a big New York audience. Almost half a century after he told me the timeless stories of an ancient Greek admiral, I was able to keep that inspirational character alive, down the long centuries, by echoing his words that we must all "row for freedom." That is a powerful lesson, and one I've carried with me, drawing upon Themistocles over and over.

What do we know of this ancient admiral, and what can we learn from his voyage of character? Various ancient sources paint a vivid but inconsistent image of the historical Themistocles. Rather than a crisp factual narrative, we have a mosaic of sharp, short vignettes of his life from two of the earliest Greek historians: Herodotus and Thucydides. Although they are described as the first modern historians, the work of neither would hold up to modern standards; moreover, their separate approaches and biases led them to draw quite different conclusions about Themistocles. Herodotus, writing about the Persian Wars which distinguished Themistocles's career, saw the admiral as a greedy swindler; Thucydides, writing about the origins of the Peloponnesian War decades later, portrayed Themistocles as a tragic hero who saved Greece only to be exiled by his own city. Both, however, are clear that Themistocles was a remarkably influential and self-assured voice in military and political life.

Themistocles was born in Athens about 524 B.C. In 508, just as he was entering into maturity, the city began its experiment in democracy by giving all free men the right to vote—a radical move for the time, but we should be careful to note that the privilege extended to only a very few of the city's inhabitants. Nevertheless, it allowed the solidly middle-class young Themistocles to enter Athenian political life on rough par with any other citizen. He grew up in a time of heady change, full of opportunity and challenge, and quickly established himself as a voice in his thriving city-state. From the earliest days of his life, he would have been part of a society that was both prideful of its position at the top of the Greek hierarchy of city-states but also a society under stress and challenge from lesser nations in the Hellenic world, as well as the "looming tower" of his day—the massive Persian Empire to the east.

We do not know much personal detail about Themistocles's life before he was elected archon, the chief administrative role in Athens, at the age of thirty-one. In that role, Themistocles distinguished himself early by his speaking ability, upon which Athenian democracy placed a high priority. Once in office, Themistocles quickly and forcefully began speaking out in favor of building Athens into a seagoing power. Crucially, as archon, he commissioned a defended port to be built at Piraeus (the nearest significant harbor to Athens, just a few kilometers distant), which transformed Athens into a sea power almost overnight and continues to serve the city to this day. His was a strategic vision coupled with a practical ability to move supporters, win public arguments, and demonstrate the long-term value in leveraging the seagoing access Athens enjoyed. I have often journeyed to the port of Piraeus from downtown Athens, and in the modern world the two ancient cities are part of a single seamless, contiguous entity. I made the trip in the 1960s as a young boy living in a suburb of Athens, headed to catch a ferry to the islands with my parents; then later in the 1980s as a junior Navy officer coming from my ship to the liberty spots of the Plaka (the strip of bars and restaurants surrounding the Parthenon); as a NATO commander—whisked along with police escorts and in hardened black cars; and most recently as a member of the board of the Onassis Foundation (and shipping company) to visit one of our ships in the harbor. On every occasion, I thought about the vision of Themistocles, who sensed early on the power that a true, defendable harbor would afford the ancient city-state. His ability to "see around the corner" and build that harbor helped save Greece's democracy a decade after his service as archon.

As would the American admiral Alfred Thayer Mahan centuries later, Themistocles understood the geopolitical context better than most, saw sea power and seaborne commerce as the natural destiny of his people, and devoted his early prime years of life to helping make that vision reality. Themistocles knew that the combination of Athens's coastal location and expanding mercantile interests, plus the ever-growing threat of the expanding Persian Empire to the east, made it essential for Athens to develop a navy as a connector and protector between it and the outside world. He also understood the value of building coalitions despite the challenges of uniting the famously fractious Greek cities into rudimentary alliance systems. And he demonstrated not only vision, but also the kind of internal strength of character that allows a leader to carry a position that is not intuitively clear or wildly popular.

When the Persians predictably attacked the politically fractured Greek mainland in 490 B.C., Themistocles was among those Greeks who helped repulse the hated enemy at the Battle of Marathon. After that desperate fight, Themistocles not only never forgot the experience of combat, but he—unlike many of his fellow Athenians—also never let down his guard in anticipation of another Persian attack. Keen observer that he was, Themistocles predicted not only that the Persians would return, but that they would bring a much more powerful navy with them when they did. To survive such an attack, the Athenians would need a navy of their own—but first they had to be convinced of the need to build one. Themistocles consistently made the argument throughout the Athenian polity that building the port was necessary but insufficient to the needs of his nation. Both his vision and his character came into play in making the case for creating real security—these were expensive propositions and there were harsh criticisms of his advocacy for sea power.

Themistocles set about the task of convincing his countrymen of the need for sea power by using his famous oratorical skills, not merely in the abstract but also by trumpeting a time-honored maritime threat: piracy. As the newly appointed commander of the nascent navy he championed, he began talking up the threat posed by pirates on the nearby island of Aegina to give the Athenians a concrete reason to build a fleet without directly referencing the Persians. Luckily for him, as this argument began gaining traction, the obvious money problem was solved by a windfall from a nearby silver mine; with one last oratorical effort, Themistocles persuaded his fellow citizens to put the additional revenue into building the fleet he so fervently sought, ostensibly for antipiracy protection. In this he demonstrated the ability to exercise pragmatic judgment to accomplish a larger purpose—so often we see leaders who lock themselves into a rhetorical position and cannot summon the flexibility to shift arguments when necessary to achieve success. Character requires both conviction *and* flexibility.

Themistocles got his fleet, and none too soon. He also saw his fears fulfilled as the Persians returned, led by the young, capable, and determined emperor Xerxes I. Xerxes assembled an army of conquest from the far corners of the Persian Empire and descended on Greece from the north—and, as Themistocles had predicted, the Persians did not neglect to bring a powerful navy this time around. The Second Persian War had begun, and the fighting quickly became desperate on both land and sea. This became a time of existential danger for Greece. It is hard to imagine how the world would have shifted from what we know today had the Persians won. Would they have continued west, choking off a nascent Roman Empire? Conquered Europe entirely? Would the superpower of today be Iran, the inheritor of that empire two millennia later? Would democracy—the greatest of Greek contributions to civilization—have emerged when it did? These are, of course, unanswerable questions. But without question, the world we know today would be more than a few degrees of separation different. We are so used to the story of history we know that we tend to think of it as an immutable force. But big doors swing on small hinges, and the fact that Themistocles built a port and a fleet, and was able to stop a Persian fleet, was a seemingly small hinge upon which a big door eventually swung to the west, not east.

Despite Athenian capabilities, Greece overall was initially unprepared for the onslaught. Political divisions and operational bickering between the allied city-states hampered a coherent response. The Greeks eventually settled on a two-pronged strategy. To counter the land invasion, the allies would hold at the strategic choke point of Thermopylae on the eastern coast of mainland Greece, where King Leonidas and his three hundred Spartans (plus a handful of other Greek warriors) would make their legendary last stand to buy time for the rest of the Greeks to assemble. Meanwhile, the Athenian navy led a blocking effort at Artemisium (a seaport on the island of Euboea, north of Athens and near Thermopylae), where they, like the Spartans ashore, delayed the Persians but could not turn them back. Greek land and naval forces fell back to the immediate vicinity of Athens, setting up the conclusive battle against Xerxes's invaders. Themistocles, who was a strong voice in any situation, continued to advocate the idea of striking a maritime blow at the invading forces. He correctly saw that they would be overconfident in their vastly larger numbers, and also were logistically dependent on supplies and reinforcement from the sea.

Rather than sacrifice the inhabitants of the city under siege, Themistocles thought it better to sacrifice the city itself, and persuaded the Athenians to evacuate. Imagine the difficulty of carrying *that* argument—give up everything you know, surrender your possessions and land, and flee into the scrubby woods around the city. Themistocles argued that Athens could be rebuilt and repopulated as long as her people survived and the Persians were defeated at sea. Abandoning their city to the Persian onslaught, civilians took to the hills while Themistocles and his crews took to their ships and sailed across the Straits of Salamis to take refuge on the island opposite the port of Piraeus. Civilians and sailors alike watched from their sheltering places in the countryside as the Persian army burned Athens and the Persian fleet gathered in its multitudes at the mouth of the straits.

This moment must have been one that demanded extraordinary character from the young admiral. Imagine him walking among his sailors as they watched all that they knew go up in smoke and were equally unsure about the survival of their wives, children, and aged parents. Themistocles would have spoken in confident, strong tones about the chance to strike a blow for Greece on the morrow, going slowly from campfire to campfire, conducting leadership at the retail level—all the while knowing in his own heart that the odds were stacked against the heavily outnumbered Greek fleet. Character.

And it was all so transparent to the sailors—each of them could easily see the Athenian navy was badly outnumbered, and some of the subordinate Greek commanders wanted to withdraw still farther, perhaps to the southern Peloponnese, to preserve the men for the defense of the Greeks' final refuges on the peninsula. Themistocles, however, wanted to fight in the straits, where the Persians' numerical advantage would be naturally constrained. They might have a larger reserve, but they would be unable to surround and destroy the Greeks as they easily could have in open water.

In his typically self-assured fashion, Themistocles not only set about making his case to his fellow Greeks, but also devised a scheme to lure the Persians into battle. He secretly sent a messenger to the Persian fleet to falsely tell them of a plan to retreat and urge them to attack now to take advantage of dissension in the Greek ranks. At the same time, Themistocles sent another secret mission to persuade the ethnic Greeks serving in the Persian fleet to turn on their masters in the coming battle. Acting quickly on their newly gained but false intelligence, the Persian fleet moved to cut off the Greeks' escape, and the die was cast. The battle would be joined in the Straits of Salamis, just as Themistocles hoped.

On the morning of the battle, the light of dawn broke over the mountains to the east of the island of Salamis, revealing the smoking ruin of the city of Athens nestled below the peaks. The light quickly crossed the narrow stretch of water between the city and the island, and a fleet of Greek triremes, powerful warships with three tiers of rowers and heavy battering rams at the prow, lay nearby, swinging gently at anchor in the morning breeze. As their Athenian crews set about cooking their morning meal, their commander, already armed for battle, stepped forth from his tent. At a glance, Themistocles would have taken in the sight of the breaking dawn, the ships at their anchorage, and the somewhat uncertain faces of the crews—many of whom were no doubt looking to the sea and the straits in which the fate of all would be decided. There must have been a mixed feeling of both anticipation and fear in the morning breezes. The morning's windless calm was a stroke of luck—stronger winds would have favored the Persian warships, which depended more on sail.

Sailing against the Persian fleet would require every bit of tactical brilliance and personal charisma Themistocles could muster—plus the unified effort of every man and every oar in the fleet. The Persian fleet was five times larger than the Athenian one and crewed by some of the best mariners in the world (including some Greek traitors). As his men finished their meals, extinguished their fires, and began moving toward their ships, Themistocles knew that they were deeply aware of the odds against them—and the consequences of failure. He also knew that he had one last chance—and only one—to inspire them to achieve a seemingly impossible victory. All that he learned and practiced as an inspirational leader had built up to this moment. Was he nervous? Or confident? We can never know with certainty, but all that we can understand about his character and temperament would suggest that his swagger was natural and unforced. It was simply part of the long sweep of his personality and experience, and would have made him feel he was in the right place at the right time for his nation—and for his glory.

Themistocles would have taken a few long strides down to the water to face his crews, who would have turned to look at him in expectation. My bet is that he would have inhaled deeply, released a tense lungful of air, then taken an even bigger breath and started to speak in a loud voice that echoed over the quiet beach and the still morning water beyond. What did he say? In my mind, I could hear him saying something like this:

"Men of Athens! Look back over your right shoulders. See it there—Athens, our home, where our families depend on us to deliver them from the Persian threat.

"Now look over your left shoulders: see the straits there, and in them the Persian fleet waiting to ravage our city and enslave our people, as they themselves are enslaved.

"Now look at each other: fellow Greeks, brother freemen, the last obstacle between the Persians and their goal. Some of you are new to war and indeed new to manhood. Many of you have fought in other battles of this long war. And all of you—*all* of you—know that if we fail today, our city will fall, our families will perish, and any who live will lose their freedom. I ask you: should we fail, would not any who survived immediately face a fate worse than death? Picture your mother and your wife and your daughters, hauled away as playthings of the Persians; your male children slaughtered in their thousands; your aged parents put to the sword.

"Men of Athens! *Free* men of Athens! When you take up your oars today, you take in your hands the destiny of our city, of our families, of our way of life. If today we fail, with us will die the hopes of all, and the hope of freedom for any. We must not fail—we *shall* not fail.

"To your boats, men—and to your oars.

"For today of all the days we will row with all our hearts.

"We will row for our home, for Athens . . .

"We will row for our children and our wives and our parents . . .

"We will row this day for our city . . .

"Today, this day, we must row as we have never rowed before!

"For today, men of Athens—we will *row for freedom!*"

After persuading his men to "row for freedom," Themistocles put to sea. As he had hoped, the narrows negated the Persians' five-to-one numerical advantage in ships, and his motivated oarsmen dealt the enemy—rowed by enslaved men—a crushing blow, sinking nearly ten times as many ships as they lost themselves. At a stroke, the Persian army that had so recently burned Athens found that it was cut off from resupply and forced to retreat hastily toward Persia. With the main body of the enemy off the Peloponnese and the rearguard defeated at Plataea not long after Themistocles's victory at Salamis, the Persian threat once again passed from Greece.

It was an extraordinary victory, and one that is still studied at the Naval Academy today. It reflects not only the tactical brilliance of Themistocles, but also his character—the ability to reach deep inside himself, at a moment when everyone around him was frightened and trembling, and rally people to his cause. His combination of vision, energy, and charisma have seldom been equaled in naval history. He won a stunning victory, and the Persians retreated, allowing the Athenians—as he had predicted—to return to their destroyed homes and begin again.

The citizens of Athens did indeed set about rebuilding their city and their democracy, but the man who had secured their preservation was not destined to enjoy the fruits of his victory. With the crisis passed, gratitude for Themistocles's military genius was quickly eclipsed by the memory of his harsh, argumentative, take-no-prisoners political style. Without fear of foreign foes, old political enemies at home were emboldened to seek their revenge against Themistocles for his arrogant style. Much as Winston Churchill was effectively tossed out by the British public near the end of the Second World War, Themistocles was destined for a dramatic reversal of his fortunes—and it descended on him almost immediately.

Before long, Themistocles found himself increasingly constrained politically as his popularity diminished. He was ultimately brought down by a handful of political opponents who accused him of trying to parlay his victory into tyranny. Exiled from Athens to the neutral city of Argos, he was implicated there in an attempted slave uprising and coup d'état in Sparta. In one of the supreme ironies of history, Themistocles was forced to flee across the Aegean to the lands of his old enemy, Persia. There he swore fealty to the new emperor, Artaxerxes. Legend has it that he learned the Persian language in a year in order to communicate with his new master. His natural charisma—and probably the ironic novelty of a Greek admiral switching sides—assured him a place in the court, where he no doubt functioned as a kind of prize put on display by the emperor. Themistocles found secure refuge among his former foes and was soon named the satrap of a province in modern Turkey, where he lived out the rest of his days.

His final resting place is unknown; legends in Greece speak of his crossing the deep azure waters of the Aegean once again in death, as his remains were perhaps illegally smuggled back to Greece and secretly buried in the land he helped save. At least that is the way my father told the story.

Themistocles's life invites a question that will haunt this book and the lives of most of these admirals: is vision a consequence of character? I would argue that vision is in fact one of the most distinctive elements of human character, and that it is so often what separates the ordinary life from the extraordinary. It is always easier to live life as a simple flowing series of events and merely react to them. Or, at the most, to look just a step or two ahead in life, settling often for the mundane outcome, boxed out from taking the bold step by a lack of vision. Oscar Wilde said, "We are all in the gutter, but some of us are looking at the stars." Indeed, one of the most valuable skills a leader of character can possess, especially in competitive fields like business, politics, or the military, is to be able to chart a course toward a fairly distant desired outcome, and in the process effectively shape what happens next. As Themistocles demonstrates, this does not require some innate or occult vision as much as two deceptively easy habits of thought that any leader can develop with some effort.

The first of these is a general refusal to be swept up in the mood of the moment. Themistocles was neither transported by the wave of euphoria that broke over Greece after its victory in the First Persian War, nor given to despair during the darkest moments of the Second Persian War. In victory, he counseled readiness and correctly planned for another battle; outnumbered in the next battle, he devised a forward-looking strategy and produced yet another victory. Both outcomes essentially flowed from his calmness of vision. All leaders can practice this style of analysis that seeks to avoid overreaction or emotional response.

The second quality we see in Themistocles was his great predictive skill, which flowed from the ability to weigh the odds and realistically forecast the possible outcomes in any given circumstance. After the First Persian War, he knew that Persia defeated might yet return in still-greater force, but that it could be successfully challenged in the right circumstances. Again, this is a learnable skill that requires a leader to consciously think about future outcomes. Doing so in analytic ways—thinking in terms of percentage outcomes for example—is a very helpful habit to cultivate.

With time and experience, leaders can learn to overcome their emotions, see their situation clearly, and calculate the odds of various possible outcomes. No leader can see the future in a literal sense, but these habits of mind can help one see one or two moves ahead on the chessboard—a tremendous advantage against any adversary. Themistocles knew that fighting at Salamis was a risk, but he accurately calculated that the Persians would jump at a chance to surround the smaller Greek fleet and overlook the danger of the straits. Thus, even without perfect certainty, Themistocles could use his qualities of vision to nonetheless predict that his motivated crews could prevail with the help of good tactics and a strategic ruse.

Predicting an outcome through vision is one thing; motivating people to respond and execute that vision is quite another. Had Themistocles failed either to persuade Athens to build a fleet before the Second Persian War or to inspire his crews to strike the decisive blow at Salamis, his story—and Greek history—might read quite differently today. And you might be reading this book in Farsi.

Whether as a Greek archon persuading his fellow citizens to invest in a navy, as a commander inspiring his crews to victory, or as a refugee persuading his former enemies to take him in, Themistocles consistently demonstrated a unique ability to *communicate* his vision to those around him. Even his detractor Herodotus acknowledged that the speech Themistocles gave before the Battle of Salamis was crucial to the outcome. The speech quickly became a feature of contemporary Greek plays and remained a feature of later Roman histories. As usual in the ancient world, each historian has bequeathed us a somewhat different version of the speech—but all emphasized its central importance to the victory that saved Athenian democracy.

Not all leaders are born rhetoricians, but even the best speakers practice their craft. Themistocles proved to be an inspirational speaker from his earliest days as archon, but we can safely assume that he put significant effort into developing whatever gifts he had during his largely unrecorded youth. Few leaders today will face such desperate circumstances as Themistocles did, but all can benefit from developing the arts of inspirational, persuasive communication. And, while today's leaders communicate across many platforms, the ability to speak well—in person, on television, by videoconference, or through tweets and Facebook posts—remains a crucial tool in a leader's toolbox. Being able to do so comes in large measure from practice, study, and most important, a sincerity of belief that is instantly discernible by an audience. Inspiration flows from character.

In the end, a fundamental part of human character is a belief in oneself. This can be expressed as quiet confidence; or, sadly, it can cross the line to arrogance. The quality of arrogance is one that we all must avoid if we are to live lives of character. Themistocles was a brilliant leader, a talented strategist, and a master communicator—in so many ways, a man in full bloom, suited to the crowded hour in which he found himself, ready to act as a savior to his nation. And yet he too often found himself straying across that vital line from confidence to conceit and a certain sense of his own power. He eventually utterly lost his way through arrogance. In politics and war, whether making the somewhat disingenuous case for building a fleet or sending a secret mission to the Persians to precipitate the Battle of Salamis, Themistocles was willing to go to great lengths to get his way. He exuded self-confidence, but over time he gradually became perceived by his countrymen as too full of himself.

In today's world especially, where there is such transparency, leaders must remember the fine line between the helpful characteristic of self-confidence (which so often becomes inspirational to others) and the toxic quality of arrogance. This is something many talented people struggle with, especially when they are young and driven by ambition to secure a meaningful role in life. Too often a justified self-confidence, which is quiet and steady, can become a boastful, loud arrogance that drives away potential followers. Often the best antidote to slipping across that line is found in truthful (and occasionally blunt) conversations with peers. In the end, it is our peers who see us most clearly and understand us best—listening unflinchingly to them can help keep all of us on the right side of the divide between confidence and arrogance. Themistocles strayed far across that line, and it led to the end of his career and a deep stain on his legacy.

This was the dark side of his visionary, inspirational character—which later in life cost him dearly. It is not too far a leap (or a bad pun) to say his is a Greek tragedy of sorts. Themistocles's ultimate failure and humiliation should not only humanize him to us, but also illustrate for us two perennial challenges of both character and leadership. First, almost no leader can sustain momentum forever: behaviors that were convenient to overlook in peacetime became problematic for Themistocles soon after his great victory restored the peace. Second, scorched-earth leaders are often humbled in this way, when the resentments they can create in pursuit of short-term victories come to a head later (often following an inevitable shift in political circumstances).

Learning to balance being right with being a leader is often a great challenge of character—especially for the most visionary and charismatic leaders. As I like to remind young leaders, the World War II fleet admiral Ernest King once remarked, "The sign of a great ship handler is never getting into a situation that requires great ship handling." Similarly, the sign of a mature leader is an understanding that a leader should avoid getting into a position where the only way to persuade an audience is by an almost magical feat of rhetoric. That trick will not bear repeating, which is the story of Themistocles. No one's luck lasts forever.

Themistocles might have been a gifted persuader, but he did not rely on rhetoric alone to achieve his goals. Recalling again the examples of his antipiracy appeals and the secret mission to the Persian fleet, it is clear that Themistocles was creative in his methods—even in a society that was very traditional in its day-to-day life. While I cannot always recommend that leaders emulate in detail the kind of political intrigue that Themistocles routinely practiced, I do want to emphasize the larger point that leaders often must "make a way" out of what appears to be "no way." This is called pragmatism on a good day and slippery double-dealing on a bad one. In both building the fleet and tricking the Persians into a fight, Themistocles outmaneuvered the opposition by superior grasp of strategy and an ability to display a certain flexibility of judgment. Judiciously applied, this type of creativity can help a leader achieve his or her goals in the face of opposition that cannot be swayed by clever words alone.

A cautionary note: as an element of character, creativity and innovation can be paralyzed by fear of failure. Too often, dynamic leaders become bound by their fears of failure, especially as they mature and have so much more of a successful track record to defend. I found this in my own career as I moved up the ladder of rank and authority, and consciously fought to keep my ideas fresh.

This does not mean swinging for the fences on every pitch, but rather being selective in what we try and recognizing that with risk comes occasional failure. Finding the courage to accept failure is part of the voyage of character and is the gateway to creativity. I remember especially as a relatively young officer finding myself starting to become more conservative in my recommendations—from how we navigated the ship to the way we employed our weapons in combat—and it hurt my ability to fully contribute to the mission of my commands. It is hard to take risk, wherever you are in life, but the rewards of success far outweigh the possibility of failure over the long throw of a life. The Battle of Salamis was not forced on Themistocles: rather, he chose it over the opposition of his fellow Greeks and developed the secret mission to the Persians for insurance. Even and especially when the stakes are highest—as they certainly were at Salamis—leaders must some-times take their own counsel and choose action.

Themistocles's decision to seek battle at Salamis shows not that risks can be fully controlled—they never can be—but rather that great leaders learn how to balance inherent uncertainty with a firm-enough grasp of context to enable decisive action. Themisto-cles did not vainly court disaster by seeking battle at sea, where the larger Persian fleet could have destroyed his own; but neither did he give in to the pessimism of his fellow commanders who could not see the opportunity offered by the straits and instead coun-seled pulling all the way back to the last redoubts. Thankfully, most leaders never have to face stakes as high as Themistocles did, but no leader can avoid taking decisive action forever.

This quality of character—decisiveness—is a good example of the adage that so often an imperfect plan executed with determination and ferocity is better than cautiously waiting for everything to fall into place perfectly. In my own decision making, I've tried to take a 90 percent rule on the really big, dangerous decisions—especially in combat. Leaving 10 percent to chance but acting decisively, from Afghanistan to Libya, has generally worked out for me as a commander; and decisiveness has the ancillary benefit of creating confidence in the team as they perceive their leader to be someone who is unafraid to weigh the options, make a decision, and actually get underway. In the Navy we say, "let's cut some steel," meaning sooner or later you must make the hard choices. Decisiveness without facts is madness; but you will never have all the facts. Finding that balance is at the heart not only of leadership, but of character as well, since in the end it is the inner voice to which you must answer for the choices you make. For all his flaws, Themistocles made those choices at the hardest of times, and his character is therefore worth studying with deep attention and respect.

CHAPTER II

A Sailor of the Middle Kingdom

Zheng He

———

BORN C. 1371, YUNNAN, CHINA

DIED 1433, AT SEA, INDIAN OCEAN

I came across the Chinese admiral Zheng He relatively late in my life and career, when I went to China for the first time in 1999 as a Navy captain and executive assistant/senior aide to the secretary of the Navy. I had previously been to Hong Kong many times, and once to Taiwan, but never to mainland China. My boss, Secretary of the Navy Richard Danzig, a brilliant global thinker, Rhodes scholar, and Oxford PhD, always emphasized the importance of learning about the history and culture of a place you were going to visit. China was no exception, and in the weeks leading up to our trip, he kept asking questions about the Chinese navy, seeking to learn about its ethos and leadership style.

I was in my mid-forties and had just finished a successful tour as a commodore in the US Navy. In that job, I had held command responsibility for seven frontline destroyers, including four *Arleigh Burke*–class guided missile destroyers (then brand-new). During my command tour, we had conducted a series of exercises and operations in the highly contested South China Sea. In leading those operations, I had learned about the Chinese territorial claims to the entire South China Sea, which the United States and the countries ringing the sea strenuously object to, believing them to be international waters. I was vaguely aware of an ancient Chinese admiral and explorer who had established the historical precedent upon which the Chinese partially relied in claiming those seas, but I had never taken the next step to really dig in and understand the biography, leadership style, and character of that admiral.

So when Secretary Danzig began to ask hard questions about why the Chinese claimed the entire South China Sea (a vast body of water of nearly a million square miles, roughly the size of the Caribbean Sea), I realized it was time I learned about the explorer upon whom these extraordinary territorial claims rested: it was Zheng He, and his life story transfixed me. I spent several weeks reading all I could find about this extraordinary man and his implausible and inspiring rise from a genitally neutered captive to probably the leading international maritime figure of his age. It is a story of remarkable resilience, creativity, and drive, and one that resonates throughout the psychology of the Navy's greatest potential opponent in our own turbulent century: the oddly named People's Liberation Army Navy (the naval forces of the People's Republic of China, commonly referred to as the PLAN).

Arriving in China with a great deal of new knowledge about the greatest admiral in that culture's history, I used my trip with Secretary Danzig to plumb the way Zheng He is viewed and how his character continues to influence the second-largest navy in the world. With my Chinese naval officer counterparts on that trip, I would always talk about Zheng He, discuss his role in the Chinese navy's psyche, and at social events often end up proposing a toast to him. This was well received, and often elicited a toast to US fleet admiral Chester Nimitz, who is also well known in a very positive way among Chinese naval officers—for having defeated Japan, a nation they view with suspicion and bitterness stemming from centuries of bad blood and the attempted Japanese conquest of China in the Second World War.

What I learned in my studies was that despite his singular background, Zheng He's approach to life, inspired leadership, and depth of character transcended his own painful history and made him famous throughout the vast Pacific region. Though little known on US shores, Zheng He's life is an important part of the larger story of Pacific peoples and the oceans that surround this part of the earth. My own personal lesson with Zheng He is a very practical one: to understand the character of other nations, regions, and cultures, we must learn their stories and legends, study in a methodical and comprehensive way, and draw lessons from the great sailors of the world—a group that most assuredly includes Admiral Zheng He.

The multiethnic composition and lingering boundary disputes of modern China are trace reminders of the great historical flux in the peoples and lands that have made up Chinese civilization across the centuries. Dynastic transitions created some of the biggest fluctuations of all, and one of these—following the proclamation of the Ming dynasty in 1368—was responsible for creating the conditions that would lead to the rise of Zheng He.

In the mid-fourteenth century—as Europe was staggering

through the medieval period and trying to rebuild after the plague years—one of the most important dynasties in Chinese history emerged: the Ming. Just a few years after the Ming formally assumed the "Mandate of Heaven," a child named Ma He was born to a Muslim family in Yunnan province, which is nestled just to the north of modern-day Myanmar, Laos, and Vietnam. The Ming were still consolidating their power over the whole region of China, and Yunnan was one of the provinces still controlled by governors appointed by the deposed Yuan dynasty. Like all new dynasties, it took the Ming some time to assert their control throughout the lands they claimed, but Yunnan's turn had come by 1381. According to legend, the Ming general who was sent to end the Yuan governor's holdout was closing in on the governor (by then on the run) when he stopped to question a ten-year-old Muslim boy. When the boy not only refused to reveal the governor's whereabouts but openly defied the general, he was taken as a prisoner of war and, in a relatively common but unpleasant practice, was soon castrated and placed into imperial service as a eunuch.

The boy Ma He's new master was Prince Zhu Di, the fourth son of the Ming emperor and aide-de-camp to the general of the Yunnan campaign. Despite the castration, Ma He became a powerful fighter and grew to an impressive height. He studied war and politics, peppering members of the court for their opinions on everything from the best weapons in a close-in battle to the navigational power of the stars. He was a standout in every dimension, and gradually became a favorite of the prince. Over the subsequent decades, the two would fight together against frontier Mongol warlords, rebellious provinces, and a claimant to the Ming throne. Ma He became a trusted confidant of the prince and, when the prince defeated the challenger to the throne and became the Yongle Emperor, he conferred on Ma He the high honor of choosing his own surname. Thereafter he became known as Zheng He, a reference to an important region in central China.

The specific path of the unlikely rise of the young boy and eunuch to court favorite and confidant to the prince is not known. The conquering Chinese dynasties were quite willing, up to a point, to provide upward mobility for conquered "barbarians," especially when they had been neutered and presumably were immune to feminine wiles and their natural ambitions curbed. This practice, also known in the Ottoman Empire, was largely successful in providing a talented pool of workers to the courts—strictly in advisory positions. But occasionally there are historical examples of such men rising to positions of significant power, albeit alongside rulers who would take advantage of their lack of outside sponsorship or affiliation. Such was the case with Zheng He, who fought alongside his master in many campaigns, earning his trust over more than a decade.

Following a period of frontier wars, the new emperor set about rebuilding and modernizing the country. He charged Zheng He with one of the most ambitious parts of this plan: building China's first deep-ocean fleet and leading it on exploratory voyages beyond the traditional range of Chinese coastal shipping. Although the emperor's original reasons for ordering the fleet's construction are lost to history—speculations range from conquest to commerce to sheer curiosity—the ruler's wishes were of course carried out, and his longtime factotum and functional chief of staff, Zheng He, was given the task of his life. The emperor picked wisely—he knew the qualities of Zheng He: skilled management, a measured temperament, an independence of mind tempered by utter loyalty to his prince, and above all, a high degree of resilience to face whatever would come in the vast maritime unknown.

A big part of Zheng He's charter, of course, was not simply sailing off into the ocean blue. He had to first build a fleet, and in ancient China, the tendency was to build big, striking structures—a tradition that is followed today in the People's Republic of China. In this case, that meant expanding existing designs and building what remain among the largest wooden structures of the time, massive warships over five hundred feet in length. Doing so successfully did not depend on military force, but on the less glamorous attributes of administration, supervision, and logistics.

It is not hard to imagine Zheng He walking through the Longjian shipyard, caught up in the shattering noise all around him. Even after several months of supervising construction, he would not have fully adjusted to the sheer din of the work: it surpassed anything he had ever experienced before. This is also the case in modern shipyards, by the way—the noisiest and dirtiest times of my own naval career were the painful months spent in ship construction or repair in various shipyards on the coasts of the United States. Even when working in wood instead of metal for hull construction, the noise would have been substantial—but each day's hammering, sawing, and shouting would bring the massive project closer to completion. In the end, the laborers of Longjian produced some of the largest wooden structures ever built by human hands. In the early 1400s, when Zheng He took command of his fleet, Europeans were struggling to build sailing vessels a fraction the size of the Chinese ships as their own age of exploration was just getting underway. When completed, the Chinese flagship would sail at the head of a fleet of dozens of "treasure ships"—all impressively large if not quite as enormous as the flagship itself—on a series of voyages that vastly expanded the Ming Empire's map of and influence in the world.

The work in the shipyards occupied Zheng He for the better part of four years. The tasks he faced included finding and transporting wood, pitch, nails, iron, and all the rest of the materials, but the most complex part of his job was leading his temperamental workers. Zheng He knew that people problems would get out of hand quickest, and with the greatest consequences. As a result, he often took personnel matters under his personal direction. Even as he sorted out the problems of construction, he was spending his nights preparing for the voyage itself—studying navigation, consulting with China's few deepwater sailors, learning the art and science of combat afloat. The enormous ships coming together under his watchful eye would require massive crews and when at sea would prove to be far more cramped and contentious than the shipyard—once at sea, no one would be able to go home at night to cool off.

The first voyage set sail in 1405. With more than three hundred vessels in the fleet and a crew of over twenty-seven thousand, the expedition was the largest naval excursion in history up to that time. As a point of comparison, nine decades later, Columbus set sail with only three vessels, which together approached the displacement of only one of Zheng He's minor treasure ships, and a full crew of only ninety sailors, less than 1 percent of Zheng He's crew. When the Yongle Emperor wanted something done, it got done in the most spectacular fashion possible. This was no simple fact-finding mission; it was the armada that truly introduced China to the world.

The treasure fleet's first mission was to reach the trading city of Calicut on the southwestern coast of India. A natural port of call for merchantmen crisscrossing the Indian Ocean, Calicut had been a commercial hub for a thousand years. Even the Romans conducted trade in this part of India, bringing glass and wool in exchange for spices. The government of Calicut mirrored China's own: wealthy, efficiently managed by a bureaucracy, and a haven for the arts. There the Ming would establish their first prolonged contact with the outside world. The voyage also helped establish China's historical claims to the South China Sea. The echoes of Zheng He's missions form part of the case China has presented to the international legal system as evidence of China's sovereignty over this vast area—echoes from centuries ago roiling the waters of the modern world.

It was an ambitious undertaking from the start. The fleet would need to sail from its home port in southern China down the South China Sea, through the Straits of Malacca, across the Bay of Bengal, and into the Arabian Sea to reach Calicut. High waves and storm winds would batter them throughout the course of their voyage. This wooden "city at sea" could not make it straight through in even the best of times. The fleet would need to resupply often, securing new food for the crew, medicines to ward off disease, and materials to make field repairs for the damage wrought by man and nature. Luckily, although the fleet was the first official representation of the Chinese government ever to reach most of its ports of call, its crew were not the first Chinese people ever to set foot there: often, the fleet was aided by members of local Chinese diaspora communities. I spent years sailing these waters in massive steel US warship hulls, pulling into ports from Hong Kong to Taiwan to the Philippines to Singapore. And everywhere I went, there were Chinese hulls: warships, trawlers, coastal steamers, waste disposal ships, and always the fishing fleets.

Piracy is one of the great consistent threads in world maritime history (recall Themistocles's original appeal to his fellow Athenians to build a navy to sail against nearby pirates). In Zheng He's day as well as our own, the desperately narrow, always-busy Straits of Malacca—at the head of which sits the gleaming modern city-state of Singapore—were subject to consistent predation by local pirates. The worst of these in Zheng He's time was Chen Zuyi, a Chinese pirate who was as much a king as he was a brigand. It took months of cat-and-mouse pursuit to bring down Chen's pirate network, but the treasure fleet eventually neutralized the most notorious raiding force of the era. Even though it was not designed specifically or even primarily for war, the fleet was proving to be an effective means of extending Ming foreign policy beyond the Chinese mainland.

The keys to Zheng He's success are not hard to see over the

centuries. He was carefully organized, calm of spirit, devoted to his prince, and willing to take risks. Combined with his resilient character, this combination of attributes stood him in good stead through the long voyages, especially the first, which was a resounding success. The enthusiastic emperor ordered another expedition to Calicut to personally invest the leadership with China's recognition. The fleet would also be used to prop up pro-Chinese leaders in kingdoms and city-states across Southeast Asia as the Dragon Throne cultivated a regional order to support its interests. In using the fleet in this fashion, the Chinese were anticipating by nearly half a millennium Alfred Thayer Mahan's theories of sea power as a crucial element in national power.

Subsequent voyages would range farther afield than Calicut, reaching the great trading cities of the Arabian Peninsula and East Africa. Zheng He would be at the helm for these voyages, generating wealth and prestige for the Ming court. The benefits were not confined to traditional objects of wealth. During the fourth expedition, for example, the fleet returned to China with a giraffe as a personal gift to the emperor from the king of Malindi in modern Kenya. The first animal of its kind ever to reach China, it bore resemblance to the mythical *qilin* of Chinese folklore, and supporters of the voyages pointed to it as proof that the heavens themselves favored China's sojourns abroad.

But the expeditions did not enjoy universal support. The cost increased markedly, as materials had to be brought from across the empire to sustain this massive enterprise. New domestic infrastructure had to be built to support the flow of goods. The eunuchs who served in the emperor's household supported these missions and the wealth they brought the court, but the professional bureaucrats who staffed the imperial ministries opposed them. These administrators subscribed to traditional Confucian views on the role of government and society—they believed that virtuous emperors focused on managing domestic politics and improving the lives of their subjects. Trade and commerce were predatory activities—societally necessary evils that fell beneath the dignity of an emperor, in their view. As with any political disagreement, these fault lines were just as much about personal power as they were about high-minded ideals. The bureaucrats did not like being sidelined by the emperor, while the eunuchs fought to maintain their privileged role.

The intense palace intrigue between eunuchs and bureaucrats brought on by the controversy over the fleet went back and forth for decades. Eventually, the death of the Yongle Emperor brought his more Confucian-minded son to the throne. The new emperor called a moratorium on the voyages in favor of focusing on domestic affairs, but he sat on the throne for only a few months before succumbing to illness. The next emperor launched a seventh and final round of expeditions. Zheng He was called back into service one last time to lead this final voyage. The great admiral, who had come so far from his provincial boyhood, died during the return voyage. His sailors committed his body to the deep.

Without their powerful patron, the court eunuchs never regained the prominence they once held. The bureaucrats won the internal struggle, and the treasure fleet was abandoned to rot in port. Perhaps saddest of all for people interested in learning about this unique period of Chinese history, Zheng He's personal logbooks were casualties of the political infighting, destroyed by those who wanted to remove the memory of the treasure fleets and prevent future adventurism. Thus we are forced to rely on secondary sources to catch glimpses of the admiral's life and adventures.

Nonetheless, his legacy lives on: Zheng He remains a folk hero among Chinese communities throughout Southeast Asia, and as I discovered on my own first trip to China, his name and memory are frequently invoked there as the country rediscovers its connection with the sea. And it is worth noting again that his voyages are part of the historical claims that China has repeatedly made in international courts to sovereignty over essentially the entire South China Sea. The treasures of oil and natural gas beneath that disputed body of water are crucial from a Chinese perspective to their nation's strategic path in the twenty-first century. Zheng He's voyages, which brought vast treasure to his emperor centuries ago, are very much a part of China's pursuit of modern-day power as well. In a very clear sense, you can drop a plumb line from the qualities of character possessed by this ancient admiral to the ambitions and accomplishments of modern China.

What can we learn from Zheng He? What were the qualities of character that shaped his life? The first of those qualities was in many ways the simplest: an organized frame of mind, tempered by a calm personality. Like Chester Nimitz, the US admiral whom my Chinese hosts toasted after I toasted Zheng He, Zheng's undeniable accomplishments as a wartime commander flowed from—and in some ways were outshone by—his organizational abilities. Overseeing the fleet's construction would have been a daunting task under any circumstance and was made all the more remarkable for being China's first large-scale attempt to put to sea. For comparison, imagine if the United States had determined to send people to the moon on the first rocket it ever built—and succeeded. This required enormous organizational ability, and the challenges did not end once the fleet was underway. Hardly would Zheng He and his crews have learned to build and sail their enormous vessels before they would have had to learn how to repair and resupply them at sea and ashore beyond the edges of any maps they possessed. If going to the moon in one shot sounds difficult, imagine continuing to Mars next—and having to ask a Martian when you arrived for spare parts to fix your rocket.

As I learned in my own first command of the destroyer USS *Barry*, much of a commander and crew's success at sea depends on how well they organize before setting sail. If communications, procedures, and training are working well before a ship leaves port, her people will stand a good chance of surmounting the challenges they will inevitably confront at sea. This is a large part of the reason that naval cultures everywhere have given ships' captains such enormous authority and commensurate responsibility: everyone helps in preparing for a voyage, but the captain is ultimately responsible for adequately provisioning and training the ship. Not all leadership cultures are quite as stark as those found in the world's navies, but all leaders need to learn how to organize and take responsibility for their people, equipment, and mission.

Organization is more than a skill—it is a quality of character. It implies a disciplined, linear, sensible approach to analysis and problem solving. It rejects spurious inputs, emotional analysis, and the kind of mental clutter that afflicts so many of us. And best of all, organization is a character trait that can be developed and practiced. Luckily, in today's electronic world, we have many devices, software, and applications that help us get organized, from simple to-do lists on our smartphones to artificial intelligence programs that over time can "machine learn" what is important to us and key our daily work along those lines. Using these tools is a simple but crucial part of building the ability to exercise organizational character skills. We can also reject the impulses leading to disorganization that come from the pursuit of instant gratification and a sort of mental laziness that afflicts much of society today. In so many ways, our character is the sum of the choices we make about the immediate moment and the course we chart into the future. Doing so in a methodical, organized way influences our character deeply.

Resilience was also a crucial element in Zheng He's character. He did not have an easy life. It is difficult to imagine the brutality of his capture and castration—yet Zheng He not only continued onward but made himself indispensable to the very people who brutalized him. The additional rigors of his bureaucratic service, his command of the treasure fleet, and his political positioning within the bureaucracy are also largely left to our imagination by the gaps in the historical record, but it is safe to say that it must have required immense resilience and tact to make his way into the emperor's confidence, command seven massive voyages, and remain in the good graces of three successive emperors with divergent priorities. His character was clearly shaped by the quality of resilience, which is perhaps the most important of human attributes for the simple reason that all of us will suffer failure repeatedly on the road of life.

Luckily, most leaders—indeed, most people—today will not have to face the kinds of challenges Zheng He did. However, all leaders need to be resilient, and resilience is most often developed by the experience of operating under pressure. Many people have worked for a demanding boss, taken responsibility for a project at the very limit of their organizational abilities, or metaphorically sailed beyond the limits of any previous experience. The important thing to remember is that resilience is a sort of inoculation against stress, and it is best developed by progressive doses. By the time Zheng He was tasked with building and commanding the treasure fleet, he had already been tested many times in many ways. The new challenge might have been the biggest yet, but he had already confronted big-enough tasks to teach the lessons he would need to lead the fleet. How can we become more resilient?

The two best tools of character an individual can deploy in strengthening resilience are stoicism and perspective. Stoicism, which comes to us from the ancient Greek philosophers, is simply developing a lifelong attitude that recognizes the world is painful and hard, and that whining and complaining are not helpful. The Stoics believed that as humans we are unable to be accepting of the present moment, and too focused on obtaining pleasure and avoiding pain. While stoicism is seemingly a simple philosophical approach, it requires a lifetime to achieve for most of us, mainly because so much of society today is based on the pleasure/pain calculus. While not strictly speaking a Stoic, the great Greek writer

SAILING TRUE NORTH

Nikos Kazantzakis's tombstone is engraved with three simple sentences: "I want nothing. I fear nothing. I am free." The degree to which we can develop that attitude in life is often reflective of the degree to which our character can be free to achieve greatly.

Second, in achieving resilience, having perspective and keeping a sense of the larger context helps. This means recognizing that no matter how difficult the circumstances of the moment, there are always far worse situations in which one could find oneself. There is much here to consider, as all circumstances are perceived in our own minds, and it is difficult to say, "Well, my child has a terrible illness, but others have children who died at birth." Some circumstances are so tragic and painful that there is no positive way to deal with them by "keeping them in context." But so often we sweat the small stuff, as the saying goes, and become deeply frustrated over a missed plane flight, a promotion that is delayed, a rude interaction at the supermarket, a lengthy line at the drugstore, and a thousand other slings and arrows that life throws our way. Keeping a sense of context while adding the sort of Stoic philosophy of the ancient Greeks helps develop the quality of character we call resilience. Practicing a little stoicism and taking note of context is a way to strengthen our character and improve our resilience for when things *really* go wrong—and they will.

One other quality that was central to Zheng He's character was a healthy appreciation of the great diversity of life, and a tolerance for it as well—this stemmed from his own experiences, but was also a pragmatic choice. A practicing Muslim throughout his life, Zheng He was among a religious minority in service to the Ming court. And the diversity of religions among his fellow courtiers was far eclipsed by that among his crews in the treasure fleet. In dealing with such an array of ethnicities, cultures, and religions, forbearance was critical to keeping the crews motivated and working together. In that sense, Zheng He's fleet resembled the modern workplace—and the admiral did what modern leaders do to adapt: he cultivated tolerance with and among his subordinates while keeping true to himself. Even as a Muslim, he built shrines honoring Tianfei, a figure from Chinese folk religion who became the goddess of the sea and sailors. He not only allowed Buddhist and Taoist rites to be practiced by his sailors, but often participated in them to demonstrate his respect for his crews' beliefs.

As contemporary research continues to demonstrate the many advantages of diversity in team performance—and as so many kinds of work increasingly involve interactions across boundaries and cultures—it is more important than ever for leaders to learn how to build tolerance, both in themselves and within the organizations they lead. It does not always come easily, but it is always worth it. Developing tolerance as a quality of character is a matter of study and practice. We must study other cultures, learn and appreciate their history, and essentially explain to ourselves why someone is fundamentally different.

Once we have studied other cultures, races, and religions, we take the step to the most challenging part of character development—practicing respect for others in a conscious, day-to-day way. Zheng He by all accounts did this throughout his life. The superb speech by the celebrated American writer David Foster Wallace, "This Is Water," explores this under the rubric of empathy, a closely related element to tolerance. "The really important kind of freedom involves attention, and awareness, and discipline, and effort, and being able truly to care about other people and to sacrifice for them, over and over, in myriad petty little unsexy ways, every day." This brilliant speech, which I read at least annually, inspires me to work harder on tolerance—something in sadly short supply in today's United States of America. I thought of it recently as I was passing through a crowded airport. A woman behind me in the TSA security line was trying to maneuver through with a toddler and a three-month-old baby. While I was simply registering her difficulty, a young man of perhaps twenty-five stepped up and gave her his place in line, delaying everyone else. You could see the annoyance in faces of the half dozen people delayed by his action. But it was the right thing to do. The echoes of Zheng He and his remarkable character can be heard in Wallace's speech and in the young man's act of grace.

Zheng He was also, by necessity, highly independent in his approach to command. In contrast to the tyranny of the modern inbox, admirals in ancient times faced the opposite challenge—that of operating with guidance that was overtaken by events almost as soon as they left port, and which could only be updated if a letter could somehow overtake the fleet at sea. Much as this might sound like a welcome respite for modern leaders who can seemingly never be out of touch with their organizations, it is worth pausing to consider the stakes—and trust—involved. For the emperor to send out an expedition without much hope of receiving more than a few updates during the entire time it was underway, he had to be able to really trust his commander's autonomy and understanding of his instructions.

At every port of call, Zheng He was confronted by new and often dangerous situations, which required him to make a range of quick decisions weighing his mission, the safety of his ships and crew, and his perception of the scene on the ground. During his third voyage, Zheng He called in Sri Lanka in the midst of a three-way civil war between a Sinhalese Buddhist kingdom in the south, a Tamil Muslim kingdom in the north, and a rebel Sinhalese warrior who fought both. His instructions to establish relations with the people on the island were silent on this unforeseen and challenging situation, which must have taken the admiral himself some time to decipher. (By chance, Zheng He's first contact was with the rebel leader, which could not have made things easier for him.) He was forced to adapt to the events on the ground without recourse to "instructions" from higher authority. He was able to establish trading relations with all three groups and kept Chinese neutrality—and opportunity for further trade—alive.

Even with the ubiquity and speed of modern communications, today's leaders still frequently find themselves called to make similar decisions: on the scene, on the spur of the moment, and on limited situational understanding. In many cases, developing the ability to operate autonomously while remaining within the intent of one's mission is an important part of a leader's developmental process—and one that today's leaders may have to develop on their own initiative. If a young leader comes to over-rely on constant and near-instant access to higher authority, he or she can miss out on this crucial maturation step.

Finding that balance—between "checking with headquarters" and acting boldly—is a crucial part of character development. At each stage of my career, I found myself making mistakes, generally on the side of acting a bit too boldly. As a young destroyer captain, I had impulsively turned my ship toward the Suez Canal during a crisis in the Gulf, assuming I'd receive orders to head that way. After we had steamed through the night for a couple of hundred miles, my commodore awoke to find my ship well off station. He sent me a message in code that when broken said simply, "Your movements are not understood." It was an old sailing command often sent via signal flags in the days before radio communication. I was quickly reeled back into station, and my next report of officer fitness was a bit less glowing than it could have been. But I learned a valuable lesson in the balance between bold autonomy and organizational fidelity.

Managing his diverse crew was one challenge and figuring out what to do in a situation like Sri Lanka was another, but those were hardly the only challenges of diversity and uncertainty Zheng He faced in the course of his voyages. Sailing beyond the edges of the map naturally meant contacting people and cultures unknown to the admiral and his crew, and Zheng He was expected to engage with these people and establish relationships with them that could conceivably outlast his own visit. To do so required from Zheng He a lightness of touch with others, and qualities of tolerance and empathy. It called for creative diplomacy of the highest order.

While it is unlikely that modern leaders will discover truly unknown lands, they will almost certainly find themselves in unfamiliar situations requiring diplomatic skills. Luckily, as Secretary Danzig taught me before my own first trip to China, modern leaders have the enormous advantage of being able to read up on the people and cultures they are likely to encounter. There is an enormous difference between reading a little Chinese history and actually going to China, of course, but I have always found impromptu diplomacy to be much easier when I have done some homework beforehand. As the Supreme Allied Commander of NATO, with its twenty-eight member nations, I made a point of reading a novel from a country before I set off for an official visit there. There is much we can learn from an evocative, culturally attuned work of fiction, such as *Broken April* by Ismail Kadare of Albania or *The Bridge on the Drina* by Ivo Andrić of Bosnia.

As the world grows ever more interconnected in every sector, it is essential for leaders at every level to develop some basic diplomatic skills (including but not limited to pretravel reading). While we are forced to imagine the specific methods that Zheng He developed to manage truly alien interactions, after seven voyages to the edges of the earth he could probably carry on a "conversation" with ease even in places where he knew not a word of the language. That takes practice and a little charm—and not a little willingness to jump right in and laugh at oneself if mistakes are made. As I have seen repeatedly during my time in the Navy, and especially as a student and dean at the Fletcher School of Law and Diplomacy at Tufts University, developing some basic diplomatic skills can help aspiring leaders make a positive impression in those unavoidable circumstances when they find themselves far out of their depth.

As I reflect on Zheng He and his voyage, I feel the power of his lessons across the many centuries: his quiet skills of management and organization; his tolerance for the full range of human beliefs and diversity; his gift for independence tempered by loyalty to his ruler; and especially his hard-earned resilience in dealing with the pain of life. There is much to discover about China and its history, culture, strategy, and ambitions in this complex twenty-first century by studying the story of Zheng He. But above all, learning about the life and times of Zheng He, as well as his qualities of character, provides a guidepost for anyone seeking the way to live a meaningful and productive life.

CHAPTER III

A Pirate and a Patriot

Sir Francis Drake

———

Born c. 1540, Tavistock, England

Died 1596, at sea, near Panama

When I was commander of US Southern Command from 2006 to 2009, I led all US military operations—Army, Navy, Air Force, Marine Corps, special operations, and Coast Guard—south of the United States. I had a beautiful headquarters in Miami, four stars on my shoulders, and my job was essentially to travel around Latin America and the Caribbean and encourage military cooperation. It was a wonderful job, especially for a Miami native like me. And everywhere I went in the Caribbean Sea, I kept bumping into Sir Francis Drake.

Drake cut a bold course through that sea in the 1600s, operating in a most piratical manner. His raids were infamous; I ran across the memory of the "English pirate Drake" in San Juan, Puerto Rico; Cartagena de Indias, Colombia; Panama City, Panama; Santo Domingo in the Dominican Republic; and many other ports. He burned more real estate and sacked more cities than Captain Jack Sparrow ever did, and the memory of his misdeeds is long indeed. The Spanish called him *El Draque* (his nickname, and today the name of a killer cocktail somewhat akin to a mojito), and mothers would frighten their unruly children into obedience by threatening his arrival. His exploits to my eye seemed the basis for the Pirates of the Caribbean ride at the Disney parks around the world. Even today, when I visit with leaders in the various nations and ports touched by Drake, I hear about him, see exhibits of his exploits in the small, dusty museums, and generally feel the dislike and fear he engendered.

Drake's character is among the most difficult to evaluate of any admiral in history. Despite his manifest accomplishments on behalf of his nation, there was a dark, cruel, and hot-blooded streak that ran like a four-lane highway down the middle of his personality. He was strategically heroic and tactically flawed. While I admired his boldness, decisiveness, and audacity, I also shuddered at some of his chosen courses of action, reflecting the darker angels of his character. Sir Francis Drake is a good example of how a deeply flawed character can still accomplish a great deal in an energetic life—for both good and ill.

Most often, his actions were morally ambiguous, richly varied, and full of a dark energy. He helped save his nation from the Spanish Armada and greatly expanded its power and reach in the New World. But he also traded slaves, tortured, and raped his way across the seas—a brutal tactician who did whatever it took to succeed.

His character became for me a roadmap of sorts, a cautionary tale. As I struggled to deepen my own sense of understanding of the Caribbean, it helped me to remember how much so many countries had suffered at the hand of colonizing raiders like Drake. Despite all his energy and evident charisma, in the end what I learned from studying El Draque was that the effects of his harsh methods, applied with brutal force, have echoed across generations. His reputation will never fully escape the cruelty of his methods. The essence of each of us—the character we show to the world—lives long after we are gone. As Mark Antony says in William Shakespeare's *Julius Caesar* at the eulogy of the fallen Caesar, "The evil that men do lives after them, / The good is oft interred with their bones." Character transcends time and lives on not only in the memories of those who actually knew us, but also through the historical record of our deeds.

Francis Drake was born into an era of conflict. He came from the small town of Tavistock in Devon, in the southwest of England. The sixteenth century was the height of religious conflict in Europe as the Reformation swept across the Continent and Henry VIII divorced his first wife, and in the process separated his kingdom from the Catholic Church. The Drakes' corner of England remained staunchly Catholic in the face of state-sponsored Anglicanism. When London imposed a change in all church services from Latin to English, the Catholics revolted—and Drake's father, a Protestant minister, fled with his family.

Young Francis was sent to live with his cousins, the Hawkinses of nearby Plymouth, one of the great English seafaring cities. The Hawkins family had been prominent shipowners and merchants for years, and quickly brought young Francis into the business. The young man took quickly and confidently to the sea—and to the business methods of the Hawkins clan, which made most of its money in illicit trade with the Spanish and Portuguese territories, and not a little more through piracy.

For as long as people have shipped money and goods by sea, other people have put to sea to steal it. From the fictional swashbucklers of *Pirates of the Caribbean* to the deadly serious Somali pirates of *Captain Phillips*, the image of piracy has not changed as much as its tactics—it is still a business condemned by the family of nations, illegal under all codes of international law. In Drake's day, English piracy had not yet entered its semiprofessional golden age of Jolly Rogers and rum-swilling roguery. Rather, it was more of a watery Wild West, in which the line between merchant and pirate was thin and frequently crossed from voyage to voyage, or even in the course of a single sailing. Like the early stagecoach and rail lines of the West, the Caribbean offered many vulnerable, treasure-laden ships and rich settlements to tempt an unscrupulous captain to turn a quick profit at gunpoint.

Drake found his calling in this frontier environment. Sailing with the Hawkinses to western Africa and on early forays into the Caribbean, Drake quickly developed as a sailor—as well as in exposure to the seamier sides of his cousins' business. During Drake's apprenticeship at sea, the Hawkinses muscled their way into the slave trade and made a small fortune, shook down defenseless cities, and eluded capture by Spanish warships. Drake learned the thrill of plunder and of the narrow escape, but also how the line between success and failure could be just as fickle as that between merchant and pirate.

One particularly close brush with the Spanish viceroy off the coast of Mexico split Drake off from the Hawkins fleet and launched his solo career. When a hasty escape from the Spaniards precluded much-needed repairs, Drake determined to sail back to England in a barely seaworthy ship. His cousin John Hawkins eventually followed, but only after losing most of his crew as prisoners of war—and learning the true cut of Drake's brutal methods. On returning to England, Drake promptly went into business for himself. The early results were not auspicious, as he made a series of dangerous and unprofitable raids, lost many of his new crew to disease, and had many close calls with the Spanish authorities. However, Drake soon recognized what he needed to do to succeed as his own boss, and ruthlessly set about doing it. First, he steeled his own will, then drilled his crew to a high state of discipline. Before too long, Drake's reputation began to rise, both among Spanish colonists fearful of his raiding and English officials impressed by his seamanship.

In Drake's day, Britannia did not yet rule the waves. That role belonged to Philip II of Spain, then the leading monarch of the powerful Habsburg family, which controlled or exploited much of the Caribbean, Mediterranean, and transatlantic trades. Around the world, Habsburg ships carried Habsburg goods from port to port, creating an enormously lucrative form of proto-globalization to gild the Spanish throne—and a model for England to emulate and exploit. Thus, when Queen Elizabeth commissioned Francis Drake to circumnavigate the globe, the none-too-subtle subtext was a growing English desire to expand their geopolitical reach and compete with the Spanish crown. A round-the-world expedition would not be cheap, but the open secret of its piratical designs on Spanish commerce made it an attractive investment for English businesspeople. Like modern venture capitalists, backers lined up to finance the voyage—including the queen herself. Drake was commissioned as captain of the expedition, and led it from 1577 to 1580.

The small group of raiders under Drake's command did not even wait to cross the Atlantic before beginning their exploits in 1577. Sailing south from England, they first raided Spanish holdings in Morocco and nearby islands, then turned west and seized vessels in Cape Verde. After the crossing, the fleet continued raiding down the coast of modern Brazil and Argentina. The money piled up, but so did the challenges: once again, Drake was chased by storms and Spaniards, and his hard-driving style of command created tensions with his own people. True to form, Drake drove his crew by the lash of his fury and made them dependent on their captain's stormy graces. He tolerated no challengers to his authority and took the extreme step of executing his business partner, the nobleman Thomas Doughty, during the brutal passage around Cape Horn. The crew rallied around their captain, but his decision to spill noble blood would haunt Drake for the rest of his life.

Rounding the Cape through the Straits of Magellan, Drake and his crew became the first English sailors to reach the Pacific Ocean, where their brutality would continue to reverberate throughout Spanish America. They plundered and pillaged up the coast of what are now Chile, Peru, and Ecuador, torturing captives and taking whatever they could carry. Reaching the top of South America,

Drake and his crew turned west again for the long run across the Pacific. Upon making landfall in the Philippines, they turned south and resumed plundering through those islands and modern-day Indonesia before crossing the Indian Ocean to round the Cape of Good Hope and head north toward England and a hero's welcome by 1580.

Drake, whose draconian and rapacious tendencies had reached new heights in three years at sea, was promptly knighted for his achievement. Not only was he the first captain to survive a round-the-world voyage (his Portuguese predecessor Ferdinand Magellan had died en route), but his exploits instantly made the humbly born Sir Francis a very wealthy man. He promptly set about the same pursuits as his new peers, becoming mayor of Plymouth, sitting in Parliament, and investing in real estate. He had amassed a fortune and spent money like—well, a drunken sailor.

But Drake's life was at sea. The queen once again commissioned him to raid Spanish shipping in the Caribbean in the mid-1580s, which he did with great enthusiasm and success. Santo Domingo in today's Dominican Republic burned. San Agustín (now St. Augustine) in my native Florida burned. His targeted cruelty against Catholic churches conjured images of a Protestant crusader hell-bent on bringing the European wars of religion across the Atlantic. In one particularly brutal attack, Drake stood on the shores of the Caribbean outside the town of Cartagena de Indias on the northern Caribbean coast of Colombia. The city was a commercial hub of Spain's Latin American empire, and rich with gold. Drake had hundreds of men arrayed around him in the fields near the beach. They carried a mixture of weapons: long pikes, clumsy harquebuses with powder and shot, swords, and cannon. They stood in front of their commander, looking intently at his face. Sir Francis Drake recognized the look: a mixture of eagerness and hesitance, optimism and trepidation. These men were afraid of the battles to come. But more than that, they were afraid of Sir Francis Drake.

In raid after raid, the historical record shows us a commander who bullied and terrified his men. In terms of killing, rape, and pillage, Drake liked to lead from the front, and any of his men who held back were treated worse than the victims in the towns he attacked. A good example was the attack on Cartagena de Indias in which he tasked his men to take the fort at Boquerón (the mouth of the harbor), but watched them fail while under the hesitant command of his second, Martin Frobisher. Drake turned them back to battle, saying he would take the fort if he had to tear the stones down with his own hands. The fire in his eyes and the threat in his voice had a predictably "inspirational" effect on his men, and they returned to the fray, took the fort, and destroyed the town— the heart of the Spanish Empire in the Americas.

But over time, the Spanish began to understand his tactics and create an intelligence network throughout the Caribbean that often gave them early warning of his approach and intentions. Despite some measure of success in harrying the Spanish treasure ships, his second cruise failed to pay off financially. As a result, Drake lost some of his sheen of invincibility, especially in the eyes of his investors. Even thus tarnished, however, Drake retained the all-important support of the crown. His next mission was to lead a squadron in support of Protestant rebels in the Low Countries who were challenging their Catholic Habsburg masters. The English-Spanish relationship continued on a downward spiral which would soon spill over into open war. Both countries prepared to invade the other by sea; Drake was put in charge of the English efforts, and ultimately determined to strike at the southern Spanish port city of Cádiz. He struck first with a brazen midday attack, which smashed the Spanish merchant fleet sheltering in the harbor. The blow set back the Spaniards' own preparations for invasion, recovered some of Drake's prestige, and provided another major financial windfall for Drake and his crew.

Despite the setback, the Spaniards redoubled their efforts to invade England. The new plan called for a massive fleet from Spain to embark an army from the Low Countries and land the troops in England to march on London. The English hastily assembled a fleet to repel this armada, and Drake was named second in command under the aristocratic Admiral Lord Charles Howard. As in the early days sailing with the Hawkinses, Drake distinguished himself as a subordinate by carrying out his assignments with characteristic dash. Drake initially wanted to attack the armada straight out of port, before it could ship the soldiers from the Low Countries, but was overruled by Admiral Howard. Nevertheless, he was typically swashbuckling in coastal defense: ships under his command were often first into the fray, and his crews took risks bordering on foolhardiness. The Spanish Armada could overcome neither the English fleet nor its own poor planning and was forced to return by way of the Scottish coast, where violent storms ravaged much of the remnants of the once-mighty fleet.

Though he shared in the glory of Spain's defeat and had more adventures ahead, Drake's best days were already behind him. Further raids on Spain and Portugal proved unsuccessful militarily and financially, and Drake went ashore again in Plymouth. There he took a seat in Parliament once more, and, in an ironic twist, was commissioned by the crown to arbitrate restitution disputes between pirates and legitimate merchants. Finally, he received his last seagoing commission in 1589, ostensibly to take control of Panama but as usual with an open charter to harass the Spanish throughout the Caribbean and South America.

This last Caribbean voyage was star-crossed from the start, and not least by the mercurial habits of Sir Francis himself. Now in his fifties, Drake had hardly changed his leadership style since his twenties, and he continued to lead fearlessly from the front, to drive his crews and himself inhumanly hard, and to chase any apparent opportunity for plunder. He eluded the Spanish until the end, but finally fell victim to the tropics he had terrorized for so long. Drake died at sea of dysentery—an ignominious end for a swashbuckling pirate—on January 28, 1596. Fittingly, his crew sealed their captain's remains—dressed in full armor—in a lead coffin and committed them to the depths of the Caribbean, whose waters and shores his memory still haunts today. His body has never been discovered.

Throughout his life, Drake's exploits at sea were defined by his personal physical courage. Whether raiding around the Caribbean, risking the wrath of the more powerful Spanish viceroys; personally leading the second attack on the fort at Cartagena; or aggressively engaging the Spanish Armada, Drake never hesitated to put himself out in front and on the line. While Drake's personal leadership did not ensure the success of all his exploits, it was always the foundation of the fear and respect he inspired in his crews, victims, and enemies alike.

As Drake's life demonstrates, courage is a powerful asset of character, but also one that can tempt a leader into trouble. Ferdinand Magellan was hardly less brave, yet his luck did not hold out as Drake's did, allowing the latter to claim the title of first known global circumnavigator. At many points, Drake's luck could just as easily have run out—especially when his near-reckless courage put him in a tactically unsound position in the first place. Good leaders know that all the courage in the world can be undone by a bad stroke of luck, or misplaced planning—and they measure their courage. "Live to fight another day" is a good mantra in most settings, and Drake was able to balance his courage and his luck—a good lesson in character.

Even though most leaders today will probably never need to demonstrate physical courage in the ways that Drake did throughout his life, there are many less-swashbuckling ways to exercise courageous leadership. First and foremost among these is moral courage, whether in making a big strategic decision or taking a stand for a deserving person or cause. And like many other qualities of character, courage is a habit that can be developed over time. In the physical sense, there are both psychological and physiological ways to improve performance under stress. Hemingway said that "courage is grace under pressure," which has been more prosaically rendered as "never let them see you sweat." Simply taking deep breaths, reflecting on calming settings, telling yourself that you are in control, stretching, speaking in a slow and measured way, and avoiding raising your voice are all physical ways to calm yourself. Another good psychological technique is simply keeping a sense of perspective on whatever you perceive as danger ahead. In all but the direst of circumstances, there is a way to make the situation safer—by concentrating on that, instead of allowing panic to dominate your mind, you have the best chance of reacting with courage as danger threatens.

The first time I faced real danger in a combat setting was in the mid-1980s as the operations officer and tactical action officer in the Aegis cruiser USS *Valley Forge*. We were operating in and out of the Strait of Hormuz during the so-called tanker war between Iran and Iraq. We would often go to "general quarters" (all hands at their battle stations, four hundred men at tense alert throughout the ten-thousand-ton warship) as we sailed under the range of Iranian missiles and Iraqi attack jets flew overhead. This was about the time that the USS *Stark*, a US Navy *Oliver Hazard Perry*–class frigate sailing in these waters, was attacked by an Iraqi jet and nearly sunk. These periods of "general quarters" began with harsh announcements on the ship's loud sirens ("General quarters, general quarters, all hands man your battle stations") and would stretch into long hours, broken only by the mess stewards bringing us soup and sandwiches on station. The tension was palpable, and many of the younger sailors were unsettled by the possibility of an actual attack.

Even as a mid-grade officer and a department head (essentially third in command as the operations officer) on the ship, I was scared, nervous that I would make a crucial mistake (I had control over the ship's weapons system), and above all, I desperately wanted to avoid showing my men my own fear. Fortunately, my vastly more experienced captain (later rear admiral), Ted Lockhart, was able to do all the things I discussed above, plus he had one other endearing habit: he would bring exotic snacks to the Combat Information Center to share during periods of combat alert—everything from French truffle pâté to caviar and smoked oysters. His sangfroid had a wonderful calming effect on us all, to say nothing of the excellent nibbles. Not everyone has the battle experience and bold personality of a Sir Francis Drake (fortunately), but building the habit of courage—no matter the venue—is within everyone's reach and is part of the voyage of character.

Drake's management style would have made Darth Vader proud. He ran his crews ragged in search of perfection and quite literally left a trail of bodies behind, having executed scores of his followers for desertion and cowardice. He cultivated loyalty by Machiavellian games designed to keep his crews divided against one another and dependent on him. As with his personal drive, Drake's harsh disciplinary methods are badly out of line with today's mores—but they got results. Still, even if we grant that times have changed, Drake's leadership style forces us to confront the extremely uncomfortable question of whether the ends justify the means. In commenting on his discipline, it is necessary to understand the context of his life and times. He was surely not "to the manor born"; he faced enormously difficult physical tasks and was in essentially constant extreme physical danger. Only by understanding those facets of his situation are we able to contextualize and possibly justify his draconian methods. So, adjusting for those factors, what can we learn about character from Sir Francis?

What is most important to remember about Drake's character in this regard is that he imposed harsh standards of discipline because he was an internally disciplined leader himself. The character lesson, when you strip the centuries-old setting away, is that only a leader who is personally disciplined herself or himself can realistically apply significant discipline to an organization. Nothing succeeds less than an undisciplined leader attempting to apply standards that he or she cannot meet—this evident hypocrisy always fails. It is worth noting that naval history is rife with examples of brutally harsh admirals like Drake; but it also offers inspiring examples of leaders who successfully faced enormous tasks and extreme danger without resorting to the sort of techniques Drake employed throughout his career. (Drake's countryman Horatio Nelson offers a particularly strong example.) Especially today, when so much *has* changed in life and work, it is essential for leaders to have the self-discipline to build and maintain healthier team dynamics than Drake did.

In the course of my career, I have seen many Francis Drakes in the ranks of the Admiralty in the sense of overdriving their subordinates. Very, very rarely have I encountered someone who has the self-discipline to impose sufficient internal discipline so that their own level of intensity is matched by their team. In one example, this led to a two-star admiral ultimately being fired; yet I judged he was no harder on his sailors than he was on himself. Today's gentler world increasingly does not permit the kind of harsh imposition of maximum discipline on the team, and we are better for it.

So as we examine the role of both discipline and self-discipline in character, we see that the ability to effectively incorporate a regime of discipline in an organization begins—as do so many things—within ourselves. Our level of self-discipline—all things in moderation, nothing in excess, a calm demeanor, a strong work ethic—is the enabler that permits effective discipline throughout any organization.

As with many leaders, the outlines of Drake's later successes were not always apparent in his early exploits. Most of those, frankly, resulted in failure or near-failure: he abandoned his cousin, narrowly evaded the Spanish, and even struggled to turn profits in his early days as a pirate. It was hardly an auspicious beginning. Despite these failures, Drake did what great leaders do: he kept going, and—most important—he kept learning. Soon after striking out on his own, he realized that weakness and waffling were likely to be hazardous to a pirate's health and fortunes; though he probably overlearned that particular lesson, he soon reinvented himself as an extraordinarily disciplined and decisive leader.

All leaders must keep learning and growing throughout their lives and careers, and many—including many of the most successful—learn most through struggle and failure. Had Drake not found a style that allowed him to become a successful pirate, he might never have succeeded in his round-the-world voyage, which required still-greater discipline. This is an important lesson not only for individuals but also for organizations. Knowing that even the best people make mistakes, the best organizations find ways to help competent people learn and improve from failures.

This was particularly true for me on my very first ship, USS

Hewitt. I was never a good natural ship handler. The first few times I attempted to drive the ship in a complex formation, I nearly managed to collide with a fellow destroyer, and as a joke, the next time I took the conn the watch team of a dozen sailors came to the ship's bridge wearing life jackets. This hardly improved my self-confidence. But I persevered by a combination of watching other, better, ship handlers; studying the classic books of the trade (several of which I later edited); and learning that in the end, so much of driving a ship is a combination of basic confidence and what is essentially eye-mind coordination—you have to watch the hull moving and constantly adjust your steering and motor commands. Driving a car is eye-hand coordination; driving a ship is eye-mind: two very different things. It took me the better part of three years, but by the end of my first tour, I was nominated by our commodore for the top ship handler in the Pacific Fleet, beating out nominees from a half dozen other destroyers—I didn't win it, but at least nobody was wearing a life jacket when I took the conn of the ship. Perseverance saved me, and it is a habit of character that can be developed as we sail along in life.

In modern terms, Drake was a master of successful personal branding—and his brand was at heart one of ruthless boldness. In his mind (and in the view of the English leadership and public), looting Spanish outposts and Catholic churches were not the acts of a simple brigand, but of a patriot striking bold blows for queen and country. As he grew wealthier, he also cultivated a story of historical connections to the nobility. Always quick with a bon mot and a good story and never overburdened by strict adherence to the truth, he bragged that his raid on Cádiz had "singed the King of Spain's beard" and consistently maintained a reputation that far outstripped the reality of his accomplishments. Through what we would call "strategic communications" today, Drake sold himself as a bold sea warrior in everything he did.

What made Drake successful in establishing his brand of boldness was a sustained pattern of seizing the initiative—"Fortune favors the bold" as the saying goes. He matched deeds to his words more often than not, although there was certainly an element of embellishment throughout. However, the great yarn of Drake's life continued to spin even after his death, and—largely truthful in terms of his character—continued as well to inspire future generations of British seafarers. Centuries later, the great maritime strategist Julian Corbett wrote one of the most popular biographies of the first great English admiral; today, Drake's beard-singeing comment has its own Wikipedia page. Boldness has many salutary qualities, especially when linked to a compelling strategic narrative that inspires others.

Oddly, I have found today's military far less bold than the public at large might think. As a newly selected one-star admiral in the days immediately after 9/11, I was charged with running a tactical and strategic think tank called Deep Blue, an homage to IBM's big computer and to the ocean itself. The Pentagon still smelled of smoke, and we were all desperate to get the Navy into the new fight. I was specifically chartered to develop "bold new ideas" for the Navy in the recently-named Global War on Terror. We came up with lots of ideas: a new structure for the old blue-water battle groups that made them more lethal in the littorals striking terror groups ashore; forward afloat staging bases at sea for special forces;

increased rotation of ship hulls into the emerging combat zones; and many others. We thought they were bold, but many in the Admiralty thought them crazy. The chief of naval operations supported us, and our ideas went forward—some were better than others. But what I learned was the built-in tendency of the very hierarchical Navy to push back on the new and the bold.

As always in life, a character trait like boldness can simultaneously be your greatest strength *and* your greatest weakness. The trick is using it to inspire others, challenge your assumptions, and move with alacrity when it makes sense. In this regard, I am in awe of the Navy SEAL community. Contrary to the public's view of them as a "let's just wing it" culture, they are, by far, the most meticulous planners in the military. What they do so effectively is couple pure operational brilliance with deep planning—and cap it with a bold approach. That is the kind of boldness that most often wins in the most dangerous of settings: a bold approach aligned with thoughtful analysis. Left untethered, as Drake's boldness sometimes seemed to be, this is a character trait that can do more harm than good. Finding the balance is the key to employing boldness as a good quality of character.

So, what is the legacy of character of that pirate, knight, leader, and adventurer Sir Francis Drake? Many victories in combat, national accolades and honors, great wealth at times, and a fierce reputation as a courageous warrior are all part of his memory. But there is a dark and sinister aura that haunts his legacy, and always will—the needless cruelty, the burning of cities and the killing of civilians, the harsh treatment of his own sailors who cowered before him. Though there is much to admire about Drake, in the end the lessons of character we take away from him are principally of the things we should simply avoid doing. Sometimes the best lessons we can study are indeed those we should not repeat: that is the case with Sir Francis Drake. Not the legacy to be wished, and of all the admirals in this volume he would be the least admirable, pun intended.

CHAPTER IV

The Band of Brothers

Vice Admiral Lord Viscount Horatio Nelson

———

Born September 29, 1758, Burnham Thorpe, United Kingdom

Died October 21, 1805, Cape Trafalgar, aboard HMS *Victory*

The worst night I ever spent at sea as a ship's captain was, ironically, close to land. It was in the so-called chops of the channel, the western sea approaches to the United Kingdom near the mouth of the English Channel, in the summer of 1993. Visibility was almost nonexistent in a whipping gale, and my ship—a nine-thousand-ton destroyer, hardly a small vessel—was seriously battered as we crashed into the wind and seas. I spent most of the night on the bridge of the ship, anxiously scanning the horizon and holding on for dear life while most of my crew were violently seasick. It was a hard, hard night.

I was a young sea captain in my late thirties in command at sea for the first time of the USS *Barry*, a brand-new *Arleigh Burke*–class guided missile destroyer on its maiden cruise. We had left our home port of Norfolk, Virginia, late that spring, and were headed for a much-anticipated first overseas port call in Portsmouth, England. I was very excited to be pulling into Portsmouth, because it would afford me my first opportunity to tour HMS *Victory*, the flagship of my idol and hero, Royal Navy Vice Admiral Lord Viscount Horatio Nelson. Throughout the long night of hammering storms in the channel, I consoled myself with the thought that soon I'd be walking on the decks of the oldest commissioned warship in the British navy, which served as Nelson's flagship at the scene of his greatest triumph at Trafalgar. It was also the scene of his untimely death in combat, and thus especially sacred ground to the Royal Navy.

I idolized Nelson for several reasons, starting with the fact that he was a man of very normal height—about five-feet-five or so, which coincidentally is my height. More important, I deeply admired his understated style of leadership, especially with his subordinate sea captains; his true compassion and concern for his enlisted crews; and his deep, instinctive love of country. Naturally, I was well aware of some of his personal flaws and failings, including an adulterous affair with Lady Emma Hamilton and a well-honed love of publicity. But on balance, his was a character and style of leadership that appealed to me deeply, and almost immediately after we finally made it to Portsmouth, having recovered from our rough approach, I literally bounded across the ancient dockyard and up the gangplank of *Victory* to pay my respects.

Over subsequent decades, I returned to *Victory* many times and was privileged when I was a four-star admiral myself to be guest of honor at dinners held in Nelson's shipboard cabin. On one of those occasions, my host—Britain's first sea lord, the equivalent of our chief of naval operations and the overall commander of the British navy—presented me with a beautiful pen stand made from wood taken from HMS *Victory*. In that pen stand today I keep a fountain pen made from the timbers of the US equivalent of *Victory*, our own beautiful nineteenth-century (and still commissioned) warship *Constitution*. These two ships, paired up so naturally in the American pen and the British pen stand, represent to me the deep, abiding, and indeed special relationship between our nations.

But above all, to know and study Lord Nelson is to sail into big and important questions about character, personality, and leadership. And doing so affords the chance to learn and improve how we navigate our own voyage of character. On the shelves of my library today are nearly a dozen biographies of the admiral, and each of them provides a different insight or two into a unique, powerful, and historic figure. I am immeasurably grateful to him for his example in so many ways. So, who was he and what can we learn from him?

Born weak and sickly, Horatio Nelson was hardly a giant among men: as I mentioned above, he stood at most five and a half feet in his stockings. Slight of build, and eventually missing both an arm and an eye lost in combat, he was also afflicted with seasickness and other illnesses on and off throughout his life. An adulterer and a rebellious subordinate in a navy that prized loyalty above all things, he hardly seems to the modern observer to be the type of leader who would be remembered two centuries after his death in battle. But his "immortal memory" (to which Royal Navy sailors offer a toast each year) is exactly that, and most naval officers of any nation would immediately name him as among the very best sea warriors in history.

He was born in 1758 to a modestly prosperous family in Norfolk,

East Anglia, and sponsored into the navy at the age of thirteen, following the traditional course of on-the-job training as a very young midshipman. Nelson rapidly ascended the Royal Navy's ranks, and by 1778 was in command of his first ship. He fought well in the battles of the American Revolution and began to develop a service-wide reputation for both personal bravery and tactical acumen. As a young midshipman, he was always small for his age, and suffered the usual abuses of the system; however, his native intelligence and leadership gifts began to emerge early, even in the midshipman's berth. He was acknowledged as a fine seaman (the sine qua non of the British maritime hierarchy) and "learned the ropes" with great rapidity.

Nelson also started to formulate the philosophical approach that would ultimately make him an international success: building coherent, seamless teams of subordinates bound together by competence and loyalty to him as a peerless commander. As he would famously write from the decks of HMS *Victory* to each of his captains before the Battle of Trafalgar, ". . . in case Signals [flag hoists used to signal friendly ships about their orders] can neither be seen or perfectly understood, no Captain can do very wrong if he places his Ship alongside that of an Enemy." He had the luxury of writing in such a spirit of independence because he knew intimately the quality of the officers under his command and had trained and bonded them together personally. Ironically, that signal—almost as famous as the one he would craft calling on every man to do his duty—implies a premium on independent action. While Nelson favored such independence, his greatest gift was building teams, the "band of brothers" in the term coined by Shakespeare in *Henry V.*

No British commander in history is more respected for pure leadership than Nelson.

After the American Revolution, like many of his brother officers, he was sent ashore and languished there until the outbreak of the Napoleonic Wars at the end of the eighteenth century. He returned to sea and fought in a series of minor battles against the French revolutionary navy, continuing to burnish his reputation. By 1797, he ascended to command of the major warship HMS *Captain*, and fought in a major battle at Cape St. Vincent under the command of Admiral Sir John (later Lord) Jervis, who became a strong patron and personal supporter. Throughout this period, he not only consistently demonstrated the skills of seamanship and war fighting that defined his professional reputation, but also displayed a skilled ability to find and impress mentors like Jervis. No British admiral could rise to the heights of command without skill both bureaucratically ashore as well as at sea.

During the Battle of Cape St. Vincent, another part of the Nelson legend was cemented in history when he chose not to precisely follow the signaled orders from Admiral Jervis but used his own initiative to do what he knew was tactically most optimal. He said later, "The Admiral [Jervis] made the signal to 'tack in succession'; but I, perceiving the Spanish Ships all to bear up before the wind, or nearly so, evidently with the intention of forming their line going large, joining their separated Division, at that time engaged with some of our centre [*sic*] Ships, or flying from us—to prevent either of their schemes from taking effect, I ordered the ship to be wore." Translation—Nelson ordered his ships to sail in essentially the opposite direction from what the admiral in command decreed, taking full initiative (and responsibility) into his own hands. While this was blatant disobedience of an order, Jervis later publicly praised Nelson for his initiative. Nelson followed that same pattern of doing what he thought was right, not blindly obeying orders, throughout his career. He managed to balance that spirit of independence nicely with an ability to keep the chain of command well informed about not only his operational plans, but his successes as well. Nelson was certainly not without a certain thirst for glory, and that trait manifested itself throughout much of the latter part of his career.

Another incident at the Battle of Cape St. Vincent involved then Captain Cuthbert Collingwood, a follower of Nelson's who would go on to become an admiral himself and was to lead the lee line of the British fleet at the Battle of Trafalgar alongside Nelson. During the earlier battle, Collingwood helped Nelson by directing his ship, HMS *Excellent*, to support Nelson's command, HMS *Captain*. After the battle, Nelson wrote Collingwood, saying, "A friend in need is a friend indeed, was never more truly verified than by your most noble and gallant conduct yesterday in sparing the *Captain* from further loss." Their careers were much intertwined over the next decade, and Collingwood was eventually buried near Nelson at St. Paul's Cathedral in London. Nelson, for all his self-publicizing style, managed to form and maintain close relationships with his peers—so often the most critical of judges for anyone in a relentlessly hierarchical organization like the Royal Navy, where everyone is jockeying for their turn at the brass ring.

Geopolitically, Nelson was fortunate to live in a period in which the British nation depended heavily on the "wooden walls" of the

Royal Navy. Had Napoleon's France not risen from the confusion of its bloody revolution to become a serious threat to Britain's independence, Nelson probably would have spent much of his life on half pay hoping for a return to sea that might never have occurred. Given the rise of the threat to Britain, Nelson's career timing was as impeccable in terms of his planning as it was lucky in terms of timing—like most successful admirals, he needed both a war to prosecute and a nation to defend at the time in his career when his skills, connections, and savvy were at their peak. In that regard, all seemed to be on track for a relatively young Rear Admiral Nelson— until the wheel of fate spun significantly against him for the first time in his life. It was a personification of something he said later, which is that "in war, much is left to Providence."

The next major battle in his career was devastating, as Nelson lost most of his right arm at Santa Cruz de Tenerife and was sent ashore for a significant period to recover. Some of his despairing letters and journal entries from this period are heartrending, bespeaking a deep depression as he contemplated the potential end of his career. His scratchy script as he painstakingly worked to learn to write left-handed is painful to read, and many biographers talk about this period as the darkest of his career. Yet within a year he was back at sea, again as a rear admiral, and in command of a significant Mediterranean force that pressed the French fleet around the Med and ultimately forced a disastrous defeat on French forces in the Battle of the Nile at Aboukir Bay in August 1798, ending Napoleon's geopolitical ambitions outside of Europe. The Battle of the Nile cemented Nelson's place at the upper reaches of the British Admiralty and marked him for future high command. It also opened the doors of British society at the highest levels to the diminutive and somewhat battered admiral, who took every advantage he could.

It also marked the beginning of the love affair with the young, beautiful Lady Emma Hamilton, which did much to define the personal side of his life. More than twenty years his junior, she nursed him back to health after the Battle of the Nile, and their love affair—hardly a secret in British society—continued for the rest of his life. While they carried on a platonic ménage à trois with Sir William Hamilton, an elder British peer, Nelson fathered two daughters with Emma—one of whom lived to adulthood. After Sir William died in 1803, Nelson intended to marry Emma, but could never obtain a divorce from his loyal wife. This scandal was well known and should have been damaging to Nelson's reputation, but the public was willing to overlook or ignore it, so long as the nautical hero continued to deliver the big victories.

Despite his personal peccadillos, Nelson's reputation professionally was assured by the Battle of the Nile. He then fought another major fleet engagement at Copenhagen in 1801, where he famously deliberately pressed a telescope to the eye that had been blinded earlier in his career, thereby ignoring the signals of his superior, and ended up winning an important victory over the Danes. The phrase "turning a blind eye" was reportedly inspired by the incident. In the Battle of Copenhagen, he is also reported to have said, "It is warm work [British naval expression for heavy combat] and this day may be the last to any of us at a moment; but mark you, I would not be elsewhere for thousands [of pounds]." Nelson's personal physical courage was a fundamental part of his character and was much remarked upon throughout his career. His victory at Copenhagen led directly to his next promotion, and the level of public acclaim increased as well.

Promoted to vice admiral, Nelson took command of the crucial Mediterranean squadron with the key mission of forcing the combined French-Spanish fleet to battle. After chasing them to the West Indies (today's Caribbean) and back, he settled in for a lengthy blockade off the Spanish coast, not far from the Atlantic port of Cádiz. He knew the criticality of a crushing victory, correctly assessing that until the Franco-Spanish fleet was destroyed, Napoleon would continue to dream of an invasion of Britain. To George Rose, a political friend, he wrote, "It is . . . annihilation that the Country wants, and not merely a splendid Victory . . . honourable to the parties concerned, but absolutely useless in the extended scale to bring Buonaparte to his marrow-bones."

In 1805, the French-Spanish fleet finally emerged to fight, and at the Battle of Trafalgar, Nelson sent his most famous signal: "England expects that every man will do his duty." And they did, winning a spectacular victory at sea. The victory was indeed a near-total annihilation of the French-Spanish fleets and ended any chance Napoleon had of invading the United Kingdom. But Nelson was killed by a sniper's bullet smashing through his spine. The last signal he sent just before the battle was joined was pure Nelson: "Engage the Enemy More Closely." The French and Spanish lost twenty-two ships, the British a single ship. It was among the most lopsided naval engagements in history, and certainly at the top of the list for geopolitical impact within the era.

While he lived long enough to know of his victory, he died soon after in agony below decks in *Victory*, surrounded by his sailors and with his loyal flag captain, Thomas Hardy, by his side. His final words, "Thank God I have done my duty," continue to echo across the centuries. Upon arriving in England, his body was borne in honor through the streets of London, and he was accorded a state funeral, an extreme rarity for a serving military commander. Monuments to his memory dot the English countryside, and in the center of London Nelson's Column dominates Trafalgar Square.

Reflecting on the lessons of character and leadership in the life of Vice Admiral Lord Nelson offers examples of gratifying success and deep personal failure. In terms of successful lessons, Nelson managed throughout his life to devote himself to the higher purpose of serving king and country. Again, and again, he built highly cohesive teams of subordinates united in common cause with high morale, paid particular attention to the needs of his subordinates (during a period when this was extremely rare), and used simple and direct tactical approaches in combat with significant success. His failures were in the personal dimension, and included flagrant adultery, betraying a faithful and devoted wife; an arrogant certainty about his superiority when compared with his contemporaries and his seniors; a complex insecurity that delighted in and aggressively sought the highest level of public recognition; and a willfulness that led him to counterproductive behavior on a variety of occasions.

There is no doubt that Nelson was truly and deeply devoted to his nation. Throughout both his writings and his reported speeches, he spoke constantly about the need for leaders to set an appropriate example of patriotism and zeal in defense of their king and country. His famous signal, "England expects that every man will do his duty," is endlessly repeated in British popular culture and official Royal Navy pronouncements. He personified the desire that many people of character have to be part of something larger than themselves, something into which they can fully invest themselves. There is an apocryphal story that when asked one freezing night if he wanted the boatswain to send below for a cloak, he was said to have replied that his zeal for king and country kept him warm. Nautical historian and novelist Patrick O'Brian's brilliant twenty-volume treatment of a fictional naval officer of the period is centered on Captain Jack Aubrey, who idolizes Nelson. In it, he has Aubrey tell this story of Nelson's rejecting the cloak, and Aubrey admits that from anyone else it would sound ridiculous, but from Nelson it just seemed to fit with his persona.

This sense of ironclad duty was a fundamental part of his self-identity and was inculcated in his personality from his earliest days in the English countryside. As we seek to reconcile the challenges of modern life—from balancing the needs of family with the role we play in our nation's destiny at any level—we can look to Nelson as an exemplar of positive patriotism and belief in the nation. This is the bedrock of character in many ways—a belief in something bigger than any individual—and it is clear in the life of Lord Nelson. He addressed this very simply, saying in a letter, "Duty is the great business of a Sea Officer. All private considerations must give way to it, however Painful it is," and "Our Country has the first demand for our services; and private convenience, or happiness, must ever give way to the Public Good." Throughout his life and career, he never wavered from this belief as the centerpiece of his character; and it is worth remembering that he was deployed at sea, away from hearth and home, throughout the majority of his adult life. He lived a life of devotion to his nation.

For each of us individually, we must learn this lesson along the voyage to character. Love of country—despite the manifest flaws and mistakes we often make as a nation—is a quality that leads to service to others and improves the society lucky enough to develop true patriots. Our national values are the right ones: liberty, democracy, freedom of speech, freedom of education, gender equality, racial equality—we execute them imperfectly to be sure, but they are the right aspirational values to hold. Patriotism, not blind to faults but believing overall in the nation, is a powerful element of character. It can lead to the kinds of acts of heroism that represent the very best that is in each of us, as when a soldier dies in combat or a Peace Corps volunteer is injured serving the nation. And we should remember that at times, patriotism drives acts of protest—like African American football players taking a knee to try to improve racial justice in our nation—that can mystify and frustrate many. But however we judge any specific act of service or protest, we should recognize that patriotism is a powerful force within the best of us that implores each of us to stand up for the country, love it for all our challenges, and work together to improve it.

Beyond his devotion to the nation, Nelson was a master of leadership and character in assembling the right collection of subordinates and motivating them to pull together as an effective squad—from a handful of sailors manning a gun when he was a young midshipman to the legendary "band of brothers" he created among his ship captains when he was a fleet commander. He was able to do this because he applied his already high level of emotional intelligence to sense the individual strengths, weaknesses, and needs of each team member. A good example of this was his melding and motivating his individual ship commanders in the days leading up to the Battle of the Nile, where he focused his captains on working together effectively while also being able to act independently. This type of team-building approach—fanatically adopted by twenty-first-century organizations as diverse as US Navy SEALs and the corporate giant Google—is at the heart of both Nelson's character and leadership skills.

Thinking about teamwork in the context of character is important. This holds true in two very important dimensions: with our peers and with our subordinates. So often in our zeal to impress our seniors and to rally our subordinates, we do not pay enough attention to our peers. And truth be told, we are often competing with our peers for a promotion, a raise, or a better slice of the organization's resources. Far too frequently, we do not build strong teams among our peers. Nelson understood this, and it is a powerful lesson of character that often we can accomplish so much more if we are willing not to take total and personal credit for it. This means being transparent with peers, organizing gatherings where peers can interact both professionally and personally, and above all helping one another in times of trouble.

The second element of teamwork is building teams among our subordinates. This is done first through demonstrating teamwork at the senior level. When I was a commander of a US Navy destroyer, I would often organize gatherings of my fellow sea captains on the waterfront, if only to have a beer and compare notes. Our subordinates watched this and over time took a similar approach. Commanders can also frequently talk about how important teamwork is for an organization and give substantive rewards—in evaluations, monetary bonuses, or promotions—to those who are using teamwork effectively. Finally, the use of team analysis can be very powerful—prebriefing big events, then debriefing afterward in group sessions with everyone free to applaud or criticize. Building teams is hard work, but again and again we see powerful benefits from doing so. No one of us is as smart as all of us thinking together.

Closely related to this quality of team building was Nelson's strong sense that one of his key tasks was taking care of his team. In an era when most captains and admirals relied on brutal discipline and didn't particularly worry about the needs of their crews in terms of provisions or medical care, Nelson was famous for ensuring that his sailors received the best possible treatment. He worked hard to make sure that food was fresh, water plentiful and unpolluted, and each ship had a competent surgeon. His crews (and his captains) returned his care by idolizing him personally, and his method of caring for his teams became known throughout the fleet as the "Nelson touch." This kind of care and concern are of utmost importance to leaders today, especially as the idea of "servant leadership" has evolved over the past several decades. For example, when one of his captains died in battle, Nelson said, "I am full of grief for the fate of poor Parker; our only consolation is, that everything has been done which was possible: the breath is not yet gone; but, I dare say, he cannot last until night." After

Edward Parker's death, Nelson paid for his funeral and helped his widow.

For each of us, learning the lesson of true compassion toward our subordinates is crucial. Today it is fashionable to speak of servant leadership, and many very senior people espouse this philosophy. But far less often do we see the most senior leaders do tangible things that are of benefit to their subordinate colleagues. This comes at a cost for organizations—in everything from the quality of food in the company cafeteria to salary, bonuses, maternity leave, and vacation days. In the long run this kind of approach provides real benefits that accrue in successful accomplishments.

Finally, we see in Nelson a highly competent and increasingly experienced war-fighting commander who is unafraid to evolve his own personal tactical approach. He became famous for encouraging initiative in his subordinates, and developed a system of tight, simple signals (most communications in that era were conducted by flag hoist) that could be easily controlled from the quarterdeck of his flagship. Nelson's tactics at the Battle of the Nile, the Battle of Copenhagen, and above all Trafalgar are still studied, debated, and imitated in fleets around the world.

Simplifying command and control, whether running a business unit at Amazon or a university economics department, is a crucial attribute for effective twenty-first-century leaders. As Nelson said to a subordinate about the need to make the right tactical decisions instead of blindly following a senior's orders at the Battle of Copenhagen, "Do you know what's shown on board of the Commander in Chief? Why to leave off Action! Now damn me if I do. You know Foley, I have only one eye—I have a right to be blind sometimes. [He then placed his telescope to his blind eye.] I really do not see the signal." His actions ultimately led to victory.

But there were darker angels at work in the character of Nelson. On the negative end of the spectrum of Nelson's character, most analysts would begin with his betrayal of his marriage vows and his highly public and deeply hurtful affair with Emma Hamilton. As both an adulterer in his own marriage and a contributor to the instability of the Hamilton marriage, he failed to maintain basic moral principles. While it did not destroy his career, it is difficult to predict how his nation would have looked upon him over time had the apotheosis of Nelson not occurred through his heroic death in an epic naval battle. The lesson here for anyone, of course, is to be true not only to marriage vows, but to the promises we make in life.

Temptations abound for us all, and Nelson failed in one of the most basic character tests most of us face—fidelity to a spouse. That is not to say he was truly evil or even deeply flawed, but rather that he was human and vulnerable. The lesson for us all is that we must try to live up to the commitments we make, recognizing the challenges in doing so and the price for failing in them. And it also tells us something about the possibility of redemption and the need to balance what we accomplish in our public lives and careers alongside the personal choices we make and the outcomes that ensue.

Additionally, it is hard to admire Nelson in terms of his elevated view of himself, which probably resulted more from childhood insecurities than from a real sense of superiority. He was quite candid about this need within himself, saying in a letter to a mentor, Admiral Jervis, "If it be a sin to covet glory, I am the most offending soul alive." While it's difficult to judge this fully from the perspective of more than two centuries, it seems reasonably clear that Nelson sought to place himself at the center of events, pursued the limelight to an excessive degree (especially given the temper of the times), found almost childish delight in even the most trivial of recognitions, and generally placed an excessively high value on the opinions of others. In an ideal world, his personality would have benefited greatly from a higher degree of modesty and a more relaxed approach to the world's view of him—a good lesson for us all.

Tied to this was a powerful sense of personal ambition. He felt he was destined for greatness, talked about it often, and at one point wrote, "In short, I wish to be an admiral, and in the command of the English Fleet; I should very soon either do much, or be ruined. My disposition cannot bear tame and slow measures." This kind of ambition is so often highly destructive for many individuals. In Nelson, fortunately, it was not only matched with genuine brilliance as a naval officer and combat leader, but also coupled to a sincere and heartfelt sense of patriotism. His ambition, while strong, was grounded in a desire to do well for his nation, even as he found a path to personal glory. Not a bad bargain for England in the end.

All quotations are taken from Joseph F. Callo, *Nelson Speaks: Admiral Lord Nelson in His Own Words* (Annapolis, MD: US Naval Institute Press, 2001).

CHAPTER V

The Influencer

Rear Admiral Alfred Thayer Mahan

———

BORN SEPTEMBER 27, 1840, WEST POINT, NEW YORK

DIED DECEMBER 1, 1914, WASHINGTON, DC

My curious relationship with Rear Admiral Alfred Thayer Mahan began in 1972, when, as a first-year midshipman, along with 1,200 of my new best friends, I was herded into Mahan Hall at the US Naval Academy to hear a lecture on sea power as part of our class's indoctrination into the Navy. At the time, I noticed a portrait of the grizzled, bald, mustachioed admiral in the foyer of the building. Despite the nineteenth-century naval uniform, he certainly looked every inch like what he was: an intellectual. The Russian writer Isaac Babel said that an intellectual was a man with spectacles on his nose and autumn in his heart. That would, in many ways, sum up Mahan, whom we would call today a "public intellectual" or perhaps a "defense wonk."

He was first and foremost a historian and a scholar. While he accomplished the minimum number of modestly successful seagoing assignments to continue to be promoted, his heart was almost entirely on the intellectual side of the Navy. His classic books about sea power, history, and geopolitics helped shape the course of his country's emergence as a global power, and Mahan's work in the early days of the US Naval Institute—the professional organization of the US Navy, Marine Corps, Coast Guard, and Merchant Marine—resonates today. In the end, Mahan's most important command was not a ship but the Naval War College; his work there continues to help chart a geostrategic course for America more than a century after his departure.

Over the next four years as a midshipman studying both engineering and English, I learned a lot more about Mahan and returned many times to Mahan Hall for lectures, performances, and debates. I started to develop my own belief that part of being a professional naval officer included an obligation to read, think, write, and—eventually—publish. Throughout my time at Annapolis, I would often sit down to write a column for the alumni magazine, *Shipmate*; an essay for the Academy's monthly literary magazine, *The Log*; or a short piece for *Proceedings*, the magazine of record for the sea services published by the Naval Institute that Mahan helped to shape early on. My classmates thought it strange that I would want to write and publish, but I firmly believed then and continue to believe now that it is through being part of a larger conversation in a profession that we can best advance the interests of our community. Mahan was the beginning of all that for me.

Today I have the honor of serving as the chairman of the board of the US Naval Institute. In my office in Beach Hall, the Institute's headquarters on the grounds of the Naval Academy, I have a sweeping view of the Severn River and the small cemetery of the Academy. Mahan is not buried there, but his spirit sails on through those gravestones, so many of them marking the final resting place of such great admirals of US naval history as Ernest King, Arleigh Burke, and James Stockdale. All of them spent more time at sea than Mahan and were vastly more distinguished in the handling of ships and sailors, but none of them can surpass Mahan in contributions—both practical and theoretical—to the profession of naval service.

One of the most prized items in my office at Annapolis is the logbook that was the original "proceedings" of the US Naval Institute, including the minutes of the founding meeting of eight officers in Newport, Rhode Island, in 1886. It is written in a spidery hand, but the names and signatures are clear—including that of Commander Alfred Thayer Mahan. He would be proud, I think, to know how the Institute has grown; today it counts more than fifty thousand members—officer, enlisted, and civilian—convenes conferences on the big defense issues of our day; publishes more than eighty titles annually; maintains a superb library with more than 400,000 images, hundreds of oral histories, and thousands of books; and features a staff of dedicated professionals who carry on Admiral Mahan's legacy every day.

My relationship with Mahan endures to this day. Over the course of four decades, I have written for the *Proceedings* magazine at every stage of my career and authored or coauthored five books with the Naval Institute Press. All of that began for me—and for many others—with Alfred Thayer Mahan. In an early fitness report, Mahan was infamously slammed with the admonition, "it is not the business of naval officers to write books." Count me grateful that he was undeterred: we are all richer for his continued writing—as a Navy, as a profession, and as a nation.

What do we know about him? Mahan was an unassuming man who sported either a mustache or a tidy goatee and a withering stare. He was a scholar, and perhaps above all a teacher, but he was certainly *not* an accomplished sailor. His nautical career progress was uneven, to put it charitably. A good example is when Mahan was assigned to the new Naval War College in Newport, Rhode Island, in 1885. Mahan's mentor, Rear Admiral Stephen B. Luce, had founded the college almost by force of will at the old torpedo school in Newport in 1884. Luce was driven by the idea that the principles of naval warfare could and should be found out by study and elevated to the level of a science, as (land-based) military science had been over the preceding century. In October 1885, he secured Mahan's appointment to the college as a lecturer in naval tactics and sea power. With the college's first academic year already underway and Mahan needing some time to prepare his lecture materials, he successfully lobbied Luce to let him live in New York with his family for ten months until the next class began in the fall of 1886. "I wish," Mahan had written to Luce, "to place myself where I can find the best material for my intended book" on sea power. Luce agreed, and let Mahan stay in New York, where he did nothing but read, think, and write over nearly a year—a great rarity in a supposedly seagoing officer's life.

Mahan's time in New York violated all the normal routines and responsibilities of naval life. There were no uniforms, no time aboard ship, no squalls at sea, no unruly sailors to discipline, and certainly no battles to be fought: just the long months of reading and writing. It was an interlude that perfectly illuminated the unique liberties this scholar-masquerading-as-sailor was permitted. Far from wanting to sail ships to war, he wanted to reshape the way the United States viewed the world, and show how the relatively new nation could best secure its strategic future. He said, "How to view the lessons of the past so as to mold them into lessons for the future, is the nut I have to crack." Mahan intended nothing less than "to raise the [naval] profession in the eyes of its members by a clearer comprehension of the great part it has played in the world."

He did all this, in large measure, by studying the past and then intensively and creatively applying the lessons of history to the unruly present. His 1890 masterpiece, *The Influence of Sea Power upon History, 1660–1783*, reshaped global geopolitics. Mahan's work deeply influenced future president Theodore Roosevelt; indeed, it laid the intellectual foundation upon which Roosevelt would build the modern US Navy and carve out a far larger role for the United States in the world. All of this evolved as a result of the tumultuous geopolitics of the late nineteenth century. The European powers were scrambling for colonies around the world, especially in Asia and Africa. The prevailing geopolitical theory of the time was that of mercantilism, which espoused the idea that a nation's wealth could be expanded by dominating vast tracts of the undeveloped world and constructing complex trading patterns that generated highly profitable trade for the colonizing power. The United Kingdom was the dominant actor in the system, and at one time controlled enormous swaths of global territory, with the Raj—what is today India, Pakistan, and Bangladesh—being the crown jewel. But all the European nations were colonial powers— notably France, Germany, the Netherlands, Spain, and Portugal; even tiny Belgium controlled territories in Africa and other parts of the world that dwarfed its small European landmass. In Asia, Japan was modernizing and emerging as a colonizing power itself.

The United States initially rejected the mad dash to divide up the world, partly from its own history of overthrowing a colonizing power and partly because it already held an enormous spread of land in its own continental-sized nation. Much of the energy of the US population was focused on simply consolidating control of the continental United States, the "manifest destiny" of the nineteenth century. It was conventional wisdom to avoid any kind of overseas engagement; the admonition of George Washington to "steer clear of . . . entangling alliances" continued to resonate. But Mahan carefully studied the history of Great Britain and its path to global dominance and concluded that the United States needed to pursue a similar path to wealth and security—through sea power. He wrote, "The history of sea power is largely, though by no means solely, a narrative of contests between nations, of mutual rivalries, of violence frequently culminating in war. The profound influence of sea commerce upon the wealth and strength of countries was clearly seen long before the true principles which governed its growth and prosperity were detected."

His prescription was simple: approach the global system as a zero-sum game in which the United States must compete; exclude rivals wherever possible; create trading monopolies with colonial authority; establish a global network of bases (the coaling stations of the time) which allow the fleet to operate with impunity anywhere in the world; maintain a technologically advanced fleet (making the shift from sail to coal and eventually from coal to oil as rapidly as possible); and—above all—possess the ability to control the sea at will. None of this necessarily would require war. Indeed, he said, "force is never more operative than when it is known to exist but is not brandished," which Roosevelt would recast as "speak softly and carry a big stick." Today the massive aircraft carrier USS *Theodore Roosevelt* (CVN-71) still carries the nickname "the big stick." Through the span of his life toward the end of the nineteenth century and the beginning of the twentieth, Mahan was able through sheer force of intellectual will to bring alive the ideas of naval power as the key determinant of national power—and convince his own nation of the vital importance of sea power.

This was not merely an academic exercise, of course. On February 15, 1898, the battleship USS *Maine* exploded in the harbor of Havana, Cuba—at the time a colony of Spain. The war fever that swept the country was fueled in part by a sense that the United States had fallen behind the European powers in colonization around the globe, and a "splendid little war" would provide the opportunity to join the competition. After a short, sharp war with Spain, the United States—for the first time in its history—acquired significant territory abroad, following the theories of Mahan. Cuba, the Philippines, and other territories fell into our hands, allowing the United States to remedy the shortage of overseas bases, which Mahan felt was critical. He had earlier written, "Having no foreign establishments, either colonial or military, the ships of war of the United States, in war, will be like land birds, unable to fly far from their own shores. To provide resting places for them, where they can coal and repair, would be one of the first duties of a government proposing to itself the development of the power of the nation at sea." Through the intellectual determination of Mahan, the United States began at last to project its power outward into the world. The effects—as well as the debate—continue today.

Ironically, the reluctant sailor who would intellectually reinvent the naval profession in the United States and around the world was born and raised on the campus of the United States Military Academy at West Point, New York, surrounded by soldiers through the early years of his life. Alfred Thayer Mahan's father was a professor at the academy, and by all accounts a figure of stentorian authority, certainly to his students if not always to his children.

Though he grew up amidst the sight and sound of Army military officers in training, the younger Mahan ultimately obtained an appointment to the Naval Academy, where he promptly set about trying to bring Annapolis into line with what he felt were the higher standards of discipline and professionalism of West Point, an approach that did not endear him to his classmates. From the beginning, Mahan's reform efforts were intellectually based, quite inconsistent, and not especially effective. He was neither socially inclined, organizationally gifted, nor politically astute, but he was quick to perceive problems and tackle them head-on. His methods were neither subtle nor well attuned to dealing with the likely political effects that resulted. All of this made for a somewhat solitary youth. In the early years of his career, his actions appear so wantonly reckless as to suggest that Mahan did not even make basic political calculations; rather, he seemed to identify a problem and righteously run straight at it with nary a pause to weigh the evidence or a thought as to what might happen to him personally. He never met a windmill at which he was unwilling to tilt.

Though he would grow better political antennae in time, his nerve endings would remain stubby and relatively insensitive for most of Mahan's life. Whereas most other admirals of modern, bureaucratic navies gave at least some discernible thought to career planning along the way, Mahan's approach could (and today almost certainly would) have cost him his career at many turns. Luckily, he survived such early indiscretions as lodging unproven accusations of malfeasance against a sitting secretary of the Navy. Over time, he was able to acquire sufficient discretion and protection to survive the most delicate part of his career, during the early years of the Naval War College and before the publication of his masterwork, *The Influence of Sea Power upon History*, solidified his reputation in the United States.

Throughout his life, Mahan had a strong religious streak. A "high church" Episcopalian (the unofficial but widely practiced religion of the naval hierarchy in his day), he was deeply influenced by an uncle who was an Episcopal priest, and proposed in an article on naval education that the sea service should aim to instill in young officers a solid knowledge of and reliance upon God. Whatever the wellsprings of Mahan's character—his martinet father, martial milieu, and mystical bent—the bottom line was that his career never seemed to mesh entirely comfortably with the cloistered world of the nineteenth-century Navy.

Though he made his home and his name in the Navy, Mahan showed little interest in actual seafaring, had a tenuous relationship broadly speaking with the Navy (as with his family and very few friends), and was never to be mistaken for a charismatic leader of men. No other admiral in this book was less naval or less a leader in the traditional sense, yet perhaps no other had such a profound or lasting effect on the practice of the naval profession.

If he so little enjoyed or practiced the seagoing side of the profession himself, how did Mahan come to have such influence on the entire Navy? His story is not unlike that of the influence of Thomas Aquinas on the Catholic Church. Mahan was never a chief of naval operations, just as Aquinas was never a pope. Neither man fit neatly within his organization, neither really led anyone in the usual sense, and neither was fully recognized in his own time; yet in the end, both were canonized for the quality of their thinking. Agree or disagree with him, all church philosophers after Aquinas were writing in his shadow; and similarly, all theorists of sea power after Mahan were working in the broad wake of Mahan's intellectual voyages.

Mahan's *Summa Theologica* (the cornerstone of Aquinas's work) was *The Influence of Sea Power upon History*, a book scarcely less sweeping in scope or ambition than Aquinas's. Fittingly, Mahan began the work while on his nine-month, essentially unsupervised sabbatical from the Navy, as noted above.

His efforts led to an early pair of books: one, on tactics, was later disowned by its author, who never taught the subject at the War College and moved immediately along to his principal métier: strategy. The other, which wended a tortuous path to publication, was *The Influence of Sea Power upon History, 1660–1783* (eventually expanded in a second volume through 1812). This was the subject Mahan was born to teach, and the lectures upon which the book was based proved popular among War College classes. But the effect of publication was not instantly electric. In fact, the book was initially better received in Europe (particularly in Britain and Germany) than in the United States. What it lacked in breadth of influence it made up for in the impact it had upon those who truly understood it.

It is not an overstatement to say that the book created a set of powerful acolytes around the globe, and deeply influenced the strategic trajectory of the late nineteenth and early twentieth centuries. Fellow naval historian and future president Theodore Roosevelt (himself the author of more than twenty books) read it in a weekend and pronounced it "a *very* good book." Indeed, as undersecretary of the Navy and especially as president, he would cement Mahan's influence in the United States by building the Great White Fleet—the first truly modern US fleet. If Mahan had laid the cornerstone, Teddy Roosevelt built upon it the foundation of US naval power that would go into World War I less than a decade after the Great White Fleet made its round-the-world cruise (and put the world on notice) from 1907 to 1909. Kaiser Wilhelm II purchased copies of Mahan's book for every ship in the German fleet and spoke about it often. Similar leading thinkers and strategists in Great Britain used it in justifying naval expenditures in the run-up to the First World War.

None of this should imply that Mahan's vision was perfect. Despite his ultimate vindication as a strategic thinker, Mahan could certainly miss on occasion, and his writing itself is difficult to penetrate. The sheer volume and density of his writing is frankly intimidating; even the two volumes of *Sea Power* are but a fraction of the whole corpus, and for readers without the photographic memory and boundless energy of Theodore Roosevelt, they are at least as heavy in the reading as they are in the hand. Mahan's writing is also riddled with errors apparent in his time and almost insuperable in ours. Not only are his social mores staunchly nineteenth-century (he was a late but fervent convert to the religion of American imperialism), but Mahan partially missed the already known and quite predictable effects of the technological advances of his own time, to say nothing of ours. Coupled with his difficult personality and lack of practical seagoing experience, he came across to many of his peers as an enigmatic figure, even as his global reputation grew.

The case for Mahan's canonization never really rested on his grasp of details, however, and he remains in the pantheon today not because of how well he understood ships or gunnery but rather because he understood better than any before and many since what a *navy* was for. Even in the United States, Mahan's influence has waned in recent decades due to a somewhat perverse focus on his obvious flaws, but to dismiss him based on his emphasis on big ships fighting big battles is like dismissing Clausewitz because armies no longer line up in brightly colored uniforms to exchange musket fire.

Mahan still has much to teach naval analysts today (tellingly, the Chinese navy has been diligently translating and reading his works in recent years), but his complicated character also contains broadly applicable lessons for leaders in many fields. Of the admirals surveyed here, Mahan's personality is one of the least worthy of emulating and his type of leadership was and is the hardest to replicate. Naturally, only a very few leaders are called to intellectually overhaul their professions, and fewer still have the opportunity to do so. Mahan's life still speaks to the importance of following one's muse with ruthless determination and perseverance—in many ways the sine qua non of character. All leaders have jobs, but those jobs exist within organizations, and organizations exist within even broader contexts. It behooves leaders to reflect on their work and the work of their organizations in their broad contexts, and to write and publish their reflections. In this way they can contribute to the ongoing conversations within their professions as well as the public conversations taking place in the wider society.

In the end, Mahan's genius was not that of the explorer, warrior, or master organizer. Rather, he was an intellectual—a position that does not formally exist in the Navy, and with which the Navy has traditionally been uncomfortable. Nevertheless, Mahan succeeded first in creating a career in spite of the institution (and often despite himself), and ultimately in teaching the Navy, politicians, and the public to think about sea power in a fundamentally new way. The Navy never quite knew what to make of Mahan, but it was never the same after him. Despite the dismal results of his earliest efforts to reshape his fellow midshipmen and the Naval Academy, all midshipmen since Mahan—and especially all students of the Naval War College, which still keeps the flame Mahan kindled—have been shaped by his thinking and writing, whether they realize it or not. Mahan might not have been much of a leader, but he was and remains immensely influential.

He retired from active duty at the turn of the twentieth century, and the accolades poured in—including honorary degrees from leading universities around the world, the presidency of the American Historical Society, and invitations to speak and consult in the United States and abroad. Promoted to rear admiral by an act of Congress, he lived mostly in Washington, DC, until the early days of the First World War, and commentary continued to flow from his prolific pen until the very end. Today, USS *Mahan*, the fourth ship bearing his name, sails the oceans—a powerful *Arleigh Burke*–class Aegis guided missile destroyer. I am sure that as he roams the endless library stacks of heaven he is hoping that the officers manning "his" ship have a good wardroom library at their disposal. He would think that vastly more important than a good sextant and chronometer.

Being an intellectual in uniform has never been an easy calling, and it was essentially unheard of in Mahan's day. With his icy personality, Mahan never seemed to make things easier on himself, either—particularly at the beginning of his career, when he was at his most idealistic and inflexible. Most leaders will have the good sense to go with the flow a little bit more than Mahan did, but it is essential to remember that—like most visionaries—Mahan made his defining contribution over the system's howling objections (as Admirals Bud Zumwalt and Grace Hopper would do in later years). Many people with better political sense would take the hint on receiving a performance review with the reproach "the business of naval officers is not to write books," but it is hard to imagine the Navy growing and succeeding as it did had Mahan conceded the incompatibility of being a naval officer and writing books. Such doggedness—politely called perseverance—always looks better in retrospect. It is a hallmark of strong character.

Perhaps in part because he was barely a mariner and not much of a leader—at least in the sense that the Navy traditionally prizes those roles—Mahan understood better than any before and many since the true purpose of a navy, and its vital role for any nation with a serious coastline. Today's culture is hardly less enthralled with individual bravado and derring-do as opposed to the unglamorous, eye-straining work of the intellectual in the library, but victory must be conceived before it can be achieved. Many leaders see strategy as too soft or inherently uncertain or just plain difficult, preferring the busyness of the moment to the hard, sustained work required to step back, see their work in context, and develop a theory of success. Every so often a Mahan comes along who understands the context better than anyone and then changes it for everyone, forever.

Visionary leadership is very hard to cultivate or emulate.

However, leaders are ultimately responsible for ensuring their organizations' success in context, which requires stepping back from time to time and attempting to see the big picture as well as possible. There is no need to spend months in the library—or to get into the business of writing books—to realize the benefits of occasional reflection and the clarity that comes from disciplined thought and writing (even if only for your own benefit).

In my own case, I learned early that in order to exercise vision, you need the qualities of character that underlie it—patience, diligence, and a willingness to send your ideas into the world knowing they will be battered and belittled more often than not.

The first time I tried to shape a vision was as a young antisubmarine warfare officer in my first ship. I was asked to brief the wardroom on how we would go about using all the tools of finding and killing submarines in an open ocean context. Drawing on my coursework at Annapolis and subsequent Navy schools, I sketched out a theory that was perhaps a bit beyond what my quite senior captain and the rest of the wardroom were willing to accept—a very risky mix of relying on long-range aircraft, our own embarked helicopters, and signals intelligence (listening for the subs' transmissions). I thought it was pretty good, and I suppose it was—in theory.

Unfortunately, that night, a US exercise submarine managed to penetrate my visionary formation, surface in our wake, and shoot an exercise torpedo that knocked us out of the fight. My captain justifiably reamed me out, and I learned that any vision has to survive contact with the real world. But over the next couple of years in that destroyer, my experience began to match my theories, and the two came together to create a reasonably successful vision for conducting the principal mission of our ship. It was a small victory in a small universe, but a powerful lesson for me that our visions need both theory and experience to be valid.

Mahan was a teacher every day of his life. The qualities in a life that give rise to a desire to teach are varied—to some degree it takes a strong sense of self-confidence, often bordering on arrogance. But it is also often a selfless act of service, as the rewards of teaching are usually vastly less than those that can be earned through other pursuits. And at times, for some, teaching is a refuge from the hurly-burly of the "real world." In the nineteenth-century US Navy, the monetary rewards were not great for anyone, but the psychic value of being a recognized "leader of sailors" in a heroic profession were great compensation. The majority of officers drawn to the Navy were there for the pride of service that derived from commanding ships, sailing into battle, and inspiring a crew—all earned at sea. But Mahan chose to be a teacher. Though he is remembered as a writer due to the lasting fame of his books, it is worth remembering that Mahan's real calling was as an educator. *The Influence of Sea Power upon History* was begun as the outline for a new course in naval history and strategy and remained the centerpiece of the Naval War College curriculum for generations. Mahan is still read and taught today, both in the Navy and in civilian schools like the Fletcher School, where I served as dean.

All leaders, especially in today's media environment, are in some sense educators: both their ideas and their delivery will teach the people in their organizations what the leader is thinking and how he or she communicates and will educate outsiders about the organization and its work. Leaders who demonstrate intellectual courage inside and outside their organizations can make a real difference in their organizations' success today through better communications and tomorrow through educating the next generation of leaders. And let's face it, teaching is not always regarded as the most important, or glamorous, or glory-filled endeavor. When I meet a good teacher, I often think of the screenplay for *A Man for All Seasons* by Robert Bolt. He imagines a conversation between Sir Thomas More and his ambitious son-in-law in which the younger man rejects the idea of teaching, because if he were a teacher, he says, "who would know it?" The exchange goes like this:

> **Sir Thomas More:** *Why not be a teacher? You'd be a fine teacher; perhaps a great one.*
>
> **Richard Rich:** *If I was, who would know it?*
>
> **Sir Thomas More:** *You; your pupils; your friends; God. Not a bad public, that.*

Great teachers shape our lives, are men and women of true character, and Mahan was indeed a teacher of enormous importance to our Navy and the nation. And he was a fine teacher, building on the foundation of his intellectual capital and enabled by his endless determination to inspire the Navy and the nation to set our sights on the world's oceans.

Like every leader in this book, Mahan had his flaws. His relationships with people and organizations were notably tenuous. A visionary is often a frustrated person; the righteousness of his or her ideas is much easier to see and accept in retrospect than in the visionary's own time. Mahan's lingering reputation for iciness bespeaks his lifelong inability to leave work at the office and come home to a different kind of real life.

Every leader has her or his own temperament, which can prove difficult or impossible to change. When difficult, highly driven personalities succeed, it is hard to prove a counterfactual about whether they could or should have taken things a little easier in some way or other. (Could Steve Jobs have done what he did if he had just relaxed a little? It's impossible to say. I'd guess not.) Still, just as in Mahan's day, there seem to be far more needlessly ill-tempered leaders than true visionaries. Vision and drive are good qualities for a leader to possess, but condescension and browbeating are not often hallmarks of successful or sustainable leadership. Vision and perseverance often result in a certain amount of isolation. Anyone would do well to minimize the difficult edges of their personality, even in the pursuit of high levels of accomplishment.

In the end, Alfred Thayer Mahan's qualities of character derived directly from his determination and intellectual power. He was simply unwavering in his determination to communicate a new strategic vision of his nation—one that fitted the times and turned America's gaze to the world. He said, "whether they will or not, Americans must now begin to look outward. The growing production of the country demands it." Despite the dangers and challenges of the world, then and today, we cannot hide from it. Mahan expounded a vision that remains a significant part of US global power today—that a strong and capable Navy is crucial to our nation's security and prosperity. He has sailed alongside me in the long voyage of my career, not always a friendly voice, but one in whose counsel I have always taken great stock. And his character of mind and utter determination to read, think, and write exactly what he thought important have inspired me and many others on the long voyage of our nation over the past two centuries.

All quotations in this chapter are sourced from Robert Seager II, *Alfred Thayer Mahan: The Man and His Letters* (Annapolis, MD: Naval Institute Press, 1977), or from Benjamin F. Armstrong, ed., *21st Century Mahan: Sound Military Conclusions for the Modern Era* (Annapolis, MD: Naval Institute Press, 2013).

CHAPTER VI

Rum, Buggery, and the Lash

Admiral Lord John
Arbuthnot Fisher

———

BORN RAMBODA, CEYLON, JANUARY 25, 1841

DIED LONDON, UNITED KINGDOM, JULY 10,
1920

I first heard of Jacky Fisher when I was at graduate school in Boston at the Fletcher School of Law and Diplomacy at Tufts University. This school of international diplomacy was a somewhat ironic place to initially learn about the admiral, as he was easily one of the most *un*diplomatic leaders in military history. Like Alfred Thayer Mahan before him, Jacky Fisher never saw a windmill at which he could resist tilting, nor a contemporary he was unwilling to lambaste for some disagreement large or small; his career was therefore a long history of confrontation and (usually successful) argumentation. He was a revolution in a bottle, and the taste could be bitter indeed despite being sugared with a great deal of personal charm when he chose to deploy it.

I encountered him on the pages of assigned readings in 1981 while taking a course in European diplomatic history from one of the most distinguished professors at Fletcher, Dr. Alan Henrikson, a silver-haired Rhodes scholar with a gifted style in the classroom.

He introduced the admiral by outlining his tempestuous relationship with Winston Churchill in the latter part of the nineteenth century. It was Churchill who charged that the traditions of the Royal Navy were "rum, buggery, and the lash," which he meant as a shot across the bow of the hidebound Admiralty. On that point, at least, the two of them were in agreement. Churchill and the older, established Admiral Fisher shared a sensibility that for the British Empire to survive, it would have to change, and change dramatically, in regard to its management of its expensive global fleet. As Professor Henrikson guided us through the complexities of global geopolitics in the run-up to the First World War and beyond, I became fascinated less with Churchill than with Fisher.

Throughout my career, I would dip repeatedly into his oddly constructed memoirs—really a series of jottings without much structure—to find inspiration as I, in a smaller way, tilted at my own share of windmills. I tried consciously to be Jacky Fisher without the bitter bark and managed in a much more limited way to effect some changes here and there as a result. But even today I think we are poorer for lacking the kind of dynamic change agents in our military that Lord Fisher represented. Our time could use a few more Fishers, frankly, if we are to reshape our armed forces for a new era of complexity—from cybersecurity to unmanned vehicles to elite special forces.

Born to a middle-class family in Ceylon in 1841, Jacky Fisher was a precocious child. His father, William, was a minor army officer who eventually bankrupted the family as a coffee grower. William also served as a local superintendent of police, all the while raising a large family with eleven children total, only seven of whom survived infancy. Due to the family's financial straits, young Jacky was packed off to his paternal grandfather in England at the age of six and never saw either of his parents again. His father died when Jacky was fifteen years old and just starting out in the navy; and while his mother, Sophie, lived a long life, he did not pursue further contact with her. He did send her a small amount of money annually until she died. Oddly, his father was a handsome, strapping man nearly six feet two inches tall, and his mother was likewise tall and attractive—yet Jacky was quite short at just five feet seven and had an oddly "Asiatic" cast to his features (in the more racist terms of the time). All of this gave rise to a variety of disparaging comments and nicknames (mostly notably, "The Malay"). The rumors were inflamed after a bout of malaria in middle age gave a faintly yellowish tint to his skin (and almost killed him). The cover of Jan Morris's beautifully written biography, *Fisher's Face*, captures the degree to which his facial features were a part of his persona. Set apart physically, he sought to set himself apart in thought and deed as well.

He began his naval career at the age of thirteen as a young naval cadet, the initial entry point for many young men in those days. Fisher was inducted into the Royal Navy on Lord Nelson's final flagship, HMS *Victory*, then stationed in Portsmouth, and sent to HMS *Calcutta*, captained by a "traditional" British commander who firmly believed in the lash. Legend has it that he fainted on his first day of duty after witnessing the flogging of half a dozen sailors. Service on *Calcutta* included a brief stint in the Crimean War, and he was subsequently transferred to HMS *Agamemnon*, another of Lord Nelson's former flagships. Promoted to midshipman in

1856, he was assigned to Asia for the next five years, serving on the China Station of the Royal Navy, first on the oddly named HMS *Highflyer*, a twenty-one-gun steam corvette, where he became an expert navigator and caught the eye of the captain. This was a pattern throughout Fisher's lengthy career—he was always noticed, appreciated, given extra attention and training, and he rewarded those mentoring him with superb performance at every level.

Fisher was not part of the naval aristocracy of the day, to say the least. As he said later in life, "'Your great career was when you were young,' said a dear friend to me the other day. I entered the Navy penniless, friendless, and forlorn. While my messmates were having jam, I had to go without. While their stomachs were full, mine was often empty. I have always had to fight like hell, and fighting like hell has made me what I am." Finances would be a problem throughout his life, and he would become resentful toward the end, pointing out often how much he had sacrificed on behalf of his nation, and mentioning lucrative offers he received to enter the private sector along the way. He constantly groused about how much more money he could be making outside the navy, and he was probably right. This, by the way, remains a not uncommon syndrome among senior military officers on both sides of the Atlantic in my experience. Yet there are very few admirals or generals who would actually trade away that rank and title for millions if offered the choice. So it was with Jacky Fisher.

In China he saw brief action in the Second Opium War, and served in HMS *Chesapeake*, a steam-powered frigate. He also briefly commanded a steam paddle gunboat, HMS *Coromandel*, and ended up by serving in and then sailing home in HMS *Furious*, a paddle sloop. The captain in the latter was a true martinet, with a highly abused crew, in significant contrast to the leadership Fisher learned from his first captain in HMS *Highflyer*. Even so, Fisher was the apple of the harsh captain's eye in HMS *Furious* and was recommended for promotion to lieutenant. His captain sent him off with a set of cuff links engraved with the captain's motto on them—"*Loyal au mort*" (Loyal to Death)—and Jacky Fisher wore them faithfully for the next sixty years and more. His was a sentimental nature in many ways, and I suspect the cuff links were more about his self-view than about the memory of his captain.

When the ship returned to Portsmouth, Fisher sat for his lieutenant's test in the fall of 1861 and achieved the highest test score in history on the rigorous navigation portion. At this point, people began to talk in earnest about the oddly featured young lieutenant who seemed to have a knack for the sea and a kind of even, steady confidence with both his superiors and his subordinates—a rare combination in the Royal Navy of the nineteenth century. His reputation was growing; over time he would become the best-known and most discussed officer of his generation—both for good and for ill. The larger a military officer's reputation grows, the greater the attendant jealousy from peers. Fisher saw that clearly, but never deigned to trim the sails of either his ambition or his intellect.

In 1862, as the American Civil War was unfolding, Jacky Fisher began the first of four tours of duty at Portsmouth, the massive Royal Navy training base in southern England, which was an important center for British naval innovation. He focused on developing a variety of innovative techniques revolving around gunnery and mines, including helping the Royal Navy make the shift from muzzle-loading cannon to modern breech-loaded weapons. Over the next twenty-five years, he had a significant impact on the evolution of naval weapons, and throughout the long span of his career he would draw on the technical skills he mastered at Portsmouth to drive the naval establishment forward, often at a breakneck pace. He possessed a very rare admixture of strategic vision and true technical skill.

Fisher returned to sea in 1863 as a gunnery officer in HMS *Warrior*, the first armored battleship in the Royal Navy. The ship carried both muzzle-loading and breech-loading guns, embodying the shift not only from sail to coal-fired engines, but also to what we would recognize today as modern, longer-range, more accurate guns. In 1864 he returned to Portsmouth and spent the next five years ashore, eventually turning his attention to torpedoes—a simple, lethal idea (underwater explosives, essentially) that created new threats to capital ships. What was called a torpedo in those days would today be referred to as a "naval mine"; today's torpedoes are underwater missiles that are guided autonomously from onboard sonar systems. In 1869 Fisher paid a visit to Germany, where he met not only Chancellor Otto von Bismarck, but also King William I of Prussia (later Kaiser Wilhelm I of Germany), whose geopolitical ambitions would create much of the orbit of Fisher's career. He was also promoted to commander and sent to sea on several ships, including as second in command of HMS *Ocean*, the flagship of the British China Fleet.

By 1876 Fisher was promoted to full captain, and over the next five years assumed command of no fewer than six different warships, largely on duty in the Caribbean and the Mediterranean, frequently serving as flagship to an admiral. While command of so many ships was not unheard of, his experience was notable in terms of both the quantity of command experience and the quality of results he consistently delivered. He also suffered the loss of his brother, a naval lieutenant who went down with HMS *Atalanta* somewhere in the Atlantic Ocean between the Caribbean and England. At the time, Fisher was in command of HMS *Northampton*, which was part of the force sent to search for the missing ship.

All of this groomed him sufficiently to provide the basis for his breakout command in HMS *Inflexible*, which he assumed in 1881. HMS *Inflexible* was a brand-new warship, with thick armor, electric lighting, and torpedo tubes—but was still equipped with sails, which she seldom if ever actually used for propulsion. Under Fisher, she became a perfect test bed for many of his tactical ideas. She had a number of advancements and innovations built into her, and Fisher took full advantage, driving the ship into action in the Anglo-Egyptian War of 1882. Fisher went ashore and saw action during this classic "small war," and was recognized by his superiors for his bravery. Unfortunately, this led to his contracting both malaria and dysentery, the lingering effects of which, including the sallow skin tone, would haunt him for the rest of his life. This skin tone change fueled even more rumors about his mixed parentage, which somehow contributed to the growing antagonism many of his peers felt about him.

Throughout the 1880s, Fisher spent time recovering from his illness, but the effects never truly left him. Assigned ashore for twelve years at one stretch, he poured his heart into further innovation, with a focus on armor, gunnery, and torpedoes. Many of the ideas he concocted became fundamental to the way the British would operate their ships for much of the next century. Perhaps more important, he inspired a group of officers who passionately believed in his concept of pushing for the new idea over the conservative path. This so-called Fish Pond included a brace of future Royal Navy leaders including John Jellicoe and Percy Scott.

The cult of personality that grew around him created plenty of antibodies throughout the Navy, and Fisher became a polarizing figure—albeit one with significant and ongoing support from the royal family. By 1890 this had translated into a posting as the aide-de-camp to Queen Victoria, and promotion to rear admiral. While in that role, he continued to face conservative opposition to many of his initiatives, but his steady ascent through the ranks of the Admiralty ultimately brought him sufficient power to dramatically change the Royal Navy. With the royal family now fully aware of the charming young admiral, his rise was assured.

Everywhere Fisher was stationed, he sponsored dances—ashore, in distant stations, on ornate flagships and small cutters. Whenever his ship would put into port, he would set up a program for visitors that would include not only excellent food and champagne, but also the opportunity to dance. And he was an excellent and devoted dancer, often whirling lady after lady around the floor, never tiring, and beaming the entire time. It was a manifestation of his almost manic level of energy, as well as his desire, as was said of Teddy Roosevelt, to be the bride at every wedding and the corpse at every funeral.

Throughout his long periods ashore, Fisher employed every

trick imaginable to drive production in the way he demanded. In one famous instance, he brought his desk and chair outside into the shipyard, insisting he would not move until production speeded up to his expectations. He is said to have observed, "When you are told a thing is impossible, that there are insuperable objections, then is the time to fight like the devil." That is an accurate summation of Jacky Fisher's approach throughout this career, an approach that preceded and aligned with Winston Churchill's simple dictum, "Never give in;" Churchill actually went on to qualify it—never give in, except to convictions of honor and good sense. Lord Fisher never qualified it—for Jacky this fundamental principle of "fight like the devil" in the face of resistance was simply bedrock.

As he continued to ascend, he moved through the crucial flag officer jobs, beginning with third sea lord. In this role, he was responsible for essentially designing, building, and arming the Royal Navy, with a special focus on taking new ideas to sea. He helped create the forerunner of the modern destroyer (a term he popularized), a small, fast, offensive ship that fired relatively lighter-caliber guns but could operate out in front of a formation of heavier capital ships.

One of his crucial innovations was support for advanced submarines. The initial British response to the technology was that its use was somehow underhanded and unethical. Fisher pushed the arguments for the new undersea systems relentlessly, correctly foreseeing that they would revolutionize naval warfare as surely as the shift from sail to coal and then to liquid fuels—other innovations he also championed. The use of torpedoes had evolved since the mid-nineteenth century from floating mines to propelled explosives, and Fisher was an early and dynamic advocate of higher-speed versions that could be launched from surface ships. He was among the first to see the possibilities of launching submerged torpedoes from bays built into the hulls of submarines. By coupling the stealth of the submarine with the range and explosive power of the torpedo, he created a true revolution in military affairs at sea.

Fisher's radical, hard-driving approach to training was also notable. In an era when most ship captains and admirals were content to polish the brass works and holystone the decks endlessly, Fisher demanded realistic and dangerous combat-oriented training. He insisted on nighttime drills, the use of real explosive charges, target ranges to measure accuracy, long hours to simulate the stress of combat, and physical fitness training to ensure readiness around the clock. All of the technical and procedural advances he drove were additive and resulted in a far higher level of overall British naval mastery at sea. Even as a senior captain and eventually as a junior member of the Admiralty, he punched well above his weight in terms of impact on the entire navy; and as he became more senior, his power to move events grew exponentially as a result.

By 1896, he was promoted to vice admiral and returned to sea as commander of the British maritime forces in the Caribbean; and after the Fashoda Crisis of 1898, a territorial dispute in eastern Africa between Britain and France, he became the commander of the prestigious, and geopolitically crucial, Mediterranean Fleet. Fisher changed the ethos of the forward-deployed British fleet from polishing the brass and obsessively painting the sides of ships to conducting high-speed, realistic war games, often at night. The shift moved from formality and "showtime" to preparing for "wartime." His enthusiasm, energy, and inspirational drive reimagined the British fleet, preparing it for the global combat to come.

While he experienced periods of frustration and seriously considered offers to step out of the navy and work in the armaments industry (eyeing the big compensation that would have come his way), he again was promoted, this time to second sea lord—in charge of manpower and personnel, with a focus on reforming naval training. In this role, he created better career paths for both engineers and deck officers, extended shore training before sending cadets to sea, added physical fitness training, added competitive examinations as nearly the sole path to a commission, and updated the curriculum for the entire officer corps to include much more science and technology. His impact was debated throughout the fleet. In the end, as always, he had his way, and the imprint of his reforms created new intellectual capital in the officer corps that matched the changes he instituted in the ships of the fleet. We so often think of innovation as improvements in physical systems and specific equipment (torpedoes, fire control systems for gunnery, submarines, engines). But in many ways the most important innovations in any enterprise are the changes we make in how we prepare human beings to perform. Fisher was the rare leader who fully understood the need to do both.

By 1903 he briefly became commander of the large naval base at Portsmouth, with Lord Nelson's HMS *Victory* as his flagship, before ascending to the pinnacle of global naval power as the first sea lord. He served in this role from 1904 to 1910, continuing to innovate while at the same time infuriating many of his bureaucratic opponents—notably Lord Charles Beresford, another senior admiral, who came to despise Fisher and conducted a significant opposition campaign, both within the navy and from a seat in Parliament. The two men's quarrels persisted throughout the latter part of their long lives and created dangerous factions in the Royal Navy.

Most important, Fisher used his power to drive the design of two important and truly modern ship classes. The first was the all-big-gun battleship, the first of which was named HMS *Dreadnought*. It was so important to Fisher that he had the word carved on his tombstone. The second class of ships was the faster but more lightly armored battle cruisers. These hybrids could outgun most opponents and outrun any heavier, longer-gunned true battleships. The battle cruisers were ultimately ill fated, and several of them were ingloriously destroyed at Jutland in the First World War. The lead ship of the class, named HMS *Invincible*, joined the fleet in 1907. Fisher also championed and began transitioning the fleet from coal to oil and ensured that submarines became a fundamental and respected part of British war plans. After a successful tenure as first sea lord, he was made a peer, dubbed Lord Fisher, and retired on his seventieth birthday.

At the start of the First World War, Fisher was brought back by the young, headstrong, politically controversial Winston Churchill. They were perhaps too much alike. Churchill, the first lord of the Admiralty, appointed the quite willing and still vigorous seventy-four-year-old Fisher for a second stint as first sea lord in October 1914. There is an iconic photograph of the two of them—resplendent in spats, top hats, and ornate walking sticks—descending the steps of the Admiralty in late 1914. The honeymoon did not last long; the relationship deteriorated rapidly over legitimate differences in strategic approach. Churchill pushed for the Gallipoli campaign, a risky invasion of Turkey through the Dardanelles, which turned out to be a bloody disaster. Fisher, on the other hand, advocated an amphibious assault in the north from the Baltic Sea as a way to damage the German fleet, something he had been pushing for more than a decade.

The story of the final meeting to make the decision, which also finally destroyed the Churchill-Fisher relationship, is telling. It was mid-spring of 1915, and after much fierce back-and-forth, the two men were at a stalemate. Churchill passionately desired the Dardanelles invasion, having given birth to the idea, and Jacky Fisher adamantly opposed it, urging a Baltic campaign instead. The two men were similar in so many ways: impulsive, talkative, intellectually dominant, and charismatic; the collision seemed inevitable and the moment eventually came for Fisher to either knuckle under or resign in protest. It was a moment that tested the character of this seventy-four-year-old whirling dervish of a man, who had never touched failure and was more vigorous than ever, but was finally matched against a rival with similar levels of energy and enthusiasm, as well as thirty years his junior and nominally his boss.

Others around the table at that fateful meeting cleared their throats nervously in some embarrassment as the prime minister, H. H. Asquith, pondered the matter—and finally made a definitive ruling. It would be the Dardanelles campaign, not the Baltic. Jacky Fisher's temper rose quickly. He tore himself away from the table, a strained and angry look on his face. Everyone knew he would resign. But next stood the great soldier Field Marshal Lord

Herbert Kitchener, who moved to intercept the admiral on his course, and the two exchanged words—Kitchener soothing, Fisher fulminating.

In the event, Fisher pulled his coat closely around him and with a shudder returned to the table, a visible sulk on his face. He continued to believe with all his heart that he was betraying something fundamental. He knew the campaign was ill conceived, and as a result, thousands or even tens of thousands would probably needlessly die. And that is precisely how it all came out. But something in his character pulled him back to the table with the rest of the cabinet. It was not entirely his devotion to his nation, although that was part of it; nor his affection for Churchill, for that had long since worn thin. Rather Fisher returned to the table to stay in the game. His ego drove him back, as surely as it gave him enormous joy some months earlier when Churchill had called him out of retirement to return as first sea lord.

Fisher knew the Gallipoli campaign was doomed and wrong. In another few weeks he would finally resign. But not yet, and this pivotal moment in his life and career—when he came back grudgingly to the table and did not seek to force a reversal of what he knew was a flawed policy decision—would be a burden he carried for the rest of his life. It is also one of the very few instances of Jacky Fisher not carrying the day in a battle of ideas. He knew it was the beginning of the end.

Over the course of his final half decade from 1915 until his death in 1920, Fisher continued to fight for new naval ideas from a variety of public platforms. He lost his devoted wife, Kitty, in the spring of 1918—they had enjoyed a truly happy marriage by all accounts—and something went out of his life that he could not replace; he succumbed himself to prostate cancer in 1920. His funeral was the most important public naval ceremony since the death of Lord Nelson, and was essentially a state event, held at Westminster Hall. Both he and his wife were cremated after their deaths, and their ashes combined at their beloved estate in Kilverstone. Their gravesite overlooks a figurehead taken from Fisher's first ship, HMS *Calcutta*.

Fisher had a fine voyage through life, always fighting against the odds, and almost always winning. He created great change, and is remembered with great respect in the Royal Navy. And through his long, controversial, confrontational, and vastly entertaining life, he always found time to dance.

Humble beginnings and physical shortcomings were the forge of Jacky Fisher's character. Joining the Admiralty ran through the family: both Jacky and a younger brother Frederic became admirals, and all three of Jacky's daughters married naval officers, each of whom became an admiral, as did his only son. But he himself—despite all the success and accolades—always seemed to feel like an outsider. His DNA placed him there, in both his short stature and the features written on his face, whose sallow complexion led to derogatory nicknames and slightly condescending attitudes throughout his life. He bore it well publicly, but it always chafed inside. In the epic battles of his prime with Lord Charles Beresford—the quintessential tall, burly aristocratic British admiral (who was even accompanied everywhere by a bulldog)—Jacky often evinced a sense of being on the outside looking in, despite all his accomplishments, high rank, and public success.

The defining character conflict of Jacky Fisher's life was the struggle between his massive ego, driven by internal insecurities, and his sincere devotion to the Royal Navy. He constantly sought to achieve success for himself alongside success for his beloved service. In most cases he was able to do both, achieving personal success while advancing the cause of the Navy—but not always.

His fierce drive to succeed made him a formidable force always. This gave him a slightly dark side, which he understood and encouraged to a certain degree. At one point he said, "I don't like perfect angels, one doesn't feel quite comfortable with them. One of Cecil Rhodes's secretaries wrote his Life and left out all his defects; it was a most unreal picture. The Good stands out all the more strikingly if there is a deep shadow. I think it is called the Rembrandt Effect."

Determination has a kind of two-edged quality to it. In the abstract, we admire a determined individual, but determination in one person's eyes can easily become bullheadedness in another's. Usually life is not an on-and-off light switch, with a pair of binary and simple choices. More often, life is a rheostat, requiring us to adjust the switch one way or the other, dialing it up or down to achieve the precise effect we seek.

It is right to be utterly determined in truly urgent matters; but be willing to be flexible and listen to the other side of the argument otherwise. The latter, of course, was not Admiral Fisher's strength. His will often became a battering ram, convinced as he was of his fundamental rightness, and largely unwilling or unable to admit he was ever wrong. In the preface to his idiosyncratic memoir, *Memories*, he says it quite simply: "a compromise (the beastliest word in the English language)." And he wasn't joking. While we admire this quality of ruthless determination, in a more temperate personality even more might have been achieved. Finding the balance between determination and an open mind is one of the ongoing tests of character for us all.

Throughout his long career, Fisher always chose the hard new path over the easy conservative course. From the very earliest stages of his life and career, he tried the new, clever solution even if—*especially* if—it flew in the face of conventional wisdom. This was true of his work on torpedoes, gunnery, ship design (above all the *Dreadnought*), ship construction, and countless other crusades upon which he launched. He summed it up nicely by saying, "You will come across some idiots whose minds are so deliciously symmetrical that they would prefer ten tortoises to one greyhound to catch a hare, and it was one of the principal articles of the ancient creed that you built ships in batches. They strained at the gnat of uniformity and so swallowed the camel of inferiority. No progress—they were a batch."

Innovation, in the end, is crucial to the development of character. First, changing something as fundamental as our inner compass requires in essence a desire and ability to innovate. Innovators are willing to look at different models, sort out personal qualities just as they would compare technical options, and make the kind of complex inner choices that result in real change. In my own case, I learned early in my naval career that sometimes—especially in moments of crisis—others resonate more to inspired innovation than to repetitious, by-the-book activities. While there will always be built-in constituencies supporting "let's do it the way we always have," more and more our world is responding to the inspiration of innovation. I particularly saw this, logically enough, in the days after 9/11. As a very young one-star admiral, I was charged with running the new operational think tank on the staff of the chief of naval operations. Our mission was to innovate and find ways for the Navy to contribute to this new war on terrorism. I learned a great deal in that posting, which I've addressed elsewhere, but above all it taught me the way big organizations can be moved by a combination of timing, necessity, and ideas. Learning this as I first became an admiral was an act of lucky timing, but it informed my ten-plus years in the Admiralty, and paid dividends over the final decade of my career when my responsibilities running NATO and other major organizations demanded it.

Jacky Fisher showed consistently that his inner course was charted squarely at change. The fight for innovation in the Royal Navy was the task of a lifetime. Toward the end of his life he said, "I fully agree with you about the Navy want of first-class Intellects. Concentration and Discipline combine to cramp the Sea Officer. Great views don't get grasped." No one ever accused Admiral Fisher of being cramped by concentration or discipline. He was the innovator-in-chief of the greatest navy in the world.

Toward the very end of his life, he was still carping about those who tried to hold him back, saying, "I believe that the vindication of a man's lifework is almost an impossible task for even the most intimate of friends or the most assiduous and talented of Biographers, simply because they cannot possibly appreciate how great deeds have been belittled and ravaged by small contemporary men. These yelping curs made the most noise, as the empty barrels do!

And it's only long afterwards that the truth emerges out of the mist of obloquy and becomes history."

An often-underrated quality of character is energy. Naturally, some part of an individual's energy level is simply a result of their physiology. Some people are naturally more energetic because of heredity, health, socioeconomic status, workload, diet, sleep patterns, and other exogenous factors. But a significant portion of how individuals attain and utilize their energy level is a reflection of their character.

In this sense, Jacky Fisher was both blessed with a strong, energetic constitution *and* able to draw on inner reserves of character to catalyze his energy. He commented over and over about the need to drive at problems, to attack with real enthusiasm, and to show others that everyone on the team must give 100 percent of their effort 100 percent of the time. In his book *Memories* he said, "Two qualities rule the world—emotion and earnestness. I have said elsewhere, with them you can move far more than mountains; you can move multitudes. It's the personality of the soul of man that has this immortal influence." By "emotion" he meant energy and passion, both of which he had in abundance.

For each of us as individuals, there are steps we can undertake that lay the physical groundwork for a high level of energy. This means getting sufficient rest and sleep, taking care of our health broadly while addressing any emergent specific physical challenges, creating a work environment for ourselves that permits the best possible level of energy, finding time for a reasonable level of exercise, sleeping well, and thinking about issues of diet in terms of how to boost energy. This truly came home for me in my late thirties, when I was a captain for the first time just as my natural metabolism was slowing a bit with age. And the opportunities to exercise and above all to sleep sufficiently were greatly diminished by virtue of the job. I adopted the idea that sleep was as important a part of my ship's weapons system as the guns and the missiles. We looked closely at sleep cycles, made sure people could take naps when they needed to, and tried to moderate watch teams on the bridge and in the combat centers of the ship in order to improve performance. I can still remember, despite all that, sailing into the Arabian Gulf in the mid-1990s for potential combat missions in a state of dizziness, dehydration, and general exhaustion. Watching our physical health is an act of character and can enormously help with our ability to perform.

Having thus worked on the exogenous variables to build a higher level of energy, we need to try to think of energy level as an internal quality of character that we can improve through a variety of means. Several ways to do this include mentally organizing tasks in a coherent, simple, prioritized way in our minds; reading and studying the stories of those who have lived particularly energetic lives (like Admiral Fisher); looking consciously for the good in the people we meet; focusing on the humor in difficult people and situations; accepting the things we cannot change; thinking about the long term and overcoming day-to-day frustrations by keeping them in perspective; and recognizing that the best end to a disagreement is the creation of a win-win outcome. A tool to consider in this regard is meditation, or simply finding time to quietly think about life while listening to good music.

Closely associated with all of this is the quality of optimism.

Admiral Jacky Fisher was relentlessly upbeat and positive. While it may seem a small thing, his love of dancing was part of how he *increased* his level of energy, even as it was a way to deal with his exuberant animal spirits. While happiness is not always a choice, an energetic frame of mind can be. And the two so often go hand in hand, as they did in Admiral Fisher. As former chairman of the Joint Chiefs and secretary of state Colin Powell, a mentor of mine, has said to me on more than one occasion, "Optimism is a force multiplier." There are lessons there for us all in terms of how we wake up and frame each day in our mind's eye.

Finally, there was that questing and relentless mind, endlessly asking the question, "Why can't we do that?" So often, the most defining issue of character is curiosity. This is the wellspring that leads directly to achievement in many of the great innovators in history. Walter Isaacson's brilliant biographies of Steve Jobs, Benjamin Franklin, and Leonardo da Vinci show this clearly in three of the most extraordinary innovators in history. Jacky Fisher certainly fits into the category of a curiosity-driven character. It appears throughout his life, and often led to his brilliant (and occasionally failed) attempts to change gunnery, torpedoes, communication, armor, ship design, fleet organization, uniforms, and seemingly a thousand other things.

For each of us individually, curiosity can be both a natural tendency and something we can develop in our own character. I asked former Speaker of the House Newt Gingrich once how he survived so many boring Washington, DC, cocktail parties, and he said to keep asking questions until you found someone doing something interesting, then ask them endless questions. Drill down and learn something. What terrific advice. A mind that gets into the habit of asking questions is the mind that will learn more, accomplish more, and be satisfied more.

If I could pick only one admiral to spend a long evening with, it would be Jacky Fisher. That combination of relentless perseverance and an unbounded desire to "seize the new" is very, very rare in leaders. When you combine it with the formidable intellectual firepower and the easy charm, deployed at will, it adds up to a remarkable figure whose qualities of character leave much to be admired. And through it all, he managed to literally dance his way through his life. Yes, a dinner with Admiral Jacky would be a delight—especially if we could organize a dance afterward.

All of the quotes herein are drawn from Admiral Fisher's two memoirs, *Memories* (London: Hodder & Stoughton, 1919), and *Records* (London: Hodder & Stoughton, 1919).

CHAPTER VII

The Admiral's Admiral

Fleet Admiral Chester W. Nimitz

―――――――

BORN FEBRUARY 24, 1885, FREDERICKSBURG,
TEXAS

DIED FEBRUARY 20, 1966, YERBA BUENA
ISLAND, CALIFORNIA

You can't be an officer in the US Navy and not know about Fleet Admiral Chester Nimitz. He hit my radar when I arrived at the Naval Academy in the early 1970s and started getting asked challenging questions about him and his various famous quotations as part of the hazing process applied to new "plebes" at Annapolis. But what I went through was nothing compared with the fate suffered by my classmate and friend Midshipman Fourth Class Steve Nimitz. There is a special place in the hazing universe reserved for the progeny of admirals, especially famous ones—and, in the US Navy, there is no admiral more famous than Chester William Nimitz. (Luckily, Steve not only survived his plebe hazing but went on to a career worthy of his famous ancestor, including command of a destroyer, nuclear power training, and the four gold stripes of a captain.)

But I really focused on the admiral a few years later as a senior at Annapolis when I was assigned to go to sea on the ship bearing his name, the proud USS *Nimitz* (CVN-72). The massive, 100,000-ton warship was then a brand-new nuclear-powered aircraft carrier—the ultimate symbol of American sea power. At the time, I was considering whether to join the nuclear Navy myself upon graduation, so a two-month training cruise on a "nuke" seemed to make sense. I arrived and was scooped up by the Reactor Department, the part of the ship's company in charge of the carrier's propulsion system. Once there I was told my job would be "reviewing logs." In practice, this meant being stuck in a closet-like office with a huge stack of log pages on which the temperature of oil lubricating the main bearings on the massive carrier's engines had been recorded in black ink. I was given a red pencil and told to meticulously go through the vast stack one by one and "circle any number greater than 180 or less than 130." Not very inspiring work.

After a couple hours of that, I snuck out, went up to the "dirty shirt" wardroom (the one where you didn't have to wear a formal uniform, frequented by pilots in their flight suits), and hung out with the aviators. It was clear to me I was not cut out for service in the nuclear Navy, and luckily the skipper of one of the aviation squadrons (then-Commander and later Admiral Leighton W. "Snuffy" Smith) arranged for me to finish out my cruise with his unit. It was a terrific summer in the end, and while I discovered that I was not a good fit for nuclear power, I learned a lot about naval aviation that stood me in good stead in later years. I chose neither nuclear power nor aviation, but settled on a traditional destroyer man's career, and loved every day of it.

In the two months I was unofficially assigned to one of the carrier's two light attack jet squadrons, I felt the spirit of Admiral Nimitz everywhere I went. While a submariner at heart, he was in every sense an officer for the entire Navy. It is highly unlikely that any admiral in the future will ever command the massive firepower and fleets that he did in the Pacific during World War II. As I walked around USS *Nimitz* on that summer voyage, I thought about his life and career and promised myself that I would try to emulate three of his best qualities: a quiet sense of humor, unshakable and sincere humility, and an unbreakable bond with my friends and peers. I haven't done any of those things as well as Fleet Admiral Chester Nimitz, but I've truly tried to do so, and became a better person and naval officer as a result. That cruise was an inflection point in my own voyage of character, and I walked off *Nimitz* a better person than when I boarded, and with a deep and lasting appreciation for the character of the ship's great namesake— all the more profound when you consider the distance he traveled to become a legendary American admiral.

The first years of the life of the admiral whose career would offer the nearest parallel to Nelson in the US naval tradition gave little hint of the shape of his destiny. Chester William Nimitz was born in the German immigrant community of Fredericksburg, Texas, which at the time of his birth was pretty much the last outpost of so-called civilization on the Texas frontier. Where Nelson was quintessentially English and grew up around the water, Nimitz's childhood was one of rural ranching and farming and culturally German American, and had nothing to do with the sea. Throughout his life, family and friends in Fredericksburg communicated in German as much as or more than they did in English, and their closest approximation of a naval tradition was the legacy of the prairie schooners that had carried their forebears into the Hill Country where they built their beloved Texan "burg."

As with the young Alfred Thayer Mahan, however, Nimitz's childhood had some powerful martial influences. During and especially after the Civil War, soldiers riding through town would stay at his grandfather's hotel, which, as it happened, the elder Nimitz had designed to resemble the prow of a great ship. From the soldiers, Nimitz developed an early inclination to apply to the Military Academy at West Point; from his grandfather, he absorbed wildly embellished tall tales of ships and the sea loosely based on his "Opa's" brief service in the German merchant marine in younger days. In another similarity to Mahan, Nimitz tried but failed to secure an appointment to West Point and only considered the Naval Academy as a second choice. There the similarities between the two end, however: Nimitz was from the start a much more outgoing, committed, and social midshipman than Mahan ever was. This was lucky, for Nimitz attended the Academy at the same time as many other future three-, four-, and five-star admirals. These men, along with Nimitz, would be instrumental in the naval campaigns of World War II. Among these classmates and near-classmates were Nimitz's future boss, Ernest King, and his two greatest subordinates, the mercurial William "Bull" Halsey and the thoughtful "quiet warrior," Raymond Spruance.

A trait that would become a hallmark of Nimitz's character, discretion, was reinforced during his time at the Academy through both public controversy and private experience. At that time, two admirals were mired in a years-long public argument, known as the Sampson-Schley controversy, about which one deserved credit for an 1898 naval victory during the Spanish-American War. The undignified spat played out in Congress and the press and accomplished little other than sullying the Navy. Deeply repulsed by the officers' conduct and the damage they caused the service, Nimitz resolved early on not to emulate or tolerate such behavior.

Shortly before graduation, Nimitz himself benefited from a senior officer's discretion. Nimitz was a semiregular participant in the unauthorized but well-established practice of buying beer from the haberdasher in downtown Annapolis, and on one such trip, he blithely filled a suitcase with beer under the apparently uncaring eye of another customer in the store. The next morning, Nimitz was shocked to encounter that same man in uniform as an officer newly appointed to the Academy. The officer gave no indication of ever having seen Nimitz before, and the young man instantly learned a lesson in whether and when to punish people who made atypical mistakes.

For the rest of his life, Nimitz went to great lengths to avoid "washing . . . the Navy's dirty linen in public," as his biographer put it, as well as to preserve the careers, reputations, and egos of well-meaning subordinates who made an occasional mistake. Indeed, Nimitz's "almost obsessive discretion" is the subject of the first sentence of his biography, and no sailor—or admiral—whom Nimitz protected ever forgot it. Nimitz's personality and self-confidence enabled him to inspire his subordinates and get every bit of effectiveness out of his peers and superiors. Named to his defining role as Commander in Chief, Pacific, or "CINCPAC," after Pearl Harbor, Nimitz took great care to do what he could to protect the man he was replacing, Admiral Husband Kimmel, and his staff ("It could have happened to anyone," Nimitz said of the Pearl Harbor disaster). Throughout the war, he would demonstrate masterful tact in managing both the admirals around him and the men below, enabling each to do his work with a minimum of friction.

Look at the various personalities with whom he worked over the senior years of his career—starting with the difficult Admiral Ernest King, of whom it was said, "when things get tough they send for the sons-of-bitches," a comment he reveled in and repeated himself. King was notoriously hard drinking, harsh on his sailors, and possessed of a towering ego—yet Nimitz managed not only to remain on his good side, but also to help King navigate the political storms of Washington with sound, measured advice. Another challenging but talented subordinate was Admiral Halsey, famous for his off-handed but highly printable and colorful remarks to the media (he was the Navy's version of General George Patton). Halsey was a "fighting admiral," and Nimitz was able to soothe his subordinate's temper and keep him on a successful course despite his occasional lapses both personally and tactically. Nimitz did this endlessly with numerous others, even putting up with the greatest ego in American military history, General Douglas MacArthur, as they ran parallel campaigns across the Pacific and competed for resources from the Pentagon.

Another great stream of Nimitz's development as an officer was his drive to acquire experience, responsibility, and expertise. From his earliest shipboard assignments, Nimitz eschewed the typical approach of seeking small roles on large ships in favor of taking on large responsibilities in small ships. This pushed him first into small surface combatants, where he quickly acquired the priceless experience of commanding a ship through a dangerous typhoon, and later into submarines, where he would spend the majority of his career before reaching flag rank.

At least as important as Nimitz's habit of seeking responsibility for himself was his practice of devolving as much responsibility as possible to the people around and below him. From two-stripe lieutenant to five-star admiral, Nimitz made the people and organizations around him better by pushing subordinates to grow beyond their own expected limitations and by preserving his own energy to focus on the decisions and actions that were his alone to make. This element of Nimitz's character can be hard to see now, since our cultural memory of him is almost invariably of the victor of World War II who carried more responsibility than most of us can imagine. However, it is essential to note that Nimitz did not meet his superhuman task with superhuman capacity: rather, he was an extraordinary delegator who was able to do his job in large part because he had the discipline *not* to insist on doing his subordinates' jobs as well—often the hardest task for a gifted leader.

Another aspect of Nimitz's professional development that is too often lost in the overarching shine of the World War II victory was his sheer proficiency as a sailor. Even if the war had not broken out, Nimitz might still be remembered today—at least within the Navy—for his technical innovations at sea, somewhat like Jacky Fisher. When Nimitz moved into the submarine community, the US Navy was still working out the design and use of the relatively primitive undersea boats; Nimitz quickly began writing about how submarine warfare might be waged and became instrumentally involved in the change from gasoline to diesel-electric propulsion.

Nimitz was also a principal inventor of the underway replenishment techniques that would be essential to the US Navy as it confronted the logistical challenge of spanning the Pacific. He was an early and frequent contributor to the US Naval Institute's professional journal, *Proceedings*. Like Jacky Fisher, he combined strategic vision and technical skill.

The final building block of Nimitz's development was his prewar appointment as chief of the Bureau of Navigation, which managed all naval personnel. (In later years, the bureau was renamed the Bureau of Personnel, or "BuPers.") Nimitz's son Chester Junior would describe that posting as the most important in his father's development. Nimitz "was a people man entirely," said his son. Not only was the elder Nimitz a good fit for the position, but it provided him with the breadth of perspective that comes with learning what it takes to manage all the Navy's people. BuNav, according to Chester Junior, was the job in which his father "learned most, and in which the evaluation of his superiors was probably most critical to his subsequent success."

It was as chief of BuNav that Nimitz sat down that Sunday afternoon in December 1941 to listen to classical music on the radio when the attack on Pearl Harbor was announced. Half a decade before, in a conversation with Chester Junior while the latter was a midshipman, Nimitz had predicted that "we are going to have a major war, with Japan and Germany," which he believed would "start with a very serious surprise attack and defeat of U.S. armed forces." Nimitz knew that no admiral in command at sea when that attack came would be politically palatable after the defeat ("though it won't be their fault necessarily"), and so wished "to be in a position of sufficient prominence so that I will then be considered as one to be sent to sea."

In that sense, Nimitz's appointment to BuNav—for which he had turned down his dream job as CINCPAC—was doubly lucky. Not only did it prepare him for subsequent success, but it also kept him from being in Husband Kimmel's position on the morning of December 7, 1941. As Nimitz had predicted, Kimmel was sacked—regardless of how much or how little he was truly to blame—and the hand of fate then turned to select a new CINCPAC. Secretary of the Navy Frank Knox raised Nimitz's name before President Roosevelt, who, after an overnight deliberation, called Knox into his office. "Tell Nimitz to get the hell out to Pearl and stay there till the war is won," ordered the president. Knox promptly returned to his own office, summoned Nimitz, and asked him how soon he could be ready to travel. "It depends on where I'm going and how long I'll be away," the somewhat harried admiral had replied. Unable to conceal his own enthusiasm, Knox gave Nimitz the news: "You're going to take command of the Pacific Fleet, and I think you will be gone a long time."

Thus, nine days after Nimitz's predicted surprise attack had come to pass, he fulfilled his own prophecy by being in position to be named to command at sea. En route to Hawaii, Nimitz was concerned about what he would find: "We have suffered a terrible defeat," he confided to a friend. "I don't know whether we can ever recover from it." But on the morning of December 31, 1941, Admiral Chester W. Nimitz stepped into the defining role of his life. He completed a journey spanning an entire continent and half an ocean to take command of the shattered US Pacific Fleet in a brief ceremony aboard the submarine USS *Grayling*. There was still oil floating on the surface of Pearl Harbor, and the smell of smoke and cordite hung in the tropical air. A few yards away, thousands of sailors were still entombed in the massive battleships sunk on December 7. It was a grim and purposeful rite, and a striking contrast to the normally happy atmosphere of a fleet change of command.

The admiral came to the microphone in the center of the deck and turned to face the small huddle of fellow officers and pressmen gathered for the ceremony. As a submariner by training and therefore one to spot the humor in any situation, the irony was not lost on Nimitz that *Grayling*, a submarine, offered one of the only floating warship decks in Pearl Harbor on which to conduct the change of command. Suppressing the hint of a smile but not the glint of determination in his eye, Nimitz took a barely perceptible deep breath and read his orders, relieving his good friend Husband E. Kimmel from command. He knew that Kimmel's life and career were shattered, and he felt deeply the hurt of his old friend.

As soon as Nimitz uttered the traditional "I relieve you, sir," the sense of irony vanished. Instantly, those four words invested the four stars newly pinned on Nimitz's collar with the full weight of his responsibility. Salutes were exchanged, the boatswain's whistle trilled, and with eight sharp dings of the *Grayling*'s bell, Nimitz went ashore. "Pacific Fleet, departing," called the boatswain, and Nimitz began the task that would occupy him for the next four years. Setting his face and his will, Nimitz—a lifelong walker— began making his way up the extinct volcano of Makalapa Hill to his new headquarters. The walk up from the harbor that day was short, but it was the beginning of a long, arduous climb back from the disaster of Pearl Harbor to the singular height of glory Nimitz would achieve three and a half years later. At that moment, he of course could not foresee that the voyage of the war would end in another harbor, Tokyo's, where he would accept the surrender of Japan. All he could think about on that final day of 1941 was the shattered fleet under the oily water.

Once on-site, however, Nimitz had the presence of mind to make several key decisions that ensured that the fleet would recover but faster than anyone could have expected. First, he stabilized the personnel situation by keeping nearly all of Admiral Kimmel's people on staff—and keeping himself ashore. Intentionally retaining a defeated and demoralized staff was not merely a matter of discretion, but a deeply practical decision that began rebuilding morale and allowed the Navy to focus on striking back rather than building a new staff. Moving his own command ashore cost him the chance to command ships at sea in combat (something he never had the opportunity to do), but was absolutely the right decision for managing a war on the scale Nimitz soon confronted.

Second, Nimitz—ever the clear-eyed optimist—had the perspicacity to see that even such a terrible defeat was not total destruction. Burning and sinking battleships were quite a spectacle, but Nimitz realized what the Japanese had missed. As he pored over the photographs of a destroyed Pearl Harbor, he focused on what was *not* in the pictures of the carnage, namely the fleet's fuel reserves and aircraft carriers. Had either of those assets been knocked out, the US war effort would have been in great peril indeed; as it was, most of the battleships sunk at Pearl Harbor would be refloated and returned to combat, but the course of the war would demonstrate their obsolescence. Fuel oil, aviation gasoline, and aircraft carriers would be far more decisive in the conduct of the war.

Finally, Nimitz was involved early and deeply in setting the strategy that the United States pursued throughout the course of the Pacific War. Working with his superior back in Washington, Admiral King, and his own staff in Pearl Harbor, Nimitz had a hand in drawing the rough outlines of the central Pacific strategy that would be the US Navy's main line of effort for the next three and a half years. Nimitz was no armchair strategist, either. Within six months after Pearl Harbor, he had made the bold decision to launch the quick (though symbolic) retaliatory Doolittle bombing raid on Tokyo; had gambled and won at Midway, inflicting a defeat from which the Imperial Japanese Navy would never truly recover; and had put Marines ashore on Guadalcanal, beginning the island-hopping campaign toward the Japanese home islands.

Nimitz later said that those first six months were the hardest, but the war in the Pacific raged on for three more years. The scale, violence, and intensity of the fighting grew in a horrible crescendo from bloody amphibious landings, to fanatical banzai and kami-kaze attacks, to the ultimate breaking of the enemy's will with the dropping of two atomic bombs. Along the way, Nimitz's responsibilities grew exponentially until he "commanded thousands of ships and aircraft and millions of men, amounting to more military power than had been wielded by all the commanders in all previous wars," as his biographer wrote.

Nimitz clearly could not be everywhere at once—and he

determined not to try to be the next Nelson by playing strategist, sailor, and warrior all at once. The war was much too big and complex for that. Instead, the secret to Nimitz's success was his skillful management of a relatively few people: those above him who managed the entire war effort, and those around and just below him who conducted the actual fighting. As his biographer put it, Nimitz's personality served as the "link and buffer" that turned this complicated group of admirals into "one of the most effective fighting teams in history." Without Nimitz as the glue holding it together, the unique abilities of each of the others might not have meshed. Perhaps equally important, Nimitz also managed to work out a modus vivendi with the most temperamental and difficult officer in the theater, General of the Army Douglas MacArthur. Probably no one save Nimitz could have maintained an even keel in working with that colossal ego.

After the war, Nimitz remained in uniform for several more years, replacing King as chief of naval operations, the pinnacle of the naval profession in the United States. It was a position to which Nimitz had always aspired. Due to an act of Congress that kept Nimitz and his fellow five-star admirals (including King and Halsey) on the active-duty rolls for life, Nimitz technically never retired from the Navy. However, he had the good grace and sense to get out of town after his tenure as CNO rather than lingering— and inevitably growing stale—in some "special advisory" role. He and his wife bought the first house they had ever owned in Berkeley, California, where, not surprisingly, tending the garden quickly proved insufficiently exciting. Nimitz accepted a position with the United Nations in which he was charged with negotiating a post–civil war settlement between India and Pakistan; sadly, the talks never happened, and Nimitz retired once more to Berkeley.

Despite many lucrative offers, Nimitz never parlayed his wartime fame into a cushy second career in business. Rather, he remained a symbol of and advocate for the Navy for the rest of his days—a decision, like stepping away after his time as CNO, which did much to cement his reputation. His voyage finally ended at age eighty; he died in a sunny room in the old naval house called Quarters One on Yerba Buena Island in San Francisco Bay. True to their mutual wishes, Nimitz was buried alongside fellow World War II admirals Spruance, Kelly Turner, and Charles Lockwood, together with the admirals' wives, in the Golden Gate National Cemetery in San Bruno, California.

The memory of this "American Nelson" lives on strongly in the US Navy today. Nimitz's name adorns the library at the Naval Academy, as well as the lead ship of the *Nimitz* class of super carriers that have projected American power and maintained the peace Nimitz won seventy years ago. When USS *Nimitz* was commissioned, President Gerald R. Ford quoted E. B. Potter, the admiral's biographer, in delivering this tribute to Nimitz: "He surrounded himself with the ablest men he could find and sought their advice, but he made his own decisions. He was a keen strategist who never forgot that he was dealing with human beings, on both sides of the conflict. He was aggressive in war without hate, and audacious while never failing to weigh the risks." In so many ways, he was the greatest of our Navy's admirals.

Reflecting on the long trajectory of his career, it feels as though Nimitz is too much remembered as the conquering hero of 1945 and not enough as the keen strategist of 1941–42. Although it can be difficult to clearly distinguish between "Nimitz the strategist" and "Nimitz the implementer" of that strategy, the crucial point is that Nimitz was at his best when thinking through the strategic challenges he faced. All leaders are responsible for setting organizations' goals and martialing resources. Nimitz was a master of this element of leadership, and his skill was crowned by his executive ability. He neither overplanned to the point of inaction ("paralysis by analysis") nor struck out blindly without a clear sense of what he wanted to accomplish and how he could realistically expect to achieve it. In addition to doing the right amount of strategizing at the right level, Nimitz firmly grasped the two elements of strategy that most often slip through leaders' fingers. First, he knew that strategy is a team sport. In his capacity as "link and buffer," Nimitz not only smoothed the rough edges of the personalities around him but—crucially—knew how to manage upward, downward, and sideways to develop and execute the best strategy. Nimitz listened to King, who also had to worry about the war in the Atlantic but was unafraid to push back (with characteristic tact) when his boss's ideas seemed off-base. Similarly, he communicated strategic objectives to Halsey, Spruance, and other subordinates with enough flexibility to allow them room to exercise their own discretion as commanders on the scene as events unfolded.

Nimitz also understood that strategy is not a one-time event but rather an iterative process. Although the outlines of the central Pacific drive were set early in the war and pursued throughout, the plan had to be constantly revised and updated as the situation changed: Americans learned (at great cost) the art of amphibious warfare, Japanese resistance stiffened, land- and sea-based air-power evolved before everyone's eyes and changed the character of the war. Managing all those factors and many more, Nimitz knew when to see things through and when to make a change. Managing "thousands of ships and aircraft and millions of men" is above all an organizational challenge. Before Nimitz could take on the Imperial Japanese Navy, he first had to master the *US* Navy, and he did so with aplomb. Like strategy, organizational design and management is something that leaders at all levels need to take ownership of at some point or another, and it is best done early. From his early drive to take on outsized responsibility in undersized ships to his essential preparatory posting at the Bureau of Navigation, Nimitz developed several essential habits of management—each of which tied to his character.

First, as previously noted, Nimitz was an outstanding delegator. This made the people and organizations around him better by identifying and growing talent quickly—and just as quickly clarifying who was in the wrong job. Being an effective delegator means first and foremost sublimating your ego and allowing others to shine in the spotlight. This reflects self-confidence and an inner sense of balance that keeps the ego in check. Second, Nimitz was supremely resourceful, creative, and humane in how he dealt with the people around him. Whether by alternating Halsey and Spruance in command of the fleet at sea or by quickly and discreetly forgiving or moving people who proved inadequate in the jobs they were in, Nimitz found ways to get the most out of everyone in the fleet and minimized inefficiency and ineffectiveness throughout the organization. Finally, and critically, Nimitz knew better than most managers where his job ended and his superiors' and subordinates' began. In communicating plans before and instructions during battle, Nimitz gave his commanders room to command and resisted the temptation to micromanage by radio. If Nimitz could stay off the radio during some of the chanciest moments of the war in the Pacific, many modern managers—with infinitely more access to their subordinate's inboxes—could take a lesson from the admiral's self-discipline.

As anyone reading today's headlines knows, leaders' personalities matter immensely. Especially in today's media environment, personality is an essential foundation piece of any leader's message. And while it is tempting to let emotion drive personality, the true acme of character is sublimating anger, pettiness, and impulse in favor of a cool, calm temperament. This was the genius of Nimitz.

Personality is naturally individual, and it is often fixed to some degree. Importantly, though, a leader can first learn what sort of personality he or she has, and then how best to express him- or herself within an organization. The world is still full of irascible Halseys, brooding Spruances, and volcanic Kings—and each type can contribute to success. However, as with those three admirals, success often depends on each person being in the right position, and especially on the presence of a Nimitz who can "link and buffer" between idiosyncrasies. While we all have challenges overcoming our emotions, the habit of a calm demeanor can be learned. In my own case, in my twenties I had more difficulty with this than later in life. I was lucky that my second captain aboard my very first ship, the destroyer *Hewitt*, had a calm and soothing personality, as did the operations officer, someone I deeply admired and tried to emulate. By the time I was a destroyer captain my-self, I consciously talked with the entire 350-member crew about the need to never lose our tempers. This anger-free zone in the ship paid great dividends as we came under pressure on forward deployments.

Qualities of personality, especially such subtle ones as Nimitz exhibited during World War II, take a lifetime to develop. The important thing is to dedicate some self-awareness and effort to nurturing them, as Nimitz did from his earliest days in the Navy. Although Nimitz might have been predisposed to become a leader of leaders, his personal evolution was neither accidental nor pre-destined. Moreover, he is not the sole paragon of success in this respect, nor was he entirely successful. All leaders have lacunae in their personalities, and no one style can fit every job or mission before it. For example, it is doubtful that King or Nimitz could have succeeded as they did if their roles had been reversed—in King's position, a brutal, ruthless driver was needed; in Nimitz's job, being a conciliator was the key. And we should also recognize the simple fact that virtually all the leaders of those days would have a great deal of difficulty working alongside women or mem-bers of minorities in a partnership of equals. Although Nimitz was a superb overall leader, he was of an era that did not recognize the contributions of women or nonwhite groups or their abilities. In order to succeed deep into the postwar era, he would have needed to adjust his approach considerably. The point is that effective leaders know that personality and style cannot be static and are prepared to adjust to changing circumstances.

Nimitz was a compassionate leader who "made every effort to

protect the feelings and reputations of his subordinates, even when they failed to measure up." Nimitz established and maintained extremely high standards, but, as President Ford noted, "never forgot that he was dealing with human beings." Nimitz's standard could both accommodate occasional mistakes—even big ones—by basically competent people like Halsey and preserve the dignity and efficacy of those who simply "failed to measure up" by promptly but discreetly moving them to jobs in which they could succeed. Nimitz demoted people rarely and demeaned them never; in fact, he was unafraid to use promotion as a tool for reassigning people from unsuccessful positions into jobs they were better suited to do.

Rather than compromising his standards, Nimitz's discretion helped him build and maintain trust throughout his command. All leaders are in the business of dealing with human beings, but not all of them know it. Especially today, when people and organizations are increasingly geographically far-flung—organized around digitally delivered messages much more than by personal touch— leaders need to put a lot of energy into building and sustaining trust. In that respect, they might do well to reflect on Nimitz's famous principle of "calculated risk," by which he trusted his people to perform to the best of their judgment and ability, and they could trust him not to demote and never to demean them if they proved to be merely human.

I've certainly made my share of mistakes in failing to be discreet. As one of the famous "Laws of the Navy" (a long poem penned by a retired British admiral which US Naval Academy midshipmen are required to memorize as plebes) puts it, "Take heed what you say of your seniors / Be your words spoken softly or plain / Lest the birds of the air tell the matter / And so ye shall hear it again." I have made indiscreet comments from time to time, and they have never turned out well. Even as a senior officer, wearing my first star and certainly knowing better, I made some loose criticisms about my three-star boss that made their way back to him. This was in the immediate aftermath of 9/11, and I was sure that my ideas for radical changes were the right prescription for the Navy, and that the chain of command was just slowing things down with timidity. My boss rightly called me to his office (which still smelled of smoke from the attack), read me the riot act, but gave me another chance. He also listened to my ideas, and the lesson I learned was simple: either have the courage to go to your boss directly, or keep your mouth shut. Far better to keep your own counsel on personal opinions about others and be careful with secrets both professional and personal. That is an element of character that is so often lacking, even in the most senior of people. And in today's world of instantaneous tweets heard round the world, it's an even better policy to follow.

Nimitz was a perpetual optimist, but a grounded, almost a guarded one. He was never a cheerleader spreading sweetness and light on his sailors, but in his quiet way he did all he could to see the positives in any situation—no matter how bleak. All leaders know that surprises and defeats are a fact of life; luckily, few leaders will face the equivalent of Pearl Harbor, but all will have to respond to significant setbacks. This has been central to my approach and was something I inherited from my father. He was a career officer in the Marines and saw combat around the globe from the end of World War II through Vietnam, yet never lost his optimistic view of the world. As I have said earlier, optimism is a habit of personality that stems from our character.

How the leader responds will go a long way toward determining how the group responds, as Nimitz understood. Though he confided the depth of his fears to his wife and one or two trusted confidants, on arrival in Pearl Harbor, Nimitz's words and actions signaled his confidence in a team that had just suffered the surprise of the century. This stopped the free fall in morale, set people back on their feet, and quickly translated newfound determination into action. Had Nimitz summarily dismissed his predecessor's staff, he would have spent his first six months or more as CINCPAC fighting the learning curve rather than the enemy.

Essential as optimism was and is in the face of crisis, it is critical that it be well founded. A leader needs to lead—but leadership needs to be believable to be effective. Pearl Harbor was as serious a crisis as they come, and feigned optimism would have been at least as damaging as defeatism. By pointing to what few others could see—namely, all that was *not* destroyed, such as the underground fuel reserves and the all-important aircraft carriers out at sea—Nimitz was able to give his people real reasons for hope at a very fragile time. I continue to reflect on the quiet confidence, calm demeanor, endless civility, and incisive judgment of Fleet Admiral Chester Nimitz. He set a high bar for character and remains a true North Star for the Navy, and the nation.

All quotations in this chapter are sourced from E. B. Potter, *Nimitz* (Annapolis, MD: Naval Institute Press, 1976).

CHAPTER VIII

The Master of Anger

Admiral Hyman Rickover

———

Born January 27, 1900, Makow, Poland

Died July 8, 1986, Arlington, Virginia

In March 1974, something historic happened at the US Naval Academy in Annapolis, Maryland: four-star admiral Hyman G. Rickover arrived on campus wearing his US Navy service dress blue uniform with a single broad gold stripe and three narrower ones adorning each of his sleeves. He was present for the dedication of Rickover Hall, which was being named in his honor, and evidently had been convinced to actually don a four-star admiral's uniform, probably under direct orders from Secretary of the Navy John Warner. This was the only generally known occasion on which he did so, despite serving in that rank for years.

Rickover famously avoided wearing a Navy dress uniform for several reasons. First, he enjoyed effectively pointing out to the other high-ranking members of the "Naval Aristocracy" that he could not be defined by their conventions. Second, he jealously guarded his concurrent civilian appointment at the Department of Energy focused on nuclear power and used it to maneuver between the uniformed Navy, the rest of the executive branch, and Capitol Hill. And finally, he preferred his baggy, nondescript suits and overlarge collared shirts for the simplicity and comfort they provided over the starched white dress shirts, beribboned blouses, and admiral's cap with copious gold braid.

I remember that March day as quite strange, even to my eyes as a "youngster" or second-year midshipman at the Academy. For starters, the venerable admiral, who as a four-star outranked the well-liked superintendent, three-star vice admiral Bill Mack, just didn't seem very happy. He had a scowl on his face throughout much of the ceremony, smiling thinly and briefly a couple of times but generally looking upset. As one of the selected midshipman "escorts," I was charged with trailing in the wake of the admiral and his new bride, a Navy commander in the Nurse Corps who was a fair bit younger than Rickover. I tried to stay out of his line of sight.

The event was a perfect reflection of the ambiguous relationship Admiral Rickover had with Annapolis. He had arrived at the Academy in 1918, part of the class of 1922. He was the son of a tailor, poor, short, slender, Jewish, and an immigrant who had passed through Ellis Island. From the moment he arrived in Annapolis, he was made to feel like an outsider, and that sense of isolation and detachment from the larger naval profession continued throughout his life. Fifty-six years after he first arrived at Annapolis, on that cold March morning when I first laid eyes on this legend, I could not help but notice that on a day when he should have been feeling honored and valued there at the very heart of the Navy, the anger and the resentment he had carried with him for decades seemed to dominate his feelings—or at least that is how it appeared to a very young midshipman.

In the end, Rickover served in the Navy from 1918 until 1982—the longest tenure in the service's history. He was a flag officer for nearly thirty years, again unprecedented. Rickover led the Navy into the era of nuclear propulsion, as important a transition surely as the previous shifts from sail to coal and from coal to oil. Yet on that blustery day, despite all his honors and successes, the feeling I had watching his awkward acceptance of the honors laid before him was not awe, but rather pity. I felt sorry for all the anger he seemed to carry with him, and all the pain it must have caused him across so many years.

He was born in Russian Poland in 1900 (or possibly 1898, as there is confusion between Navy records and birth records found by some researchers), named Chaim (derived from the Hebrew for "life") Godalia Rickover. His family came to New York City in 1906, refugees from anti-Jewish pogroms, and moved on to Chicago, where his father found work as a tailor and where young Hyman, as he was now renamed, worked for low wages outside the house from an early age. He went to the Naval Academy on a congressional appointment in 1918, and graduated with the class of 1922, close to the top 100 in his class of 540—high but not signal honors.

After well-regarded service on the destroyer *La Vallette* and the battleship *Nevada*, he was sent for graduate school in electrical engineering at both the Naval Postgraduate School and Columbia University, where he met his wife, Ruth, herself a graduate student in international relations. They were married in 1931, and the event seemed to catalyze Rickover to convert from Judaism to the Episcopal faith, the unofficial high church of the Navy's Admiralty. He remained a strong supporter of what today is called STEM (Science, Technology, Engineering, and Math) for the rest of his life, and throughout his career, he emphasized the need for naval officers to be formally trained to be technically proficient. (He also maintained that the social sciences, literature, history, and politics were unworthy of serious formal study: they could be "picked up" by personal study and reading.)

The next step in Rickover's career was pivotal: the decision to serve aboard submarines. This probably stemmed from his desire to be in a smaller, more controlled environment where he could exert greater influence. Despite being somewhat senior (at twenty-nine years of age) to transition from surface destroyers to diesel submarines, he received support from his former commanding officer aboard *Nevada* and, in the early 1930s, made the jump, training as a submariner and eventually qualifying for command of a diesel boat, although he never actually took command of one. His work translating the book *Das Unterseeboot* (*The Submarine*) by the German admiral Hermann Bauer had significant tactical impact on the US Navy.

In the late 1930s, he "surfaced" briefly to take command (his only command at sea) of a minesweeper on the China Station. After only three months in command, his request to become a specialized engineering duty officer was approved, and in late 1937 he headed back to Washington for an assignment in the Navy's Bureau of Engineering. He became fascinated with the idea of serving as an engineering duty officer so that he could drive new ideas, saying later in life, "Good ideas are not adopted automatically. They must be driven into practice with courageous impatience." As an engineering duty officer, Rickover was shifting over to the "restricted line"—meaning that he would never be in line for another command at sea but would be guaranteed a string of jobs focusing on the design, acquisition, construction, and repair of ships and their systems.

After the entrance of the United States into the Second World War, Rickover was dispatched to Pearl Harbor in the spring of 1942 to help with repairs to the badly damaged battleships. With the acceleration of promotions in wartime, he pinned on captain's rank in June 1942 and continued to work at a variety of key engineering and support positions throughout the rest of the war, eventually being awarded the first of his several Legion of Merit medals. As he moved along in the Navy, it was clear that the rules-based system of order was increasingly chafing him. He said, "More than ambition, more than ability, it is rules that limit contribution; rules are the lowest common denominator of human behavior. They are a substitute for rational thought."

After the war, Rickover was named inspector general of the Navy's West Coast fleet and began to work in earnest on nuclear propulsion. He mastered every element of the developing technology, saying later in a speech delivered at Columbia University that "the man in charge must concern himself with details." This became his personal mantra, and eventually the philosophical heart of Naval Reactors, the organization he would build to direct seagoing nuclear power. His initial work in the immediate postwar years was with General Electric, and he was sent to Oak Ridge National

Laboratory in Tennessee, which became the epicenter of the Navy's efforts to create nuclear propulsion. Of note, he helped the Navy see the powerful potential of using nuclear power on submarines, fundamentally changing the need for submarines to surface and recharge their oxygen-hungry batteries. Previously submarines were all diesel-powered and therefore extremely limited (and endangered) by the need to regularly surface. Despite frequent pushback from seniors, Rickover persisted with his single-minded vision of nuclear propulsion at sea and found a champion in fellow submariner and five-star fleet admiral Chester Nimitz.

With both Nimitz and Secretary of the Navy John Sullivan championing the effort, the first nuclear-powered vessel, USS *Nautilus*, a submarine, was built, named for the submarine in Jules Verne's *Twenty Thousand Leagues Under the Sea*. Rickover occasionally said that the true father of the nuclear Navy (a sobriquet that Rickover relished) was in fact Navy secretary Sullivan. Regardless of how initial credit is divided, it is simply a fact that the ultimate development of nuclear power at sea was germinated, nurtured, led, and matured by Hyman Rickover. His work in the late 1940s and early 1950s at the Atomic Energy Commission was seminal, and his selection to lead the development of nuclear submarines in the 1950s cemented the powerful role he would play for three more decades. This was the key point in his upward trajectory. The Atomic Energy Commission was civilian led and completely separate from the Navy. Rickover was able to use his position there when he wanted to go outside the Navy chain of command. It was a critical element in his success, and it illustrated one of his key principles. He said, "What it takes to do a job will not be learned from a management course. Human experience shows that people, not organizations or management systems, get things done." The adoption of nuclear power at sea reflected the personality and drive of Hyman Rickover.

By 1958, Rickover was wearing three stars, and despite the ongoing difficulties of pretty much everyone in getting along with him, he managed to completely consolidate his power over the Navy's now-prestigious nuclear program, becoming its single point of entry and personally interviewing nearly fifteen thousand applicants over the years. He accepted this responsibility as he did everything else in life—with grinding determination to succeed. As he said about responsibility, you can "share it with others, but your portion is not diminished. You may delegate it, but it is still with you. If responsibility is rightfully yours, no evasion, or ignorance, or passing the blame can shift the burden to someone else." Because he felt that responsibility so keenly, and because he always focused on the talent of the nuclear corps of officers, he spent endless hours deciding who would enter his program and who would not.

Some of the stories from these interviews are priceless, demonstrating the stereotypical Rickover: angry, foul-mouthed, irascible, and utterly unpredictable. Most are the stuff of legend and difficult to verify. One that has been verified is from Lieutenant (later Rear Admiral) Paul Tomb, who was interviewing with Rickover in hopes of entering the nuclear propulsion program. Tomb told the admiral his name was pronounced "Tom." Despite this the admiral persisted in calling him "Toom" throughout the interview, even after the lieutenant tried several times to correct him. When Rickover asked him when he became interested in the program, he said, "Right after the first atomic 'boom' went off, Admiral." He was accepted. But plenty of midshipmen were rejected from the program for reasons that seemed odd, from being unwilling to postpone their planned weddings to being related to senior naval officers. And in fairness, some of the candidates balked at entering the program after undergoing the interview. It was certainly a "fascinating experience," as future chief of naval operations Elmo Zumwalt wryly described it.

From time to time, the admiral used a chair with the front two legs sawed off short, so the candidate was leaning forward and unbalanced throughout the conversation, which could last a couple of hours. Other times, the officers were dragged in and out of the admiral's office, locked in small cupboards nearby, given math problems to solve, yelled at by teams of senior captains, and generally harassed. The one consistent thread was a desire to put the applicant under stress and measure the reaction—then decide his fate. What Rickover was after were officers who would stand and deliver without fear or favor in the crucible of pressure. He said once, "Free discussion requires an atmosphere unembarrassed by any suggestion of authority or even respect. If a subordinate agrees with his superior, he is a useless part of the organization." Finding the right candidates was an obsession for Rickover, essentially because he fervently believed that it led to safer operations at sea.

During his decades-long stint as the head of Naval Reactors, the Navy's powerful nuclear shop, Rickover focused above all on reactor safety. He correctly foresaw that even a single significant radiation leak could doom the public's confidence in the nuclear program. Rickover understood the uneasy confusion the public had between nuclear weapons and nuclear propulsion, even though it is literally impossible to coax a full-blown nuclear detonation out of a shipboard reactor. Interestingly, he was the only engineering duty officer to hold the position as head of Naval Reactors; all the other officers who followed him in this powerful job—nearly all of whom he selected personally to enter the nuclear program—have come from a line officer background and commanded submarines at sea.

In the late 1970s, despite powerful friendships on Capitol Hill in the Senate and House armed services committees, Rickover's clout was beginning to wane. With the election of Ronald Reagan in 1980, he faced a new, young opponent—Secretary of the Navy John Lehman. In his blunt memoir, *Command of the Seas*, Lehman lays out what he calls "the Rickover problem." In essence, he believed Rickover had already made the contributions he was going to make and was a sort of dead man walking who kept the nuclear Navy in perpetual fear of his explosive temper. Lehman correctly viewed the nuclear community as a kind of elite Navy within the Navy and felt its resource needs would detract from his overarching strategic objective of achieving a six-hundred-ship Navy.

By 1982, Lehman had assembled what he viewed as a compelling case to ease out the formidable Admiral Rickover. In addition to his advanced age and acid-tongued treatment of everyone in his path, Rickover was at the center of a badly handled submarine test event in which his actions personally caused a loss of ship control. With great reluctance, Rickover finally retired as a four-star admiral after sixty-three years of service under thirteen Presidents, from Woodrow Wilson to Ronald Wilson Reagan. The story of how that came about is priceless and says a great deal about Rick-over's character.

In January 1982, Rickover was so angry his hands were shaking. He buried them in the pockets of his suit as he rode to the White House. He arrived just a few minutes before the new, young, and handsome secretary of the Navy, John Lehman. The two men de-tested each other and were long past the point of hiding it. Even as Rickover was settling into the waiting room to the Oval Office, the new secretary of the Navy was staring moodily and tensely out the windows of his limousine, going over in his own mind the script he had crafted for the small meeting with President Reagan. The objective of the meeting was to be simple: for the president to con-genially thank Admiral Rickover for his long decades of service and accept his retirement. Lehman had convinced the president that this was the only course of action to deal with the difficulties of Rickover's excessive domination of the Navy's vast nuclear power program. Rickover, on the other hand, had absolutely no intention whatsoever of going gently into that good night, and came into the White House and the Oval Office with a plan to blow the meeting apart and put the relatively inexperienced secretary of the Navy in his place, establishing again that only one man could run the Navy's nuclear program. It proved to be an explosive meeting.

After clearing security—a quick process in those distant and innocent pre-9/11 days—the secretary and the admiral were ush-ered into the White House, then into the Oval Office. At this point in his presidency, Reagan was still like the sun shining on his visitors. The smile was broad, open, and sincere; the handshake was firm, confident, and friendly. They moved to sit around the coffee table in front of the president's desk, and Secretary Lehman began his well-rehearsed pitch, thanking Admiral Rickover for his long decades of service and for his gracious decision to retire. Rickover sat silent, fidgeting a bit until there was a brief pause as Secretary Lehman threw the conversational ball to the president.

Before President Reagan could begin his amplifying thanks, the wizened admiral launched his own broadside. He told the president that he had most certainly *not* agreed with this idea of retirement, and only came to the Oval Office to plead his case to stay directly with the president. His voice raised in passionate intensity, Rickover told Reagan, "That piss-ant [pointing at Lehman] knows nothing about the Navy. He's a goddamn liar, he knows he is just doing the work of the contractors." Reagan was befuddled at this strange turn of events.

At this point Lehman was arriving at the unpleasant realization that he had personally persuaded the president, Reagan's chief of staff James Baker, and Lehman's boss, Secretary of Defense Caspar "Cap" Weinberger, to set up this meeting. He had assured each of them that the admiral had accepted his fate and was ready to finally retire. Everything had been arranged, including the offer of a new job for Admiral Rickover as a special assistant to the president on nuclear power, an office at the Navy Yard, administrative support, even a car and driver in perpetuity.

Yet Rickover felt only anger at being treated badly. He began literally shouting at the president, "Are you a man? Can't you make decisions yourself? What do you know about this problem? These people are lying to you. Don't you think people are already using this against you? They say you are too old, and that you're not up to the job either." The tirade continued unabated for long minutes, ending at some point with Rickover telling the president, "Aw, cut the crap," and demanding a one-on-one with him. Lehman remembered thinking that if it turned out to be a brawl, Reagan looked strong and could probably handle himself.

Secretary Lehman said later that he was working hard to suppress a powerful urge to lunge across the coffee table and strangle the seemingly unhinged admiral. The meeting descended further into chaos, and finally Rickover got his way—he was granted twenty minutes alone with the president of the United States while Secretary Lehman, the chief of staff, and the secretary of defense cooled their heels outside the Oval Office. Lehman felt his stock slipping minute by minute. No one knows exactly what transpired in that one-on-one meeting, but the consensus is that Reagan merely did what Reagan did best—smoothed things over. Rickover probably left the White House thinking he still had a chance to remain in his job. But the wheels of bureaucracy continued to turn, and in the end, despite some support from Capitol Hill and his own determination to stay, the writing was on the wall. Leaving the White House that day, Lehman realized that the battle to remove Rickover would be harder than he thought; and more important, that the nuclear Navy culture built by Rickover over the decades was here to stay. But in the end, Admiral Rickover did indeed retire, although his influence continues unabated to this day, decades after his death.

Despite the extraordinary achievement of bringing nuclear power to the Navy, his career was far from perfect, including various investigations into ethical missteps (accepting gifts of more than $60,000 from several contractors, for which he received a nonpunitive letter of caution). But he was ultimately afforded the unique honor of having a nuclear attack submarine named after him while he was still living. The warship, USS *Hyman G. Rickover* (SSN-709), was commissioned in 1984, two years before Rickover died. Fittingly, the massive Rickover Hall at the US Naval Academy today houses the technical disciplines of mechanical, ocean, electrical, aerospace, and aeronautical engineering. Rickover was also awarded the Presidential Medal of Freedom in 1980, while still on active duty, as well as two Congressional Gold Medals in 1958 and 1982.

His health declined through the early 1980s, although he still made occasional forays into public speaking, accompanied by his second wife, Navy nurse and retired commander Eleonore Bednowicz. He is buried at the National Cemetery in Arlington, Virginia, next to his first wife, Ruth Masters, who died in 1972.

What drove him? No one ever worked harder than Hyman Rickover. Every book about him; every subordinate, peer, and senior official who met the man; every news story and obituary all begin with his work ethic. This manifested itself not only in the sheer number of hours he put into his job, but also in the lack of outside interests or hobbies and a single-minded focus he maintained throughout his career on his professional work and goals. Where does that wellspring of truly hard work come from? It is certainly a part of what we think of as character, and in the case of Rickover it most likely emerged from his immigrant background. Coming to the United States as a refugee at the very beginning of the last century, he was raised in a culture of hard work both from necessity, growing up in a poor neighborhood in Chicago, but also as an ethical choice. Like so many new Americans, he was born into a household that held hard work as both the path to success and a clear moral and ethical imperative.

Is it something we can develop, this appreciation for hard work as a mainstay in our character? Somewhat. Certainly, circumstances play a role—being born into a household with both a significant need for work as well as one in which there is a culture of doing so matters. But this is not in any sense purely socioeconomic. I have seen both the hardest-working people and the laziest and most self-contented people come from very wealthy families. The generations of sailors I have worked with at sea, most from lower-middle-class backgrounds, have included both hard workers and slackers. One aspect of developing a character that relishes hard work is simple: choosing to do something you love. Rickover certainly did that, trying first the surface Navy, then submarines, but finally settling on pure engineering. For any of us who would improve our own desire for hard work, the first step is choosing work that is personally rewarding and fulfilling—regardless of how the world weights it in the résumé of life. A second step is to look at examples of people who have truly worked hard to achieve something worthwhile. Reading the life story of someone like Hyman Rickover and understanding the depth of his efforts to simply grind it out can be inspirational. Indeed, in the Navy's nuclear force the expression "nuke it out" means doing everything it takes to succeed—a legacy of the irascible admiral who built the program. Finally, serving on the team of someone who is a truly determined hard worker literally builds character. The boss you want in this regard is one who works harder than you do every day. As a three-star vice admiral, I worked for over two years as the senior military assistant to Secretary of Defense Donald Rumsfeld. His work ethic mirrored that of Rickover. Before that assignment, I had thought of myself as a hard worker. Watching Secretary Rumsfeld, I came away from those two years realizing I needed to amp up my game if I was going to have real impact on my nation and the Navy. Studying the life and times of Hyman Rickover will reinforce that important lesson of character for anyone.

Each of the admirals we have discussed in this book was a visionary in some regard. Each of them showed the ability to look some distance into the future, appreciate its complexities, see beyond the horizon of their contemporaries, and chart a course to either achieve a goal or avoid a catastrophe. Some of them evinced this in more tactical ways (such as Lord Nelson's approach to battle); others were quite strategic in a geopolitical sense (Themistocles in his diplomacy and use of the sea against the Persians). Several were innovators in a technical sense, including Rear Admiral Grace Hopper and Admiral Elmo Zumwalt, whom I will describe shortly. In each of them we find an ability not only to look into the future, but also to do something about it. Still I'll argue that no admiral in this book was more visionary than Hyman Rickover.

The very idea of using nuclear power *on ships* at sea is inherently crazy. The difficulties of packing such technology into relatively small spaces; the need to protect sailors operating the systems who are essentially living, eating, breathing, and sleeping on top of reactors; the enormous potential environmental dangers not only to the oceans but also to coastal life in the case of a breach—all of these would have been deal breakers to any sensible person. But Rickover correctly saw that nuclear power would change everything in the ability of a massive seagoing fleet (especially submarines) to operate globally. As he surveyed the post–World War II world, his vision allowed him to see the need to face the emerging Soviet fleet on a global basis. The interesting question in terms of character is how a leader uses vision to motivate and inspire subordinates, peers, and seniors. In this sense Rickover—despite his uncharismatic personality and awkward presentational and interpersonal skills—was able to use vision to drive events. This was at heart one of the two pillars of his character, the other being an incomparably strong work ethic and sense of personal drive. No one ever outworked Hyman Rickover.

So often leaders have vision but fail at implementing it successfully. In my own case, as a newly selected four-star admiral I was put in charge of US Southern Command—essentially all military operations on sea, air, and land south of the United States. My vision, which I believe remains accurate, was that we would never go to war in Latin America or the Caribbean. As a result, I desperately wanted to reform the command from its Cold War incarnation of being prepared to invade Cuba to an international, interagency, private-public entity designed to focus on humanitarian operations, medical diplomacy, counternarcotics, rule of law, and other "soft power" applications. I had power and I had a vision. I pitched it to my boss, Secretary of Defense Bob Gates, and he supported me, although he was skeptical. Unfortunately, I was lacking two things that Admiral Rickover had—a long time horizon and a sense of how to ensure that a hidebound bureaucracy didn't dismantle my work. While at the Southern Command, I completely revamped the organization, created a new culture, overcame both internal and external objections to the idea . . . and then was posted to Europe as the NATO commander. From five thousand miles away in Brussels, I watched my successor take it all apart and revert to the previous version of US Southern Command. The lesson I learned was that vision without staying power and bureaucratic skill is insufficient to drive the tent poles into the ground far enough. You also need the deepest reserves of character—strategic patience especially—to implement vision. Rickover was a curious combination of someone who was supremely *tactically* impatient, to the point of real anger, but had deep reserves of *strategic* patience to implement a long-term vision—a very rare combination in terms of character, and it served him well.

For each of us, the takeaway is that vision matters. And whether you are a born visionary (and there aren't many) or simply want to improve this aspect of your character, vision is something you can exercise and develop. First and most obviously, thinking longer-term matters. This is in the context of an individual's life (New Year's resolutions, five-year financial plans, creating trusts and a will) or professionally (setting goals consciously for your portion of an enterprise, sharing them as defined goals with subordinates, measuring progress). It is also important to apply vision to the world around us. We do this again in very conscious ways as we survey the global world. Reading books and magazines that are predictive in their nature, especially those examining the distant future—for example George Friedman's *The Next 100 Years* or the issues of *The Economist* that look into the midterm and distant future annually. Writing and speaking about the future is also important in crystallizing vision. Whether that is at a dinner party or in front of a big gathering, in publishing an op-ed in the local newspaper or blogging online, opining on Twitter or doing a YouTube video, sharing vision improves your own ability to exercise that part of character. Indeed, taking the long view through our exercise of vision helps us over the day-to-day frustrations and turmoil. In the long run, of course, none of us is getting out of here alive. But by focusing ourselves on a vision for the future—both through a personal vision and a local, national, or global outlook—we can calm and center ourselves, become better family members, friends, and colleagues, and hopefully contribute in meaningful ways.

Finally, and this may be counterintuitive, we have to understand that perhaps our vision is wrong. This means challenging ourselves even as we implement the vision, ensuring that circumstances don't change or being prepared to learn that the facts that we believed in formulating the vision are inaccurate. Admiral Rickover said, "To doubt one's own first principles is the mark of a civilized man. Don't defend past actions; what is right today may be wrong tomorrow. Don't be consistent; consistency is the refuge of fools." Finding that balance between creating a vision and implementing it, alongside constantly refreshing and updating it as necessary, is the hardest part of being a visionary. It was the genius of Rickover that he could so consistently find that balance.

In ancient Chinese mythology there is a minor deity, Yu Shi, who was the god of rain. He was also known as the Master of Rain and represented the capricious nature of the weather. In many ways, I think of Admiral Rickover as the Master of Anger. He used anger like a kind of psychological rain, seeking to create growth from all the tension and pressure he could (forgive the pun) rain down on his subordinates. And like a rain god, he was the one in control; but he was also endlessly temperamental and unpredictable. All of this begs the question, is there a role for the use of anger in character and leadership?

All of us who have spent significant time in the world have worked for difficult leaders at one time or another. In my case, it was the first commanding officer for whom I served in the late 1970s, who had a titanic temper, did not suffer fools gladly, and often used sarcasm to spark a response in his subordinates on a new destroyer. While there were times when I felt the spur of his temper, I also appreciated that his anger derived more from an impatience to achieve important results—a successful search for a Soviet submarine, correct and instantaneous communications procedures, a crisply executed tactical maneuver of the ship in a tight formation with other US warships moving at speed just a hundred yards away. The Greeks—especially the warlike Spartans of ancient times—often say when a child is born, "May the gods grant my child the gift of fury." Anger can be the catalyst that drives subordinates (or peers and occasionally seniors) to greater results. In Admiral Rickover, it was on frequent display, from the interviews with frightened midshipmen to his tempestuous rejection of authority from nominal bosses like the secretary of the Navy or the secretary of energy. The question to consider in the sense of how anger plays in the formation of character and the achievement of results is ultimately both a moral and a pragmatic one.

Morally, the use of anger (call it extreme and visible impatience if you like) is a failure. It is too often an indulgence by someone in a position of power to simply ease tension on them, not a clinically applied technique to improve performance. Anger violates the basic tenets of civility, creates either slavish subjugation or internally hidden reserves of resentment that will ultimately play out. It opens up a chain of behavior that pays forward all the wrong moral cues and leads so often to a cycle of bad behavior. Like hazing at a fraternity or a military academy, all too often, the moral cycle becomes one of "I was abused, therefore I shall abuse." Even when dressed up as a leadership technique, the use of anger fails in the moral dimension. Pragmatically, the question is more difficult to answer as we think of leadership and character. Every angry leader I have known can point to subordinates who "never would have amounted to much if I hadn't shown them the error of their ways through harsh treatment, anger, and impatience." And often, I must admit, some of the subordinates buy into that vision themselves. I have been told repeatedly by supporters of Admiral Rickover that they became vastly better people through experiencing his impatience and anger. This becomes, in the end, a very personal question that leaders must ask themselves, and it sits squarely at the nexus of leadership and character.

As we all seek to find the right balance for ourselves in terms of character, we need to ask, are we truly using anger and impatience as tools of leadership? Or, when we lie awake at night and review the events of the day before drifting off to sleep, do we admit to ourselves that it just felt good to yell, to dominate, to be sarcastic to subordinates who had little power to respond? For me, on the occasions when I have lost my temper and used raw anger and power to spur a response, I must admit that in the end a significant part of it was a need inside me to find release from the fear, tension, and failure that a subordinate was allowing to come close to me. In the end, if we give Admiral Rickover the benefit of the doubt, I would say that he used anger and impatience to create truly important, significant, and meaningful outcomes—operating nuclear reactors at sea in the service of his nation most obviously. But were the anger and impatience used clinically as an appropriate tool of leadership? Or were they rather a character flaw that he could not control? He was not the most openly self-reflective individual (to say the least), and I am not sure there is anyone in a position to answer the question on his behalf. My view: I suspect that this diminutive, complicated, driven, utterly brilliant leader used anger consciously to achieve results; but the fearsome temper also met some dark need in his own heart. He was at once the Master of Anger and a leader of brilliance as well.

All of the quotes by Admiral Rickover come from Rear Admiral Dave Oliver, USN (Ret.), *Against the Tide: Rickover's Leadership Principles and the Rise of the Nuclear Navy* (Annapolis, MD: Naval Institute Press, 2014).

CHAPTER IX

The Angel of Change

Admiral Elmo R. "Bud" Zumwalt Jr.

———

BORN NOVEMBER 29, 1920, SAN FRANCISCO, CALIFORNIA

DIED JANUARY 2, 2000, DURHAM, NORTH CAROLINA

I n the spring of 1999, I sighed loudly as I settled into my well-appointed desk on the legendary E-Ring of the Pentagon as the newly installed executive assistant and senior naval aide to Secretary of the Navy Richard Danzig. Having just left sea duty in San Diego as commodore of Destroyer Squadron 21, I was missing the roll of a destroyer under my feet as well as the thrill of being able to lead 2,500 officers and sailors on the eight ships under my command. In short, I was feeling sorry for myself after giving up major command at sea to take command of a desk.

The only thing making me feel better about the job was the quality of the secretary I would be serving: Richard Danzig was a brilliant Rhodes scholar, PhD, and distinguished lawyer who had just finished up four years as the undersecretary of the Navy. He was also kind, generous, funny, and an innovator of the first order. I knew I would learn a lot. I was also cheered as I looked at the photos of the previous executive assistants on the wall beside my desk—an impressive rogues' gallery, most of whom would go on from this captain's assignment to wear an admiral's stars. I was cautiously optimistic I would do so as well, although it is a slippery ladder in the Pentagon and I was not a typical E-Ring denizen—having published too many controversial articles and certainly standing a few inches short of an admiral's normally imposing stature.

As I looked around and tried to focus on the positive aspects of my new job, a flustered staff assistant burst into my office just a step ahead of a jaunty older man in a beautifully cut suit. "Sir, Admiral Zumwalt is here and wanted to say hello" was all the aide got out of his mouth before I leaped to my feet to greet my visitor. He had a pleasant smile on his face, but the first thing I focused on were his strong and quite unruly eyebrows, a visual trademark I remembered well from the time when Zumwalt was the Navy's most senior officer and I was just about its most junior midshipman starting my studies at Annapolis.

I invited Admiral Zumwalt to sit, ordered coffee from the mess, and thought to myself how lucky I was to meet a legendary chief of naval operations and someone who had completely reshaped the Navy in which I sailed. He was early for a scheduled chat with my new boss and decided to stop in to see me because he had held the same job I was now in—back when I was in grade school. Over his shoulder, I could see his black-and-white photo from his time working for the secretary of the Navy. Suddenly, the job looked a lot better to me.

We talked for half an hour, mostly about his time as a former executive assistant to Secretary of the Navy Paul Nitze in the early 1960s. He told me how formative that tour had been for him, and how Secretary Nitze (who was still alive then and in his nineties) had helped him understand the complexities of the Washington interagency environment. I could not help wondering how the job had also shaped his view of the need to drive change hard, something he did better than any other flag officer in the Navy's history. And I thought also about the terrible sorrow he must have felt having lost his son to cancer, most likely as a result of exposure to Agent Orange. In one of the most painful father-son ironies imaginable, Admiral Zumwalt had ordered the infamous chemical sprayed along Vietnamese riverbanks to save sailors like his son from sniper fire only to see many of those sailors, including Elmo III, succumb to cancers years later.

At the end of our chat, he gave me a copy of his superb memoir, aptly entitled *On Watch*. I'd read it before, but when I opened the copy he gave me, I saw he'd inscribed it, "To Captain Jim Stavridis, with whom I share a desk, and with respect." I am lucky enough to have many signed memoirs in my library, but there is none I treasure more than *On Watch*, nor one I more frequently dip back into for renewed insights. He lived a big life, full of both accomplishment and failure, with plenty of triumph and tragedy along the voyage. Admiral Elmo Zumwalt was not only an innovator, but also a thoughtful leader whose character left indelible imprints on the Navy, and on the countless officers and sailors he met.

He died not many months later, in the early winter of 2000. The cause was mesothelioma, a common occurrence in Navy personnel of his age—many of them had been exposed to asbestos in older ships. I attended his memorial service at the Naval Academy Chapel on January 10, 2000, and I watched with awe the countless admirals, ambassadors, and other dignitaries who joined the president of the United States in honoring Bud Zumwalt. In subsequent years, I've had the chance to tour the massive destroyer named in his honor, USS *Zumwalt* (DDG-1000). Like him, it is a ship built on the idea of innovation.

Throughout the two years I served in his old job, I thought about him frequently, and continue to do so. The qualities of character he demonstrated in his life and career shine on. My boss during that time, Richard Danzig, summed it up nicely after Admiral Zumwalt's passing when he said, "At a time when racial hostility and discrimination particularly afflicted American society, he fought these problems with special ferocity in the Navy he loved so dearly." Ferocity indeed, from his eyebrows to his ideas—he was one of a kind.

Elmo Russell Zumwalt Jr., known as "Bud" from the moment his older sister met him, was in many ways an "accidental admiral." Born in San Francisco and raised in Tulare, California, he initially intended to follow both of his parents into medicine and spent much of the first half of his naval career toying with the idea of getting out and going to medical or law school. From the moment he received an appointment to the Naval Academy in 1939, however, opportunity always knocked and kept him in the Navy. In the end, Zumwalt climbed the ranks faster than anyone before him to become, at age forty-nine, the youngest-ever chief of naval operations. At every turn, and especially in his transformative tenure as CNO, Zumwalt applied youthful vigor and almost superhuman energy to reform the Navy.

If Mahan taught the Navy to think and Nimitz won its greatest victory, it fell to Zumwalt to teach the Navy that no victory is ever final or absolute. Zumwalt graduated with the wartime class of 1943 and saw action as a newly commissioned surface warfare officer in some of the biggest battles of the conflict, including Leyte Gulf in 1944. Like Mahan, Zumwalt showed a penchant for reform early, but he was personally and professionally much more like Nimitz: he sought and acquired responsibility early, demonstrated a genius for organization, and got along much better with people than Mahan ever did. Of the three, Zumwalt probably had the most highly developed bureaucratic-political sense, but it cut both ways. Zumwalt's career path was much smoother than Mahan's, and strong political cover put him in position to make his definitive contribution as CNO; but, like many reformers—and unlike Nimitz—he badly overreached at times, and never worse than during the dark final days of the Nixon administration. And his brilliance and exuberance created jealousies among his peers.

Looking back, Zumwalt's career path resembled what mariners call a "great circle" route, which looks oddly curved on a flat chart but is actually the shortest distance between two points on a round globe. His time at the Naval Academy echoed Mahan's in his early desire to make the system around him better and Nimitz's in his studiousness and fun-loving spirit—but Midshipman Zumwalt had a flair all his own. If the outlines of their defining characteristics were already apparent in Academy days in Mahan's aloof brilliance and Nimitz's steady character and sheer competence, so, in their way, were Zumwalt's. Nimitz rose early to study because he wanted to make up for a missed year of high school; Zumwalt did so because he had generally been out so late the night before pursuing his latest infatuation. Mahan's idea of the Navy led him to enforce the rules on his peers in violation of long-standing tradition; Zumwalt's idea of the Navy embraced the spirit of "it is better to beg forgiveness than to ask for permission."

Commissioned into destroyer duty, Ensign Zumwalt immediately became one of the millions of men on the thousands of ships under Nimitz's command. He saw furious fighting during the Battle of Leyte Gulf and saved his own destroyer from going aground by alerting the conn (ship driver) to a navigational error. Young Zumwalt was recognized for his bravery and his alertness, and quickly came into much greater than usual responsibility immediately after the war when he was appointed prize captain of a Japanese river gunboat and its two hundred crew. He and a small crew of US Navy sailors, all armed to the teeth, took charge of the Japanese ship and sailed upriver to Shanghai, where Zumwalt was promptly smitten by an infatuation that eclipsed any he had ever experienced.

Mouza Coutelais-du-Roche, daughter of a French father and exiled White Russian mother, did not speak any English and Bud Zumwalt barely spoke Russian, but, in his words, "both spoke the international language of love," and in that language understood each other perfectly. He proposed within days and they were married within weeks, immediately before Zumwalt had to sail from Shanghai. Mouza, already pregnant, sailed for the United States months later, where she was warmly embraced by her new in-laws in California while Zumwalt was still on duty on the East Coast. Bud and Mouza's love affair lasted for the rest of their lives, through the births of three more children and the tragic death decades later of their first child, Elmo III. Like his romantic life, the great circle of Zumwalt's career was picking up steam. From 1946 through 1952 (and despite lingering wishes to leave the Navy for medicine or the law), Zumwalt progressed rapidly and with increasing responsibility through a series of early command positions at sea and ashore. Like Nimitz, his years teaching in a Naval Reserve Officers Training Corps unit (in North Carolina) were among the happiest of his life, and he would ultimately elect to be buried in the community in which he taught as a young officer.

After a year at the Naval War College, Mahan's legacy and still an important stepping-stone for naval officers on course for high rank, Zumwalt reported for the first time to the Bureau of Personnel and the assignment that would define the rest of his career. BuPers, as it is known, is the direct organizational descendant of the Bureau of Navigation as the Navy's HR department. As a tour at BuNav had been instrumental to Nimitz en route to his defining work as CINCPAC and CNO, so that first tour with BuPers would shape the latter-day organizational genius of Zumwalt—who at first despaired of the assignment as a "career killer." Not surprisingly for someone of his energy, as long as Zumwalt was going to be in the Navy, he wanted to command ships rather than shuffle people around.

Far from killing Zumwalt's career, however, that tour at BuPers turbocharged it. In the first place, it forced him to confront the immense challenge of people management in an organization as big and bureaucratic as the Navy, as well as the institutional racism and sexism that then governed so much of the Navy's personnel system. Before long, Zumwalt discovered that applying his creativity and energy to reform the bureaucracy and improve sailors' lives was a different but no less fulfilling form of service than being on the bridge of a destroyer. Second, by making that shift in the way he worked, Zumwalt made his reputation with the chief of the bureau, who put a note in his files to bring Zumwalt back after his next fleet rotation.

After two years of highly successful sea duty, Zumwalt returned to BuPers in 1957 and promptly resumed burrowing into and reforming the bureaucracy, first for six months at BuPers and then for a further year and a half as an aide in the office of the assistant secretary of the Navy. In that time, Zumwalt renewed his appreciation for the problems of naval personnel management and his commitment to solving them and developed an increasingly high-level perspective on naval operations as directed by the senior-most civilian and naval officials. As his bureaucratic and political skills and connections also began to blossom, Zumwalt was unknowingly building the institutional launchpad and political support tower that would enable him to rocket to the top of the Navy within a decade.

The last decade of Zumwalt's career was a crowded series of big assignments of about eighteen months each, building to his four years as CNO. After BuPers and the assistant secretary's office, he commanded the first purpose-built guided missile frigate, USS *Dewey*, for eighteen months, then reported to the National War College for a yearlong capstone course. There, Zumwalt—who had joined the debate team on a lark as a midshipman and promptly distinguished himself—gave a talk that so energized his fellow students that, a few days later, they peppered a guest lecturer with more questions about Zumwalt's remarks than his own. More intrigued than incensed, that lecturer—the assistant secretary of defense for international security affairs, Paul Nitze—demanded to meet this Zumwalt character. Thus, in 1962, Socrates met Plato—and Zumwalt truly launched.

After Mouza, the relationship with Nitze was the most important in Zumwalt's life, and the connection between them was similarly instant. From the moment Nitze hauled Zumwalt into his office to take the measure of the man whose speech had overshadowed his own, the conversation between the two of them never really stopped. Immediately upon graduation from the War College in 1961, Zumwalt was assigned as a desk officer in Nitze's shop at the Pentagon; when Nitze was named secretary of the Navy in December 1963, he informed the Navy in no uncertain terms that Captain Zumwalt would be transferring to the Department of the Navy as executive assistant to the secretary.

As Mahan learned the hard way, few reformers can succeed without powerful patrons and strong political cover. Beyond the incomparable experience, mentorship, and institutional vantage that Nitze offered Zumwalt, the most important effect of their relationship was to immerse Zumwalt in the networks of the civilians who really controlled the Navy. Five years later, when those civilians decided the Navy needed a serious shaking up, they knew just the man for the job—and their continued support would allow Zumwalt to fight his intramural war against the hidebound traditions, odious practices, and institutional inertia of the Navy.

The years flew by. In 1965, Zumwalt pinned on his first two stars and took command at sea of Cruiser-Destroyer Flotilla Seven in San Diego. Continuing the pattern of previous shipboard commands, Zumwalt energized the flotilla during his year at the helm, then headed back across the country for a first tour in his future office as the director of the systems analysis division in the office of the CNO (OP-96). Two years there further broadened Zumwalt's perspective on and deepened his experience in naval administration (this time within the uniformed hierarchy). Following that, he headed west again—all the way to Vietnam, where he took a command nobody wanted in exchange for a third star.

In an ironic echo of Nimitz's practice of sometimes promoting away his problems, Zumwalt was ordered to Vietnam on the assumption that it would tame if not eliminate an overeager upstart whose energy the current CNO was tired of channeling. (Like most Young Turks, Zumwalt made powerful enemies nearly as quickly as he made powerful friends.) Not for the first time, Zumwalt was taking over a command in which no predecessor had flourished; he relished the challenge.

The first-ever three-star commander, naval forces Vietnam—a literal backwater position in charge of the so-called brown-water navy which, upon Zumwalt's arrival, was viewed with equal disdain by North Vietnamese enemies and fellow American forces alike—wasted no time in getting his command pointed up. In his last combat command (and his last prior to taking the CNO's job), the old Zumwalt energy and personal magnetism were on full display, and new relationships were struck that would remain influential in his subsequent tenure as CNO and beyond. (One such was a lifelong friendship with the South Vietnamese CNO, whose family would later be sponsored for US citizenship by the Zumwalts.)

The tour was also tinged with tragedy, however: taking the fight to the enemy, which Zumwalt's brown-water navy did with gusto, had the immediate consequence of getting more sailors injured and killed, and the long-term consequence of exposing many more to the carcinogenic effects of Agent Orange, a defoliant which Admiral Zumwalt ordered sprayed along riverbanks to eliminate cover and thus save his sailors from snipers. One young sailor exposed to the defoliants was Lieutenant Elmo Zumwalt III, who had requested duty in Vietnam and commanded his Swift boat with panache worthy of his famous name. The admiral ordered Agent Orange into the fight convinced that it was not dangerous to humans, and the decision ultimately cost him his son and namesake. Like many in that legendary brown-water navy, Elmo III died of aggressive lymphoma in 1988.

Toward the end of his time as the naval commander in Vietnam, Zumwalt was summoned to Washington. He was ordered to drop everything, leave command of his beloved brown-water navy along the coast of Vietnam, and catch the next flight back to the capital. His orders specified, strangely, that he was to make the journey in civilian clothes. He pondered the possibilities en route. He knew he had been one of the Navy's rising stars for years—a kind of enfant terrible, with all that connotes. He knew very well that he was something of a lightning rod: hard-charging, iconoclastic, and annoyingly effective, he had arrived in Vietnam a year and a half before, in October 1968, when his boss thought he could promote Zumwalt away by putting him in the career-killing position. Zumwalt had taken the job—and the attendant promotion to vice admiral—with gusto. With typical flair, he had pulled his new three-starred shoulder boards from his pocket the moment his flight reached cruising altitude over the Pacific and pinned them on as the flight crew poured champagne for everyone on the plane. As he made the return journey, he thought to himself, the good news was that the odds of being fired were low; but the bad news was that no matter how hard he tried to peer into the fog of the future, he couldn't see the shape of what was about to happen.

He knew that in terms of the possibility of yet another promotion, he had a good chance. He had hit the job in Vietnam full-on and achieved quite a bit. After a quick tour to get a grasp of the situation on the ground and inland waters of South Vietnam, he ordered his sailors off the sidelines and into the fight, built a brilliantly effective command team, and started innovating. Everyone—his own sailors, his fellow US commanders from other military services, and most of all his Vietnamese enemies—felt the results of "Zumwalt's Wild Ideas," as the new boss's brazen schemes became known. Far from disappearing, Zumwalt had jolted a backwater command to sudden life and lethal effectiveness.

As it turned out, Zumwalt had himself become the "wild idea" of the civilian masters of the Navy. Believing the whole service needed the kind of shake-up Zumwalt had delivered in Vietnam and at every previous command in his career, they had—without his knowledge—"deep-selected" him for a fourth star and the Navy's top job: chief of naval operations. Over the near-unanimous objections of the current CNO and the rest of the service's top brass, a group Zumwalt called the "naval aristocracy," the secretary of the Navy persuaded President Nixon to send for the wild young reformer. Upon landing, he was driven to the secretary of the Navy's home in Georgetown, still without a uniform or any hint as to what was about to happen. There he learned he would become the new CNO. The Navy was about to undergo a massive reorganization.

The years 1970 to 1974 saw Admiral Zumwalt's revolutionary term as chief of naval operations, the position to which he had aspired ever since he finally dropped consideration of a legal or medical career to fully commit himself to the Navy. As he had been at several key points earlier in his career, Zumwalt was "deep-selected" for the position: vaulted over the heads of many seniors and peers. Like the papacy, the CNO's job tends to be obsessively watched, and the watchers tend to have a strong sense of the likely candidates for elevation when the top job comes open. Zumwalt was not on any of the watch lists, even as a dark horse; when he was ordered without explanation to fly in mufti from Vietnam to Washington, DC, the only lists on which he appeared were those of Secretary of the Navy John Chafee and President Nixon, whom Secretary Chafee had persuaded to appoint Zumwalt. Not a single active-duty admiral supported his promotion to a fourth star. That Zumwalt became Chafee's candidate for CNO in 1970 was the culmination of the trends that had defined the admiral's personality and professional history. Also like popes, CNOs come in two basic varieties: institutionalists and reformers. In both roles, leaders of the former type far outnumber those of the latter, and their respective institutions rely on that conservative trend for long-term viability. However, all big bureaucracies tend toward inertia, and must periodically be renewed in their vitality by an energetic reformer.

In understanding the Navy's problems in the early 1970s, it is important to consider the underlying racial prejudice that was part of the ethos of the service at the time. For decades, the Navy had used African American and Philippine sailors as its cooking, cleaning, and valet force. It had ingrained in the heads of many officers a sense that those racial groups were a kind of "servant class," and their possibilities for advancement were very circumscribed. Even as late as the early 1970s when I reported to Annapolis, you could feel a sense of this bias. The huge mess hall at the Naval Academy, where all four thousand members of the Brigade of Midshipmen sit together three times each day for meals, was serviced by stewards who were overwhelmingly minorities, while there were very few midshipmen from minority groups. I was given a photograph around that time of a beautiful Navy destroyer at the pier in 1949, with the crew in ranks in the front. It was beautiful all right—until you looked very closely at the second rank of the photo where all the chief petty officers were arrayed. It had a gap where three chiefs were missing. When I got out a magnifying glass and looked at the picture, I eventually found them—in the very back row, with the most junior sailors. They had clearly been directed to get out of ranks and go stand figuratively at the "back of the bus." Zumwalt knew that the long-term future of the Navy required changing that mindset and set about doing so aggressively.

Indeed, his gravestone bears the one-word epitaph "Reformer." He came into his job like Pope John XXIII: reading the signs of the times, committed to renewal, and determined to "open the windows" and let some air and light into the institution under his charge. Although he was an accomplished warrior and couched many of his reforms in the context of the growing threat posed by the Soviet fleet, the greatest battles of Zumwalt's career were fought within the Navy itself. Nimitz, for all his compassion for sailors and skill at forging the Navy into a winning team with a shared sense of purpose, could never countenance the idea of women in uniform and seemed unperturbed by the Navy's racial policies. A quarter century after Japan's surrender, it would fall to Zumwalt to use his Nimitz-like organizational abilities coupled with his own high-energy style to clear away bureaucratic overgrowth. He was able to ultimately update racist and sexist personnel policies hardly changed since Nimitz's day and grossly out of step with the society the Navy recruited from and served.

Not only did Zumwalt's reform efforts resemble Vatican II in their scope and ambition, they also caused similar institutional controversy and their legacy remains similarly seminal but unsettled today. Zumwalt's most famous method was the so-called Z-Gram (or "zinger"): messages sent directly from the CNO's desk to the entire Navy directing specific changes in policy or operations. Detractors deplored Zumwalt for destroying the good discipline essential to a functioning navy and colorfully impugned him for bringing "beards, beer, and broads" into their comfortable old-boys' club; Zumwalt fired back and pressed on, wryly writing to one critic, "I'm sure that when flogging was abolished in the Navy there were those (in uniform and out) who regarded that as a fatally 'permissive' move."

Probably the two most important targets of Zumwalt's reforms—and predictably the most controversial—were the Navy's deeply ingrained racism and sexism. Energy alone would not be enough to bring these long-held but shameful traditions in line with the times; the effort required all the political and bureaucratic wiles Zumwalt could muster. Fortunately, as expected, Zumwalt had not only the courage to tackle these problems head-on, but also the wisdom to get the best possible advice and make the most specifically targeted policy changes he could. Two examples from my own career showed the long echoes of Zumwalt's reforms, the first illustrating the need and the second the result.

In 1980, a few years after Zumwalt had concluded his time as CNO, I became the boilers officer on USS *Forrestal* (CV-59), a tired, broken-down carrier home-ported in Mayport, Florida. My assignment was to lead about 150 of the toughest characters on the ship, the engineers who worked in the boiler rooms well beneath the waterline where temperatures often soared well above 100 degrees Fahrenheit. It was brutal, demanding, and largely unrewarded work in the least glamorous spot in the ship. I found my division of sailors rife with racial tension, malingering, disciplinary violations, and a pirate spirit that "anything goes." This was hardly what four years at Annapolis had prepared me to tackle on my own. Fortunately, I was blessed with a newly promoted boiler technician chief petty officer, one Clevon Jones. An African American standing six feet five inches tall and with a girth to match, he towered over this young, skinny, short lieutenant. We bonded instantly in our shared desire to improve morale in the division, and quickly settled on a division of labor—the lieutenant would do the paperwork, commend the few sailors who were actually doing a good job, encourage the others constantly, and run interference with the chain of command. The chief would discipline the malcontents by whatever means necessary (you could get away with a lot more primitive methods of discipline in those days), make sure the plant was running smoothly, and work to get our deserving sailors advanced in rank. We agreed that we would simply spend as much time together as we could—an odd-looking couple perhaps, but one that symbolized, "in this Boiler Division the leadership team believes in one team, one fight," and "we stand together with our shipmates." We were able to tap into the spirit that Bud Zumwalt had begun a decade earlier and build what was eventually a highly effective force of carrier engineers who performed superbly on several forward deployments.

Flash forward another decade, and in the early 1990s I became the captain of USS *Barry* (DDG-52), a brand-new *Arleigh Burke–*class destroyer based out of Norfolk, Virginia. I was in the middle of my command tour when *Barry* was selected to be one of the first combatant warships to have a mixed-gender crew. About 15 percent of my 350-man crew were transferred and replaced by women at the stroke of a pen. This raised a fair amount of consternation not only in the minds of the crew, but among the wives of this previously all-male crew who were skeptical about sending women to sea with their husbands. I spent six months going from work center to work center (about ten sailors per group) explaining why this had happened (the fleet needs more sailors, these are top-notch, highly trained shipmates) and how we were going to integrate women into the ship (they are here to work as your shipmates, not be part of your potential dating pool). It was hard leadership at the retail level, but it worked. Within a month or two, everyone looked around and realized we were a better, more talent-laden ship than we were before the transfers. Again, you could drop a plumb line from that transition back to the reforms of Elmo Zumwalt.

Always what the Navy calls a "deck plate leader," someone who is highly visible and close to his subordinates, Zumwalt as CNO continued to listen widely and well to sailors and officers throughout the service in the belief that they knew best what changes needed to be made. Several he hired directly, such as Lieutenant Commander William Norman, who was about to resign his commission because he could no longer reconcile "being black with being Navy." Norman was a principal author of the Z-Gram Z-66, issued on December 17, 1970 (about six months into Zumwalt's term), which concluded: "There is no black navy, no white navy—just one navy—the United States Navy." Zumwalt promulgated Z-66 with a personal endorsement in which he stated that "Ours must be a navy family that recognizes no artificial barriers of race, color, or religion."

Later, Zumwalt mused that "although the Navy was a racist institution, I found it easier to deal with racism than with sexism." Indeed, it took more than eighteen months and fifty more Z-Grams for Zumwalt to serve Navy-wide notice on "Equal Rights and Opportunities for Women in the Navy" (the title of Z-116). Twenty-five years after the end of World War II, women not only were still barred from combat positions but still bore the World War II–era classification of Women Accepted for Volunteer Emergency Service

(WAVES) when Zumwalt took over the CNO's office. Z-116 and subsequent efforts tried to change that, but the bureaucracy was already fighting back hard. In two more years as CNO, Zumwalt issued only five more Z-Grams.

Where Mahan's legacy was contained in his *thought* and Nimitz's shone most clearly in the *team* he built, Zumwalt's impact—like that of all reformers—shows most clearly in his long-term *innovations* which continue to be shaped by his successors. As transformative as his reforms were, he ritually revoked them (in line with long-standing tradition) upon his relief as CNO, and his successor quietly but firmly refused to institutionalize the vast majority of them. Though things are much improved, today's Navy heavily restricts beards and beer, and still has a way to go toward full equity for women and minorities. Nevertheless, Zumwalt showed what might be possible, and many evolutions the Navy has made in his wake—however reluctantly or tentatively—are echoes of his enormous energy.

Essential though it was, Zumwalt's tenure was not unblemished by scandal. As with most reformers, it was in his nature to push harder and farther than the bureaucracy was prepared to go—and sometimes he pushed too far. In 121 Z-Grams addressing a wide range of controversial issues some examples of overreach and correction were inevitable.

Zumwalt served out his full term as CNO and retired from the Navy in 1974, at the still-youthful age of fifty-three. Like his predecessor Chester Nimitz, Zumwalt busied himself in retirement with all manner of public projects. He wrote a book, ran and lost a US Senate race in Virginia against the incumbent Harry F. Byrd Jr., and remained a passionate and tireless advocate for the sailors who had served under him in Vietnam and the processes of reconciliation that followed the conflict both within the United States and between the United States and Vietnam.

Poignantly, much of Zumwalt's post-Vietnam advocacy was directed at securing public recognition and benefits for US service members harmed by exposure to Agent Orange and other defoliants. Zumwalt became firmly convinced that both his son Elmo III's cancer and his grandson Elmo IV's severe learning disabilities were attributable to effects of Agent Orange. Though he never recanted his decision to order the use of defoliants, Zumwalt (and Mouza) never fully forgave himself for his son's death, either.

More happily, Zumwalt personally advocated for and his entire family volunteered to sponsor Vietnamese refugees seeking resettlement in the United States after the war. The greatest reward of this effort was the resettlement of his onetime counterpart, the former CNO of South Vietnam—whom Zumwalt considered "a brother"—and his family.

Zumwalt passed away in 2000, surrounded by his family. His funeral was held at the Naval Academy, where President Clinton delivered a eulogy. Zumwalt and Mouza are buried together beneath a single black tombstone at the Naval Academy Cemetery. Fittingly, the admiral's gravestone bears the one-word epitaph "Reformer"; under Mouza's name is written "His Strength." Zumwalt's legacy lives on in the Navy, which in 2014 conferred his name on the newly launched USS *Zumwalt*, lead ship of the newest class of destroyers—the ultimate institutional honor for a destroyer man like Zumwalt. Fittingly, *Zumwalt* is in a class by itself. It is just as singular a ship as its namesake was a person. She proudly sails the Pacific today, in the waters where Bud Zumwalt's career began.

Like all great reformers, Bud Zumwalt was great in vision; bold in challenging old customs, ideas, and assumptions; and both willing and able to make the bureaucracy howl. Zumwalt combined an absolute devotion to the highest ideals of the Navy with an impish streak running at least as far back as his Naval Academy days, when he was known to pull pranks and push the rules at least as far as they would go. Throughout his career, he skillfully wielded both sides of this personality as he continually dragged inherited traditions into line with contemporary culture while remaining true (in his mind, at least) to the best of the old. He was in many ways a classic iconoclast, an instinctively contrarian thinker. That is a quality of character that can be very helpful, especially when wielded in an entrenched bureaucracy. It is also so often a quality that destroys a career before it truly gets underway. So often the enfant terrible becomes the figurative baby strangled in the cradle.

As with most energetic reformers, however, Zumwalt's iconoclasm could cut both ways. It fell to Zumwalt to reimagine the Navy, particularly in terms of its people, in a way that felt both true to long-cherished tradition and tenable in the context of modern society. Zumwalt was appointed CNO because a series of traditionalists had dug in their heels in the face of modernity, making an iconoclast painfully necessary. However, just as not all the old ways were necessarily the right ways, some of Zumwalt's innovations proved unsustainable or misguided.

Particularly considering today's focus on "leading change"—and the overall context of changing norms in society in the workplace that appear hardly less significant than those Zumwalt and the Navy faced in the 1970s—modern leaders need to think about how to put just the right amount of iconoclasm into their organizations and their own worldviews. After all, leaders are responsible for keeping their organizations supple, and a little innovation today is often the best insurance against epochal change tomorrow. I often ask—and especially encourage young leaders to ask—what any organization I lead is doing right now that is going to look really wrong fifty years in the future. Zumwalt had a real gift for doing this, and for knowing *whom* to ask in his organization to find the right answer. It didn't take too many conversations with black, Filipino, Latino, or female sailors for Zumwalt to spot a lot of ongoing practices that already looked fifty years out of date. As a leader, particularly a senior leader, it's a very good practice to seek out and listen to the perspective of people in your organization who don't look like you (including younger people).

In the course of my career, I worked twice on the inner team—as a quasi–chief of staff—to a pair of truly original thinkers, and they could not have been more different save for sharing that originality. The first was Secretary of the Navy Richard Danzig, who shared many of Zumwalt's qualities, including not only truly original thinking but also a lightness of touch and a fine sense of humor for pranks. He pushed the Navy hard to change everything from its outdated personnel policies regarding promotions to assigning women for the first time to submarines. He picked his fights well, won more than he lost, and ended up making real change over several years at the top of the massive Department of the Navy. And his early work on allowing women to serve in submarines, although not adopted during his tenure, eventually carried the day a decade later—showing that being an iconoclast sometimes means waiting to see the fruits of your labors.

The other truly original thinker, who literally challenged everything anyone said to him, was Secretary of Defense Don Rumsfeld. I was his senior military assistant for more than two years, and it was an exhausting time in my career. Despite being a three-star admiral myself and having just finished a two-year tour at sea commanding a carrier strike group centered on USS *Enterprise* (CVN-65), I just couldn't keep up with my boss. He outworked, outfought, and outthought everyone in his orbit and left those of us on his staff literally staggering to keep up with him. While he made his share of mistakes in terms of policy choices, overall, he drove the Department of Defense hard and made real changes—from putting in place a Combatant Command for Homeland Security (Northern Command) to reorganizing intelligence functions in the wake of 9/11 to reducing US dependence on overseas Cold War bases. And he did it by thinking originally about every proposition put in front of him. He would challenge the assumptions in every proposal, argue with briefers about seemingly small points until they either proved their point or changed it, suggest completely different recommendations, and—above all—insist on new ways of approaching old problems. I always warned briefers, "Remember, you never get a free one with the secretary," meaning don't say something you can't fully back up, from the altitude of a satellite to the test depth of a new submarine design. I learned a lot about the power of original thought from watching Rumsfeld and Danzig.

Whether or not it had anything to do with being born in

California on the edge of America's Pacific world, Zumwalt was an admiral straight out of central casting. Even as a young officer, candid and posed pictures show him to be every inch the physically impressive leader—and his effect in person was even more intense. Zumwalt possessed natural charisma in spades, but he also took care to nurture in himself the arts of personality and persuasion: from debate contests as a midshipman to intentionally working in the Bureau of Personnel, essentially running human resources for the entire uniformed Navy, Zumwalt melded tremendous people skills onto a naturally compelling personality to forge the character that would become the youngest-ever chief of naval operations and take on the staid Navy "aristocracy." Not every successful leader has Zumwalt's natural charisma, of course: look no further than Fisher, Mahan, Rickover, and Hopper in these pages for far less charismatic examples from the pantheon of historical admirals. Still, it is important to remember that, Hollywood affect aside, CNO Zumwalt did not spring forth fully formed like Athena from Zeus's skull. Yes, he started with more charisma than many people, but Zumwalt recognized this as a unique gift and took steps throughout his life to develop that gift and put it to work.

It is also worth noting that there are quieter, subtler forms of charisma as well. In typically extreme fashion, Zumwalt once concluded a keynote speech with a Tarzan yell that brought down the house, but that was credible only because of his gargantuan personality. (That kind of primal scream, for example, doomed the presidential run of Howard Dean in 2004.) Few leaders can effectively channel such raw energy, but everyone can work on refining the forms of communication that best fit their own character and circumstances. Zumwalt was frequently and widely regarded as a sailor's admiral. Extreme loyalty to subordinates was one of the hallmarks of his career. Particularly when he commanded at sea or in combat, Zumwalt drove his people hard but also did what he could to share their experience and make life a little easier on them. As commander of all US naval forces in Vietnam, he was a frequent visitor to both frontline combat units and hospitals, and his efforts to improve life for his sailors ran the gamut from delivering cases of beer in his personal helicopter to spending real time with wounded sailors in hospitals.

Zumwalt's compassion for his sailors extended well beyond his time in uniform—and indeed beyond his own wartime allegiance. Not only did Zumwalt become a national advocate for service members who had been harmed by exposure to Agent Orange, but he also became a proponent of reconciliation with Vietnam. He visited the country as a guest of his onetime foe and personally sponsored South Vietnamese refugees seeking citizenship in the United States.

Today's leaders can emulate Zumwalt's compassion for his people in several key ways. First, leaders should constantly be on the lookout for systemic injustices in their organizations. As Zumwalt demonstrated in forming advisory committees of younger sailors or by hiring Lieutenant Commander Bill Norman to help him resolve the contradiction between "being black and being Navy," as Norman put it, truly effective compassion as a mark of character does not consist in random acts of kindness but in an active approach to leadership. Second, compassionate leaders not only look for problems, but recognize they do not have all the answers.

Zumwalt was quickly convinced that not-so-little things like shipboard food and cosmetic offerings were not enough for minority sailors, but he empowered the sailors themselves to suggest acceptable changes rather than presuming to provide solutions on his own initiative. Finally, leaders need to recognize that an actively compassionate style also requires having the courage to act, even when the necessary changes are difficult or painful to make (as they so frequently are).

Of the many leaders for whom I've worked closely, I'd say that Secretary of Defense Robert Gates had the highest level of compassion for the troops under his command. Strange perhaps to think of that coming from someone who served so effectively as the spymaster of the United States during a long and successful career in the CIA, culminating in his service as the director in the early 1990s; but I saw him repeatedly make decisions that were ultimately grounded in a deep and abiding concern for the troops. And despite the fact that he wanted out of the job as defense secretary, he ended up serving both Presidents Bush and Obama in the most important and exhausting job in the cabinet. When I asked him once at a reception in my quarters at US Southern Command, where I was the combatant commander, how he was doing with the evident strain of the job, he took a sip of Grey Goose vodka, smiled wanly, and said, "I can't just walk away from the troops. They are giving it everything they have, and I have a duty to them to continue." It is not coincidence that the title of his fine memoir of those days is called, simply, *Duty.* It was a sense of duty in his case that stemmed from his compassion for his troops. That is a fine element of character, and one worth thinking about for each of us. Zumwalt had it as well.

Zumwalt was not only comparatively youthful, but throughout his career, demonstrated boundless energy in everything he did. He relished tough assignments in the belief that "if you start at the bottom, there's nowhere to go but up." He infused his own energy into his commands, raising everyone's esprit de corps. And, particularly in leadership positions, his work ethic was a living monument to the idea that successful reformers need to work both smarter and harder than the opposition.

Zumwalt's energy allowed him to outwork the entrenched bureaucracy, but much of his success depended on his ability to direct his energy against the right targets. From early actions like changing his destroyer's limp-sounding radio call sign to something with a lot more pop to his "wild ideas" and Z-Grams, Zumwalt's reforms always seemed to address just the thing that needed to be changed to shift the whole culture of an organization. As any leader should recognize, this did not happen by luck. However wild his ideas might have been, they were almost invariably developed through friendly but frank debate with advisers Zumwalt trusted to tell him what he needed to hear. This allowed him to make well-crafted, specifically targeted policy changes rather than boilerplate, bumper-sticker statements. As with compassion, leaders cannot get by on responsiveness forever: sooner or later, they must *lead* by striking out ahead of the crowd—and striking at the right target. As "Zoomwalt" discovered early on in his career, focused energy skillfully applied can put the opposition back on their heels and swing momentum around to the reformer's direction.

Charisma plus energy plus skill gave Zumwalt great self-confidence—but, like all truly great leaders, Zumwalt did not rely on confidence alone. Using the furnace of his energy and the hammering of excellent mentorship (particularly by Paul Nitze), Zumwalt forged his enormous raw talents on the anvil of experience and was rightfully confident that the results would prepare him to succeed throughout his career. Like the iconoclasm it supported, however, Zumwalt's confidence was a double-edged sword. He could not have succeeded as a reformer if he were overburdened with timidity or trepidation, but supreme self-assurance and a reformer's crusading tendencies often lead to overreach. Although the collective effect of his Z-Grams changed the culture of the Navy forever, few of Zumwalt's specific changes stayed in place after his watch ended. Today's Navy, while miles ahead of where it was before Zumwalt's tenure, is still in so many ways restrictive and lagging behind many organizations in the private sector.

As mentioned earlier, the "admirals' spy ring" scandal that happened on his watch is no doubt a blot. The activity was a grave violation of US law and custom, and even his principal biographers find it hard to believe that Zumwalt did not know what was going on. While this was certainly under the responsibility of the chairman of the Joint Chiefs of Staff as well as the CNO, it tarnished his reputation. All might be fair in intramural bureaucratic war, but there are certain lines that a leader must never cross. No amount of frustration or Nixonian subterfuge can justify breaking laws or violating the strongest cultural taboos.

Nonetheless, taken together, there is an overwhelming amount to admire about Bud Zumwalt. I have admiration for every admiral in this collection to one degree or another, but my deepest affection is reserved for this energetic, enthusiastic, highly original, and idealistic leader. His character is the one I've most sought to emulate throughout my own voyage of character.

All quotations are sourced from Elmo R. Zumwalt, Jr., *On Watch* (New York: Quadrangle, 1976), or from Larry Berman, *Zumwalt: The Life and Times of Elmo Russell "Bud" Zumwalt, Jr.* (New York: Harper, 2012).

CHAPTER X

Don't Go Near the Water

Rear Admiral Grace Hopper

———

BORN DECEMBER 9, 1906, NEW YORK CITY

DIED JANUARY 1, 1992, ARLINGTON, VIRGINIA

I met then-captain Grace Hopper in 1976 at Annapolis in my senior year of studies, hoping to wrap up successfully and get out to sea on a destroyer. She came to give a talk to a group of midshipmen engaged in primitive computer programming, using punch cards to coax the bulky machines at the Academy into esoteric calculations. A tiny person in an elegantly tailored service dress blue uniform, she hardly cut the figure of the swashbuckling seagoing naval officer we so often saw when visiting lecturers arrived. But she had a piercing look and clearly enjoyed being the center of attention in a group of athletic young men. Hopper was both an inspiration and an enigmatic figure to midshipmen; she was as far from the typical heroic naval leader as could be imagined. But her reputation as a pioneering thinker preceded her, and we listened closely.

She spoke about innovation, and the need to take chances. Those of us in the highly regimented system of the US Naval

Academy in the mid-1970s could not imagine anything more exciting than a senior officer urging us to try something outside the norm. To hear such encouragement from a legendary scientist and nationally known naval officer was intoxicating. Years later she would say, "The contemporary malaise is the unwillingness to take chances. Everyone is playing it safe. We've lost our guts. It's much more fun to stick your neck out and take chances. The whole attitude is to protect yourself against everything, don't take chances. But we built this country on taking chances." That was the heart of her talk in 1976, and her admonition stuck with me throughout my own career.

She never spent any significant time at sea, let alone led carrier battle groups into combat. Rear Admiral Grace Hopper was a gifted mathematician and computer scientist (although the term was not in existence at the time she became one) who helped lead the Navy into the computer age. Her work was central to the concept of using words instead of mathematical symbols to compile data, and she was often referred to as the "mother of COBOL" (Common Business-Oriented Language), one of the earliest computer languages.

Admiral Hopper was above all a woman of enormous character who followed her own instincts in an era when women were not often granted the privilege of leadership. She radiated the kind of blended self-confidence and humility that is magnetic, and in many ways the best indicator of character. It is no exaggeration to say her talk that day was memorable in every way and served as a touchstone for me and many others as the Navy changed to the computer-based organization we know today—as significant a change from the analog days of my youth as was the shift from wood to steel and sail to coal a century earlier. After meeting her, I continued to follow her voyage until the day she died, by which time I was a full commander and had been the captain of a destroyer. I used a lot of what I learned by watching her in each of my commands, and even today I vividly remember that elfin figure so full of big ideas.

Rear Admiral "Amazing" Grace Brewster Murray Hopper was the great-granddaughter of a Civil War Union admiral, a fact of which she was very cognizant. She often wove her nautical legacy into stories she would tell, notably one about nearly drowning as a child on the family's lake after a small sailboat in which she was embarked capsized and her mother yelled at her to "remember the admiral" from the dock. ("Swim, Grace, dammit" might have been better advice. And I say that as an admiral myself.)

The essence of understanding the enormous impact of Admiral Hopper on the US Navy lies in appreciating the sweep of technology that occurred over her lifetime. She arrived into the world at a time when the Navy still had ships with "backup" sailing masts and had only recently emerged from the smashing victories of the Spanish-American War. There were effectively no submarines or maritime-operated aircraft. Communications relied on the use of signal flags in most cases. Ships were fired by coal, and much of early-twentieth-century strategy (developed, of course, by Alfred Thayer Mahan) centered upon the perceived need for coaling stations where warships could stop, refuel, conduct voyage repairs, and continue their endless patrols establishing control of the seas for America. They were not terribly complex machines, and their primitive fire control systems to direct their massive guns relied mostly on line-of-sight observations. There were few technological demands on a warship, and the essence of operating a ship at sea was simple seamanship, engineering, and gunnery.

The First World War drove many advances in warship technology, including the advent of submarine warfare, some maritime patrol aircraft, and the use of dirigibles for observations, which were based on larger ships. The business of maritime warfare was still relatively simple. But the post–World War I period saw technology advances in a wide variety of disciplines, and by the time Grace would join the Navy in the mid-1940s, much had changed across the fleet. Radio communications had become the norm, ships were all oil-fired and their engineering plants far more resilient and sophisticated, submarines were better equipped with offensive weapons, fire control systems had better means of using inputs from radars, and carriers brought relatively high-performance aircraft to sea. But there was not yet a need for the truly complex systems that would emerge following the Second World War that would drive the need for a computer-based fleet. As Grace Hopper entered the Navy and the long trajectory of her career began, the beginnings of the computer revolution appeared in the emerging need for high-speed missile fire control, analysis of complex undersea acoustic signals, satellite navigation and communication, gunnery systems that automatically engaged incoming targets, advanced propulsion including eventually nuclear power and gas turbines—on and on. Hopper's voyage through the second half of the twentieth century ran parallel with the need for big tranches of data analysis, high speed of response, and seamless integration of complex combat and engineering systems—in other words, the need for digital to replace analog. Her career reflected that shift and enabled the even more complex warships of today.

She was born in 1906 into a loving family, her parents discovering and encouraging her attraction to technology early on in their New York City home and their New Hampshire retreat. She frequently took things apart to understand how they worked—beginning with seven alarm clocks she disassembled at the age of seven. She recalled it later, saying, "What happened was that I'd taken the first one apart and I couldn't get it back together, so I opened the next one. I ended up with all seven of them apart. After that I was restricted to one clock. It's that kind of curiosity: How do things work." Always academically inclined and precocious, she entered Vassar at seventeen and graduated in 1928 with a Phi Beta Kappa key, having studied both mathematics and physics. Two years later, she completed a master's at Yale, and went on to pursue a PhD in mathematics, completing the degree in 1934. She began teaching math at Yale in 1931 and married fellow academic and NYU professor Vincent Hopper—taking and keeping his name for the rest of her life—although they ended up divorcing in 1945. As she said, "I was very fortunate that my father believed his daughters should be given the same opportunities as his son, so my sister and I both went to Vassar. It was a little unusual back in those days."

Her life might well have continued on a comfortable academic track if the United States had not been forced into the Second World War by the attack on Pearl Harbor on December 7, 1941, around the middle of the day on the East Coast. Grace and her husband Vincent were sitting in their study in New York City on

Ninety-fifth Street in Manhattan on opposite sides of a big double desk, surrounded by books and with the windows letting in the watery early winter light. If so, she would likely have been reading while chain-smoking Lucky Strikes. There were always books in her world. She would eventually spend her final days in a small apartment filled with cartons of research papers and magnetic tapes, a portable television set, and stacks of books numbering around ten thousand volumes—from murder mysteries to complex electrical engineering textbooks. She was a deeply gifted mathematician, of course, but at the heart of her character was a huge sense of curiosity about nearly everything—which she satisfied by reading voraciously and widely.

At the start of the war, Hopper was in a troubled marriage. Her husband Vincent, a gifted writer and teacher, loved her, but something simply did not work in their marriage—some fundamental quality was missing from their connection with each other, a piece of wiring across which the electrons of love never freely flowed. She was also very concerned about finding a way to serve her country and longed for a bigger life than the academic world seemed capable of providing. When she heard the news of Pearl Harbor, the world spun around, once, twice, and again, she would later say. In an instant she knew her life would change forever, and in her heart, she also knew her marriage was over. The attack somehow blended and crystallized the discontent she felt throughout her married life. She would later say that she knew immediately that she would walk out of the marriage, and that she hoped to join the Navy. After their divorce, her husband eventually married one of her bridesmaids and went on to a distinguished career as a professor and scholar at New York University—exactly the life she wanted to avoid. She continued to use her married name and virtually never spoke of the divorce. After a time, people began to assume she was a widow, perhaps of a World War II veteran.

At the time of the attack on Pearl Harbor, there were no women in the US Navy. In a certain sense, the attack figuratively blew her life apart; and when the pieces came back together, she was forged anew in the crucible created by a national crisis that enabled for her a new calling and a new life—in the US Navy. While she would never sail on warships at sea for any significant number of days, her service as an admiral of the twentieth-century Navy was vital to her nation in ways she never could have imagined on December 7, 1941.

After the conflict broke out, the Navy began to accept women into its ranks, but at only 105 pounds, she was well below the Navy's minimum weight of 120 pounds and was initially denied the chance to serve. The rejection was possibly also related to the fact that her work as a professor at Vassar was considered important to the war effort and that she was in her mid-thirties at that point. But as much as anything it was the physical appearance of frailness that held her back. But by 1943, her persistence paid off; after training with the Reserve Officer Training Corps at Smith College, she was commissioned into the Navy in 1944.

Her initial assignment as a WAVE—Women Accepted for Volunteer Emergency Service—was under the auspices of the Bureau of Ships at Harvard. Along with her boss and mentor Howard Aiken, a towering, hard-driven Navy captain, she cowrote papers on primitive computational devices. After graduating from the initial entry school, called "Midshipmen's School," she hoped to be assigned to the Navy's code-breaker unit, the Naval Communication Annex. She felt her training in mathematics made this an ideal first assignment. But during her time at Midshipmen's School, an innovative computing device was produced by IBM and sent to Harvard under the authority of the Navy. Young Lieutenant (junior grade) Grace Hopper would not go to the Naval Communication Annex; instead, she would become one of the first several people to program the world's first computer.

This massive (eight feet in height and more than fifty feet long, weighing five tons) primitive computer was essentially an automatic calculating machine. But using a paper tape mechanism, it could accept instructions from a human. Under the direction of Aiken, Hopper began to work on what eventually became known as the Mark I computer (a Navy term for a system simply meaning it was the first version, much as we use 1.0 or 2.0 today). It would be used to study trajectories for missiles, solve complex weapons and fire control programs, analyze radio waves, validate ship construction, and many other war-critical tasks. Hopper was at the heart of these efforts, part of a small, elite, and highly visionary Navy team at Harvard.

The work environment was a long way from the ocean. Located in the physics lab at Harvard, it was guarded by armed sailors, and both her boss—the formidable Captain Aiken—and the tasks were challenging. Aiken immediately put her to work calculating arctangents (complex mathematic functions that are essentially the inverse of a normal tangent function). Since such work could not be done with extreme accuracy without a massive calculating machine, she was forced, essentially immediately, to "program" (the word did not exist in 1944 in terms of computers) the IBM Mark I. Like Aiken and the handful of coworkers (all naval personnel and all male), Hopper had to make it up as she went along. Even as she took over the job of programming the Mark I (along with a new ensign, Richard Milton Bloch), Hopper knew she was solving important problems in the effort to win the war. Her work specifically enabled far higher degrees of accuracy in radar and missile technology, a significant contribution to the war effort. What she could not know at the time was how her initial work would reverberate today in the everyday process of humans directing machines to solve problems.

It is important to note that Hopper understood that to make the idea of "programming" work, she would have to understand the mechanics of the machine. The Mark I had close to a million distinct parts, and she spent a great deal of time looking through blueprints to truly comprehend the functionality of the machine. She then had to develop the means via punch tapes to direct the movements—the raw computational work—of the Mark I. Naturally, this first "computer" was primitive compared with modern devices, and therefore it was even more challenging given that commands often had to be inputted in real time to force the necessary computations. Through sheer determination, she was able to improve the machine's performance. At heart, the extraordinary accomplishment of Admiral Hopper was taming this mechanical beast, and thus embarking on the great voyage of modern computer science during her wartime experiences in the Navy.

Hopper also spent a good deal of time outside the lab, engaging with other nascent computer efforts supporting the war. All of this was happening as the war entered its critical phase, including the landings at Normandy, the crucial island battles of the Pacific, the final bombing campaigns into the heart of the Germany, and ultimately the surrenders of Germany and Japan. You can directly connect her work with the Mark I computer to some of the tactical successes in the war, as well as to the longer-term entry of the US Navy into the computer age.

It was during this period that the term "bug" emerged in the context of early computers. At one point, Hopper described literally finding a bug—an enterprising moth—inside the Mark II, the follow-on computer to her beloved Mark I. She said it was about four inches in size, and was the cause of the machine "conking out." They took the moth out and taped it into the logbook describing the night's events; it is part of the Smithsonian museums' collection today, perhaps the most famous moth in history. After that, when anything went wrong with the computers, the entire Navy team would talk about the "bugs" in the program (or the machine).

After the war, Hopper remained committed to the Navy, turning down tenure at Vassar to stay with the Navy Computational Lab under the irascible Captain Aiken well into the late 1940s, long after the war ended. Despite the pressure-cooker environment he created at the lab, she would later describe Aiken as the best leader she ever met. Both Lieutenant Hopper and her dedicated sidekick Ensign Richard Bloch continued their work even as support waned somewhat within the Navy—although Aiken was able to obtain funding for the Mark II and Mark III computers. In order to ensure continuity, the key members of the project were shifted over to the Naval Reserve (so they could not be transferred to high-priority active-duty assignments). As other civilian team-mates joined in, the naval feel of the project diminished somewhat, and tensions between the "plank owners" (a Navy term for those who had been there from the beginning, such as Hopper) and the new arrivals increased. Luckily for Hopper, she was a favorite of Aiken's and able to continue her pioneering work with a minimum of interference. She and Richard Bloch worked on the frontiers of programming, driving the use of subroutines and using magnetic drums instead of paper tapes.

When she eventually departed Harvard to go her own way after the Navy's contract expired in 1949, she stayed in the Navy reserves, but was interested in more private-sector experience. By the early 1950s, Hopper was becoming a pioneer in working with UNIVAC computers, the first powerful computational device that was commercially produced in the United States. She worked closely with two men, J. Presper Eckert and John Mauchly, and their legendary work together was fundamental to the chain of events that would eventually lead to Hopper's central role in bringing the Navy into the computer age. It was not easy. Looking back on it, she recalled, "I can remember once I went to the general manager of UNIVAC to get some money or people. He said no, and I said, 'Okay, I'll quit. I'll clean out my desk and leave this afternoon.' He beckoned me to come back and said, 'Wait a minute Grace, you've already done that once this year, you can't do it again.' You must stand on your own two feet. That's half the fun." There were also challenges, including an arrest on drunk and disorderly conduct, accompanied by dark thoughts of suicide, according to several biographers. But the overall trajectory of her life continued upward, and her innovative course remained true north for her.

She was also an early advocate of creating computer languages that were approachable by nonmathematicians. By the early 1960s, the language known as COBOL, which she helped develop, was gaining in importance as the industry realized the value of more accessible language-based systems of control for computers as opposed to numerically based ones. As her reputation grew, the Navy found new uses for her: for a decade, from 1967 to 1977, she was director of the Navy's Programming Languages Group. She came to Annapolis often in those years to encourage the use of both COBOL and Fortran (Formula Translation), as well as mandatory coursework in computers for the entire Brigade of Midshipmen. It was the influence of Rear Admiral Hopper on the Navy that opened the door for basic computer science in the hidebound traditional curriculum of the Naval Academy. It was also during this period of her service that I met her, and the impression was indelible.

By the late 1970s, her work had pushed not only the Navy but the entire Department of Defense toward creating smaller and more distributed networks. The early forerunners of the systems in use today on all Navy ships were the direct result of Grace Hopper's determination to innovate and drive the Navy forward. For example, via her work with the Naval Reserve, she was the first to coherently and forcefully advocate for the use of computers on ships at sea. Regarded as a foolish notion at first (much as the ideas of airplanes operating from ships was once dismissed), the concept grew in her mind as technology permitted more computational power in smaller and more stable machines. She correctly foresaw the limited utility of massive mainframe devices and the resultant need to connect numerous smaller systems. In this sense, she was ahead of many of the later pioneers in the revolution in personal computing, from Ed Roberts to Steve Wozniak to Steve Jobs. Perhaps most important throughout the 1970s and onward, she articulated the idea of a "computer age," and the synthesis of humans and machines. Taking all that she had learned in the Navy Computational Lab about how humans could efficiently communicate with massive calculating machines, she was able to extrapolate forward to envision endless uses for the techniques and technologies she pioneered. She was also instrumental in helping lay the groundwork for the universal standards developed for connecting physically disparate computational systems, today under the auspices of the National Institute of Standards and Technology. This work was part of the vital technological leap that permitted the internet to evolve (from the Department of Defense systems, by the way). At every turning point in the computer age, Rear Admiral Hopper was present and central in her contributions.

Having served throughout the post–World War II decades in the Naval Reserve (where she remained very connected to the Navy, participating in many conferences, weekend drills, and stints on active duty), she was required to finally retire as a full commander at the age of sixty in 1967. But the Navy was experiencing difficulties implementing COBOL, and she was once again activated. Initially "called up" for a six-month assignment, she quickly proved indispensable. The six months turned into a year, then another, and eventually ended up lasting twenty years. As a result, she was able to continue to be promoted. She was first promoted to captain in 1973 and was "pinned on" by the chief of naval operations, Elmo Zumwalt—two kindred spirits, each supporting innovation in every way. Her fame continued to grow, as she was more and more the subject of media profiles, including one on *60 Minutes*. She was increasingly in demand as a speaker at military and industry conferences all over the country. All of the attention culminated in a special act of Congress in 1983 that approved her promotion to one-star rank, at the time called "commodore," and later rear admiral (lower half); rear admirals (upper half) have two stars. In the end, her Navy career spanned forty-two years, and she retired in 1986 in a well-attended ceremony on board the world's oldest commissioned warship, USS *Constitution*, in Boston Harbor, at the age of seventy-nine. She was among an elite handful of admirals to have served to such a senior age, along with Nimitz, William Leahy, and Rickover.

During the final segment of her career, she was assigned to the Naval Data Automation Headquarters in Washington, DC, holding that position for six years, beginning in 1977. It allowed her to be on top of the integration of computing into Navy systems broadly. Of note, she was instrumental in developing the first fleet-wide system for sharing tactical data (course, speed, contacts in the area, etc.) with submarines. After her assignment at the Naval Data HQ, she was sent on a three-year nationwide tour conducting lectures and generally pushing the idea of advanced computers at sea. When she finally retired as a rear admiral in 1986, she was the oldest active-duty officer in the US Navy.

After retiring from the Navy, Hopper worked for Digital Equipment Corporation (DEC), but spent most of her time as a national spokeswoman for the Navy, for the role of computers in our society, and for the need to increase the impact of women in science and technology. She was famous for handing out cut pieces of telephone cable of about a foot in length to demonstrate the distance light travels in a nanosecond, illustrating why it takes so long for satellite communications to synch up. And for every lecture, no matter the audience or location, she would wear her service dress blue uniform. While permitted by Navy regulations, it is not the norm for a retired officer to do so. I once asked Admiral Mike Mullen, a former CNO and chairman of the Joint Chiefs, if he ever wore his uniform after retiring, and he said, "I'll wear it one more time and that's when they bury me in it." Yet for "Amazing Grace" it just felt right. She was beloved by the Navy and seeing her in a uniform only brought credit to the service.

Rear Admiral Grace Hopper, USN (Ret.), died in her sleep in Arlington, Virginia, not far from the Pentagon, at the age of eighty-five. She was buried with full honors at the Arlington National Cemetery nearby. In 2016, she was posthumously awarded the Presidential Medal of Freedom, the culmination of dozens of national and international awards she received throughout her long life, including more than thirty honorary degrees from universities around the country. Although she made her mark on the Navy ashore, the nation honored her contributions in 1997 when the guided missile destroyer USS *Hopper* was placed in commission.

Hopper was a patriot who loved her country. Deep within her was a desire to be part of something larger than herself. This led her to push so hard to join the US Navy after Pearl Harbor, and it illuminated every aspect of her life and career. Despite being turned down time and again, Hopper kept reapplying, refusing to take no for an answer. It also was central to her decision to forsake a traditional path of marriage and children, and instead devote herself to the US Navy and the nation.

Patriotism is a fundamental quality of character. Are patriots born or made? The answer, of course, is both. Character is often expressed in sacrifice; the willingness to give unstintingly of oneself has often been described as "the price we pay for the right to serve." As is so often the case for those who have a deep love of their country, Rear Admiral Grace Hopper's patriotism had an associated level of cost. The character qualities that lead to that level of personal sacrifice are at least in part inherent in an individual, but they can also be nurtured and developed. Grace Hopper's parents and close relatives set a strong example for her, encouraged her desire to serve, and created the conditions for her to step up for her nation after Pearl Harbor and afterward. Well before anyone coined the phrase "thank you for your service" to say to active-duty and veteran members of the military, Grace Hopper was the beneficiary of parents, friends, and relatives who thanked and encouraged her to serve. This is a very valuable quality of character, the seeds of which can be planted early in a young person's life.

There is a lesson for our often-cynical time: the case for service must be made—it is not innate. Too frequently, our society defaults to the idea of the military as the beau ideal of service. I am constantly told, "Thank you for your service," and believe me, after four decades in uniform, I appreciate it deeply. Yet there are *so* many ways to serve this country—diplomats, CIA, FBI, civil servants, police, firefighters, emergency medical technicians, Peace

Corps volunteers, Teach for America, schoolteachers in low-income districts, nurses in downtown clinics, volunteers at hospitals and food banks, and on and on. I speak often about the value of service to nation, and my thinking was shaped by watching the career of Grace Hopper. Admiral Hopper's life continues to be an example to each of us that patriotism and service are inextricably intertwined.

Another fundamental quality of Rear Admiral Grace Hopper was her instinctive sense of mentorship. She constantly pushed others to excel. In doing so, she consistently demonstrated the ability to speak at the level of her audience, whether in a casual conversation in the laboratory or before hundreds of international scientists. Throughout her long and purpose-driven life, she took time to encourage, educate, and mentor others. Toward the end of her life, she would often remark that her greatest accomplishment was *not* the creation of computing languages, programming the Mark I computer at Harvard, or attaining high rank in the Navy. Her greatest accomplishment was the teaching, mentoring, and advancement of so many young men and women. In the end, they represented the very best of Admiral Hopper, and the gorgeous trajectories of their lives were what gave her joy. In later life she said, "The most important thing I've accomplished, other than building the compiler, is training young people. They come to me, you know, and say, 'Do you think we can do this?' I say, 'Try it.' And I back them up. They need that. I keep track of them as they get older and I stir them up at intervals, so they don't forget to take chances. People in a way are very much waiting for someone to express confidence in them, and once you do it, they'll take off."

The way in which she did this mentoring affords us valuable lessons. True instinctive mentors take the responsibility of mentorship seriously and go about it in a systematic and organized way. Too often, "mentors" pay lip service to the idea of helping others up the ladder, but don't truly follow up or remain consistent in their approach. Mentorship should include keeping a file of good people to draw upon for key assignments, following up with mentees frequently (at least every six months) on both professional and personal aspects of their progress, actively seeking to place mentees with other outstanding role models, and providing honest and thoughtful advice to ensure that mentees make intelligent career and personal decisions. Being a mentor is hard work that is quite often not rewarded with obvious and consistent reinforcement and is a perfect example of the way in which we must pay it forward to say thanks to others for what they have given us. When I think of mentoring I have received over the years, I am humbled—and I always vow to pay it forward whenever I can. People like former chairmen of the Joint Chiefs General Colin Powell and Admiral Mike Mullen, as well as former secretaries of defense Bob Gates and Leon Panetta, have always been willing to slow down, take time, and give me the course corrections I needed. They were also there when I stumbled to help me recover my bearings and move forward. Like Admiral Hopper, I've tried to do the same for others coming along, and a part of that was observing her do so for countless young people.

Grace Hopper was also endlessly kind and considerate, with a clever sense of humor that she was unafraid to deploy in tense situations. She was also a practical joker, although not a mean-spirited one. For example, knowing that one of her coworkers was going on an important date, she would hide his uniform dress cap in the pipes in the ceiling—a grave difficulty as naval personnel cannot venture outside without a hat on when in uniform. Whenever she traveled, she returned with spoils for her staff and friends, often carrying a pair of matched string bags that would be filled up with her gifts.

Of the comparisons that are often made of Navy innovators, the least accurate (though often heard) pairing is that of Admiral Hyman Rickover, the "father of the nuclear Navy," with Rear Admiral Grace Hopper, "the mother of COBOL." Rickover was irascible, irritable, famously difficult on an interpersonal level, and often full of anger. Hopper was just the opposite; she managed to win legions of friends wherever she went in her life, despite being employed in tense and challenging work environments in which she was often not taken seriously at first because of her gender. She was also modest and humble. As she once said, "I never thought about what I wanted to accomplish in life. I had too many things to do. I was so deeply involved in things, I just kept on going. Then something came along and changed the direction. I went off with it. I didn't know where it was going to lead me. It just keeps on leading me." As we've seen, some believe there are times when righteous anger can be an effective tool of leadership. But both my own life experience and many empirical studies demonstrate that an angry, fearful workplace is a vastly less effective workplace. In all her leadership roles, Admiral Hopper's fundamentally decent, kind nature served her extremely well in creating a sense among those around her that their efforts and abilities were valued and consciously appreciated.

In addition, Hopper was loyal. Wherever she worked, and no matter how demanding her immediate boss, she tried hard to support him (and it was always a him). She well understood that the opportunities for women were severely circumscribed simply as a matter of gender, but despite this, she never let frustration, or a sense of injustice overcome her innate loyalty to the larger Navy. She was also a believer that it was loyalty to principle that mattered, not blind loyalty to any given boss. Several times in her career, she was willing to tell her chain of command that they were simply wrong—either in their leadership approach or in their technical judgments. Admiral Hopper managed to be loyal without being slavish or obsequious. She showed us that in terms of character, loyalty is in many ways a two-edged quality. At times it is the most important character quality an individual can manifest. We naturally esteem it as a highly prized attribute in our subordinates; but it is worth remembering that loyalty must run both up *and* down any chain of command. More senior people need to be as loyal to their subordinates as they hope their subordinates are to them—a kind of golden rule of character. But there is another side to loyalty, and it is a darker one. When is it appropriate to be loyal to a boss who is simply a bad leader? Or demonstrates ethically unacceptable views? In this sense, we owe not blind loyalty to the individuals above us in the chain of command, but rather loyalty to the larger values of an organization or a nation. When members of the US military are promoted, as Grace Hopper was many times, they do not swear allegiance to their chain of command, but rather to the Constitution of the United States—the ultimate repository of our system of values and our inalienable rights. In today's morally challenged world, I often think "how low can we go?" in terms of the character failings in some of our leaders. It feels like athletics turned upside down—in sports, records are made to be broken, as the old saw goes, and they inevitably are improved upon. Sadly, our ethical and moral standards are becoming a lower and lower bar to surmount, and that should give us pause. What I take away from Admiral Hopper is that loyalty is a quality of character that has to be thoughtfully but not blindly given.

As a senior officer, Admiral Hopper always had her eye on the distant horizon. Along with many of the other admirals in this volume, she thought not only about the present and the immediate future, but about the very long term. She would often challenge her subordinates and even audiences she was lecturing to think not about tomorrow or next year, but about the hundred-year future. Intimately tied to this kind of approach was her endless drive to stay current about the world of complex computing, even in ripe old age. At the very heart of Admiral Hopper's character was her sense of vision. From the moment she started working on naval problems in the Second World War until her improbably long career finally ended, she had a consistent vision of moving the Navy into the computer age. She knew that the post–World War II Navy would continue to grow in complexity and absorb new technologies, and that the tools of which she was a master—mathematics and computer science—needed to be the drivers of those advances.

For any good leader, vision is the quality that makes the most difference in terms of inspiring subordinates. Only through an abiding sense of vision can other important character traits be fully embodied over time. Vision shows us how what we do today will shape the future. A vision of the distant future allows a valuable sense of perspective, and can enable the humor, thoughtfulness, mentorship, and loyalty that come together to create the long-lasting outcomes that really matter. It was Hopper's ability to push the Navy forward that enabled the truly advanced systems we put to sea today: the vaunted Aegis combat detection system, which can track hundreds of targets at almost infinite ranges including into space; our constellation of integrated satellites for seamless global navigation and communication; gunnery and missile systems that are "hands off" in high-speed combat; unmanned vehicles both in the air and under the sea that can maneuver with complete autonomy; the use of artificial intelligence in maintenance to predict casualties before they occur—the list goes on and on. So much of it ultimately stems from the vision of this slight, mischievous, and thoughtful visionary.

Finally, it is worth remembering in terms of her character that Rear Admiral Grace Hopper was not a charismatic person in a physical sense. Her diminutive stature and small voice never allowed her to step into and dominate a room in the way so many other leaders have been able to do throughout history. She was no Themistocles striding to the front of the Greek rowers to inspire them to defeat the Persians at Salamis, nor a stately Chester Nimitz blessed with a strong and pleasing appearance complemented by a powerful physical presence. But throughout her life, people who spent time around Grace wanted to be on her team. They came to value her character, seeing in it the fundamental goodness of a curiosity-driven dreamer with the practical skills to achieve powerful and meaningful results. Her devotion to change inspired those around her again and again: "I have insatiable curiosity. It's solving problems. Every time you solve a problem, another one shows up immediately behind it. That's the challenge. Nothing ever stays the same, it's always new and different." When I met her at Annapolis so many years ago, I was mesmerized not by her appearance, nor by her mannerisms, but by her obvious goodwill, enthusiasm, and vision. For Admiral Hopper, the combination of character attributes she developed and deployed throughout a long and eventful life reflected a powerful and highly refined mixture, and she put it to good use—changing the Navy profoundly and permanently. As she said at the end of her life, "Wouldn't it be dull to do things that ended? I'm having a heck of a good time and contributing a little bit here and there to solving problems." Not a bad epitaph for Amazing Grace.

All quotes by Grace Hopper in this chapter were taken from Lynn Gilbert with Gaylen Moore, *Grace Murray Hopper: Women of Wisdom* (self-published, 1981).

CHAPTER XI

Resilience
and the
Modern Admiral

T hus far, our sea stories have centered on ten admirals who now sail on the great fleet plying the seas of the heavens. But a study of character in the modern world would not be complete without a few observations about admirals (and generals) who are still with us today. One key element of each of the stories we've discussed is *resilience*. Each of the ten admirals we've examined demonstrated deep reservoirs of resilience over the course of their careers. It is clearly a central element of character, perhaps the most important one of all. So as we turn to modern admirals, let's look at some stories of resilience in a few more recent sea stories.

The stories of modern admirals are illustrative of what can happen to anyone given the complexities of commanding powerful fleets while facing a variety of significant personal challenges. And of course, while not everyone is a fleet commander, we all face similar personal challenges in terms of our lives and the voyage of character. These can range from the medical issues we all must eventually face to the societal barriers that confront many of us as we move forward as leaders. And ego can play a part in the voyage of character. Indeed, it is often said that the true test of character is not how we perform in adversity, but rather what happens when we are given power. This is certainly true of senior military officers.

Let's begin with power. Many wonderful things come along as you rise through the ranks of military service. If you are lucky enough to become an admiral (or a general), you get to travel to fascinating places, meet interesting people, and participate in events that would have been unimaginable before you put on those hard-earned stars. With all those benefits come burdens, although I know it is hard to generate much sympathy from the public in that regard. Believe me, though, the burdens are real. Along with the spotlight comes a microscope. Everything you do and don't do is scrutinized in minute detail. For the most part, it comes with the territory. As Luke 12:48 says: "For unto whomsoever much is given, of him shall be much required; and to whom men have committed much, of him they will ask the more." Keeping that biblical wisdom in mind sometimes requires more than the patience of Job.

In my memoir of my NATO days, *The Accidental Admiral,* I spoke about the challenges and need for resilience that stemmed from career-changing highly public negative events in the lives and careers of fellow four-stars Army General David Petraeus, Army General Stan McChrystal, and Marine Corps General and Naval Academy classmate General John Allen. Stan McChrystal was fired while serving as our commander in Afghanistan over comments some of his staff made about civilian leaders in DC. It was a highly public and embarrassing end to a brilliant career. Dave Petraeus was caught having an affair with a reserve officer who was writing a biography of him, and—more seriously—caught passing her classified information. Charged with a felony, he eventually pled guilty to a misdemeanor and had two years of probation and a $100,000 fine. John Allen was accused of having an inappropriate relationship with a socialite in Tampa based on emails that came to light in the investigation into Dave Petraeus's affair. He was ultimately exonerated but chose to retire instead of taking another four-star assignment. I also underwent my own trials and tribulations in dealing with accusations of travel violations from which I was ultimately exonerated. In my case, there was an anonymous complaint that I had taken a trip to France while NATO commander for a "wine tasting," when in fact it was a widely attended gathering with the chief of the French Armed Forces at which I gave a formal speech (in full dress uniform and in French) about the value of NATO. The investigation dragged on for months and put a cloud over my final months in uniform. But all four of us have recovered from those embarrassing moments and moved on in our lives in positive ways: Dave is a partner at a huge private equity firm, KKR; Stan runs a successful consulting business; John is the president of the Brookings Institution; and I went on to serve as dean of a top graduate school of international relations and today work at the Carlyle Group, a large international business firm. There are good lessons in terms of the need for resilience and how to cope with the most demanding circumstances from each of those cases, and they are described fully in *The Accidental Admiral*.

But as I reflect on the need for resilience as a fundamental part of our character, there are two other stories of individuals who have faced far more challenging scenarios. Both are contemporaries of mine—both retired as four-star admirals in fact—and their stories are worth mentioning briefly. One is Admiral Michelle Howard and the other is Admiral Bill McRaven.

Let's begin with Admiral Michelle Howard. As the first black woman four-star admiral, her career at first glance could seem to be one of unbroken success. Yet as an African American in a very white, overwhelmingly male Admiralty, she faced numerous obstacles. From the school playground to the highest levels of military service, going first is a universal mark of leadership, and Admiral Howard has gone first over and over again throughout her career.

Between entering the Naval Academy in 1978 (two years after the Academy first opened to women) and retiring in December 2017, she became the first African American woman to command a ship, the first member of the class of 1982 to make admiral, the first woman to graduate from Annapolis and reach flag rank, the first African American woman in any service to reach three stars, the first female four-star in the Navy, and the first woman and first African American to serve as vice chief of naval operations.

Like many of the other admirals profiled in these pages, Admiral Howard's drive and determination appeared early. Daughter of an Air Force master sergeant, she knew the rigors and frequent moves of military life from a young age. Undeterred, she decided at age twelve that she would attend a service academy—none of which were open to women at the time. Her mother, who has long been one of Admiral Howard's heroes, backed this ambition to the hilt, telling her daughter that they would file suit if necessary to make the Academy a possibility. In the event, gender integration of the service academies was one instance in which Howard did not personally have to go first. Congress ordered all of the academies opened to women in 1976, and she secured an appointment to Annapolis upon graduating from high school in Colorado in 1978. From the moment she arrived on campus, however, Howard began leading and breaking barriers. I met her first when she was a midshipman at the Naval Academy, playing a role in the Masqueraders (the drama performance troupe at Annapolis), in a Shakespeare play—I think it was *A Midsummer Night's Dream*. Though she stands only about five feet tall, Michelle dominated the stage from the moment she set foot on it. She radiates both confidence and grace and has a powerful command voice packed into her relatively compact frame. *That is someone to watch,* I thought to myself. Over the subsequent decades of her career, I did exactly that, helping at several points as a mentor, while always observing how she consistently paid it forward to the younger officers coming behind her.

After graduating from the Academy in 1982, Howard commissioned and qualified as a surface warfare officer. She quickly distinguished herself in the surface Navy, beginning a meteoric rise in rank and responsibility. Only five years after commissioning, her capability as a leader resulted in service-wide recognition as the 1987 recipient of the Captain Winifred Quick Collins Award, which is jointly awarded by the Navy and the Navy League to one outstanding woman officer each year. At that pace, it is hardly surprising that she became the first member of her class to pin on an admiral's shoulder boards.

Yet it was not easy. As I moved up through the ranks, I would hear from peers, seniors, and even subordinates about Michelle. It was often commentary plainly driven by resentment of her success—jealousy. While I hope it was not racially based—and I never heard overt comments along those lines—it was clear that many people regarded her success as simply an outgrowth of "being the first black woman." That is a heavy burden to carry, and it made it necessary for Michelle to be even that much better in how she drove her ship, the way she carried herself, the tactical war-fighting decisions she made at sea, and the way she imposed disciplinary proceedings on others. For any fast riser in the Navy, there is a special level of scrutiny, and Michelle carried an extra burden. To her credit, she maintained an even keel despite provocative comments that leaked back to her ("You should know that Captain Smith is not a friend of yours, Michelle," and the like). She kept her head down, drove her ships well, made the tough leadership decisions, and earned her way. That is character, and Michelle demonstrated it over and over again.

Although Michelle Howard shone brightly by any measure, her achievements are even more notable for the obstacles she confronted along the way—and the gritty resilience with which she surmounted them. To contextualize the challenges she faced, it is worth recalling Bud Zumwalt's revolutionary four years as chief of naval operations from 1970 to 1974. Though he fought hard against the Navy's deeply ingrained racism and sexism (which in his view ran deeper still), Admiral Zumwalt's tenure ended without long-term solutions to either problem. Many of his most ambitious reforms were rolled back immediately after his tenure too, which only raised the stakes for women and minorities like Michelle Howard. For example, women were not allowed to serve permanently on nonhospital ships until 1978 (the year Howard entered the academy), which would have made it impossible for her to qualify and serve as a surface warfare officer.

In many ways, Admiral Howard's career fulfilled and institutionalized some of the tantalizing promise that had appeared in the Navy under Admiral Zumwalt, whom she admires. Fittingly, she still has one of his business cards and keeps it close as a memento to this day. One of the most inspiring elements of her story is that she was given neither more nor less than the opportunity to prove herself at every level—and proceeded to do so repeatedly in spite of all manner of suspicion, resistance, and sheer obstructionism. As her mother helped her to see during a moment of self-doubt and frustration along the way, timing was both a blessing and a curse in her career: due to the time when she entered the Navy, her story made history at every step, but constantly going first often felt like going forward alone.

At one particularly low moment, Admiral Howard has said, she called her mother to voice her frustrations. In addition to the increasing nominal responsibilities of her successive jobs—each of which test even those leaders who have everything already going for them—she was constantly under public scrutiny both in the Navy and beyond. Within the service, where her performance each time she went first would set the standard for all who followed, people plainly wanted to see what she was capable of. Meanwhile, she was fielding a stream of publicity requests from beyond the Navy, as more and more people in the public wanted to be inspired by all that she obviously *was* capable of. "You are where you are historically," her mother said. "As long as you stay in the Navy, this will not stop. Embrace it now or leave the Navy."

Thankfully, Admiral Howard chose to stay in uniform, and her faith in the Navy was rewarded by its faith in her. As she progressed into senior leadership roles, she collected some truly impressive firsts, notably becoming the first African American woman to command a warship (the amphibious landing ship USS *Rushmore*), an experience she has called her favorite in the Navy. Later, as an admiral, she commanded Combined Task Force 151, one of the Navy's dedicated counterpiracy forces afloat. Just days after her appointment came news of the MV *Maersk Alabama*'s capture by Somali pirates, which resulted in the events made famous by the story of the ship's master, Captain Richard Phillips. In those trying days, Admiral Howard was responsible for organizing the Navy's response and ultimately authorizing the high-risk SEAL mission that resulted in Captain Phillips's dramatic rescue.

All leadership can feel lonely at times, but the sort of trailblazing leadership that Admiral Howard has exercised for four decades can feel loneliest of all. At the top of the mountain, the strongest winds blow. For her, the lights were always brighter, the microscope closer, and the path steeper. Going first always requires an extra measure of courage and grit, and Admiral Howard had to sustain both nonstop.

What is her legacy? Too modest by nature to think of this herself, Michelle will nonetheless serve as a superb example of resilience. All leaders leave legacies, but not all of them think about the legacies they leave along the way. As a trailblazer, Admiral Howard has not had the luxury of not thinking about her legacy until late in her career. With every forward step she made for women, minorities, and leaders generally within the Navy, she knew that the example she set would become the standard applied to those who followed along the path. Leaders are constantly setting the standard for those around them, and those who come after them. In that way, leaders' own characters are constantly shaping the character of the people and organizations they lead. Admiral Howard's experience offers an acutely public example of the importance of character and legacy development for leaders to consider. The grit, grace, and resilience with which she has met and conquered the challenges she has faced offer a powerful example to us all.

MICHELLE HOWARD'S CHALLENGES WERE UNIQUE. LET ME SPEND A minute on a challenge that is very, very common. Many of us—indeed, the majority of us—will at some point face a significant medical crisis in our lives. Especially as we head to the wrong side of fifty years old, the chances of a medical setback increase significantly. But hardly any of us will go through such an experience while shouldering national responsibility as the four-star admiral in charge of the Navy SEALs. One flag officer who earned my highest respect in this regard is Admiral Bill McRaven.

Bill McRaven is best known as the man who led the operation that killed Osama bin Laden. As a close second, he is known as the retired admiral who was shamefully attacked by President Trump for having spoken his mind. But I first met him when he was a newly selected captain and I was a brand-new one star. We were in my office in the Pentagon a few months after 9/11 (he was recovering from a horrific parachute accident), talking about the Navy's response to the attack. The smell of smoke still hung heavy in the air of the badly damaged Pentagon, as it would for weeks afterward. Bill has a kind of laid-back intensity. A proud graduate of the University of Texas, with the sturdy build and height of a middle linebacker, he is also well read, thoughtful in speech and demeanor, and kind to all he meets. Our meeting was the beginning of a friendship that continues to this day and has included both operational and social interactions across several continents and war zones and in the battleground of Washington, DC.

As a fellow combatant commander toward the end of his career, he shared with me the story of his battle against leukemia. We were sitting on a bus being driven from the Pentagon to the White House for a dinner with the president. It came up in a discussion of how long we would each stay in uniform. I had already decided to get out relatively soon after my NATO command tour ended that spring, but I urged Bill to stay on active duty and put his hat in the ring for chairman of the Joint Chiefs—the only higher job either of us could anticipate taking. He told me about his condition—a life-threatening form of leukemia—in a very nonchalant fashion, despite the obvious dire potential consequences. "Hey, it's just another mission, right? They can blast the cancer back now, and when it comes back they can do it again. It won't work as well the next time, but after that I know they will have figured out something new." No fear, no sound in his voice of anything but quiet confidence. That is the kind of deep resilience that is so powerful for leaders at any level. Knowing the challenges that were coming, he decided to retire and focus on his health.

Fortunately, he regained his health after an extensive treatment regime and took up new challenges as the chancellor of the University of Texas system around the time I became the dean of the Fletcher School of Law and Diplomacy at Tufts University. We often compared notes on our new lives in higher education. Bill departed that job after three very full years in the summer of 2018. So far, he has continued to deal with his ongoing health issues with grace and courage. The medical world is still "finding something new," and not only for his sake, but for that of our nation, I hope they keep doing so. Our country needs people like Bill McRaven.

It is worth knowing about Bill that well over a decade earlier, in August 2001, then-captain McRaven, as commander of all West Coast SEALs, was gravely injured in a parachute training exercise. With his legs caught in his own canopy lines as his chute deployed, the opening shock instantly broke his back and pelvis in midair. Emergency surgery saved his life and his mobility but left him with the noxious prospect of months of bedridden convalescence and career uncertainty. Just a few days after that potentially life-changing accident, on September 11, 2001, Captain McRaven watched on live national television from a hospital bed installed in his own home as the character of warfare changed in an instant.

Still recuperating in his bed, McRaven spent the days, weeks, and months after the 9/11 attacks galvanizing the naval special warfare community for the fight he knew was coming. As soon as he was ready to go to work, McRaven transferred to Washington to take an appointment in the White House as a deputy national security advisor and strategic planner for counterterrorism. In that capacity, he literally wrote the book on the coming fight as principal author of the 2006 *National Strategy for Combating Terrorism*. In the remaining eight years of his career, he moved back into the operational world and helped the US special operations forces take the fight to the terrorists in Iraq, Afghanistan, and elsewhere. We collaborated closely in those days while I was at Deep Blue—the Navy's post-9/11 strategic and operational think tank—and he was in the White House on the NSC team. He recovered fully and could not wait to get back to the field, which he did.

A decade later, long after Osama bin Laden had plunged the United States into war, Admiral McRaven's career came full circle. In the spring of that year, as the commander of the Joint Special Operations Command, he helped plan and execute the daring Operation Neptune Spear—the raid on Osama bin Laden's compound in Pakistan in which JSOC operators killed the world's most wanted fugitive. The operation was at least as risky in its conception and execution as Operation Eagle Claw, the terribly failed effort to rescue the American hostages in Tehran, had been in 1980. Its overwhelming success (despite a helicopter crash eerily reminiscent of the debacle in the Iranian desert) helped banish some of the lingering ghosts of the failure that ushered US special operations into the modern era. It helped vindicate JSOC's decades of effort to ensure interoperability among those forces.

In the wake of that mission, during which he had provided real-time commentary on the operation on the live video link to the White House situation room, Admiral McRaven and the SEALs stepped into the public spotlight, a place they had assiduously avoided for decades. The admiral was profiled in national newspapers and quickly approved for a fourth star and command of US Special Operations Command (JSOC's parent organization), while the Development Group and its operators' derring-do became fixtures of the national imagination.

A final point on this note, which Admiral McRaven does make explicitly, is that these health situations can easily feel not merely inconvenient but deeply unfair. "Why me?" we are tempted to ask, even when we know the answer is simply, "that's life." Admiral McRaven illustrates this with the concept of the "sugar cookie," a common and sometimes apparently random punishment for SEAL trainees in which they are ordered to get wet and sandy on a beach. "Sometimes," he says, "no matter how well you prepare or perform, you still end up as a sugar cookie. It's just the way life is sometimes." In order to lead, you've got to be able to "get over being a sugar cookie and keep moving forward."

There could not be two people more physically different than Admiral Michelle Howard and Admiral Bill McRaven. One is a tiny African American woman and an Annapolis graduate, serving in the least glamorous part of the Navy, its surface warfare cadre. The other is a tall, white, square-jawed University of Texas track star who led the most prestigious force in the US military, the legendary Navy SEALS. On the surface, they don't have a lot in common. Yet knowing both of them well, I would say that each embodies one of the most important qualities of character, and one that is at the heart of projecting leadership: resilience. Both Michelle and Bill, despite enormous differences in style, personality, and circumstance, evoke for me the words of Isaiah 40:31: "But they that wait upon the Lord shall renew their strength; they shall mount up with wings as eagles; they shall run, and not be weary; and they shall walk, and not faint." Resilience, whether you are a believer in the good book or not, is the quality that allows you to run and not be weary. Both of these two modern admirals faced hard challenges, and both met them with deep resilience and true grit. Their character is part of today's Navy, and a fine example for us all.

The oceans show us this day after day. As a captain on the bridge, you can be driving the ship on a perfectly sunny day, the seas calm, standing a relaxed bridge watch and contemplating a good dinner in the wardroom. Suddenly, the boatswain mate will say, "Sir, the quartermaster says the barometer is falling," and the intercom from the combat information center will pipe up with the unwelcome news that a squall is directly ahead. There is no time to turn the ship, the storm breaks hard on the bow, lines are snapping and two sailors are blown over the side. You are uncertain of the ability of the deck division to get a boat in the water, and afraid it might be lost if you get it there. Should you launch the ship's helicopter? Are you on the right course to make that a safe operation? A thousand things flow through your mind in that moment, from deep concern over the lost sailors to real fear that you will make the wrong decisions. And whatever happens—whichever way you turn the ship, how fast you get a boat in the water, if you decide to take extra time to launch the ship's helicopter—the decision is yours, and yours alone. Fighting your way through those moments requires real resiliency. And whether you are applying it in a tactical moment or in the long throw of your career like

Michelle Howard or in responding to a life-threatening personal medical crisis like Bill McRaven, how you respond is a measure of your inner resilience.

Part of resilience is inherent in your character, shaped by your upbringing and the examples your parents and others have put before you, which you do not control. But a significant part of developing resilience is based on three key elements of your life that are in fact under your control. The first is the company you keep—the peers around whom you spend time. Seek out and bind yourself to those who both dare and succeed after failure. Too often, we undervalue the importance of our peers in setting examples of resilience for ourselves. Second are the books we read. There are so many powerful tales of resilience in literature, including *The Odyssey* of Homer, about the long voyage home by the wandering king of Ithaca; *Gates of Fire* by Steven Pressfield about the doomed Spartans of Thermopylae; *The Red Badge of Courage* by Stephen Crane, set in the American Civil War; *The Cruel Sea* by Nicholas Monsarrat, about the small warship *Compass Rose* in the Second World War; or Cormac McCarthy's dystopian masterpiece *The Road*. Find books that inspire that sense of resilience. And finally, in developing real resilience, it is important for all of us to have the inner conversation that says, "I refuse to be a victim. I will not blame others. I will prevail over the hardest of circumstances. And if I don't succeed initially, I will try again and again and yet again." Remembering the words of Churchill—never give in—is helpful. But this is a conversation that has to be part of our deepest sense of self. All of us fail—but we are so often given choices about how to respond. Be resilient.

Conclusions

I want to conclude with a few thoughts on my own sea story, which may provide a glimpse of one sailor's experiences, both good and bad, in wrestling with the challenges of character. In the course of nearly four decades of life at sea, I learned that a handful of character traits were at the heart of both good character and effective leadership. I think they are echoed in the successes and failures of the ten admirals in this volume, and I offer them below, each with a brief vignette of my own.

At the top of my list is *creativity*. Again and again in the stories of the ten admirals, we see the importance of a willingness to embrace the new, despite the difficulties and challenges of doing so. Especially in the cases of Admirals Fisher, Zumwalt, Mahan, and Hopper, we saw the challenge and the ultimate success of pursuing innovation—but not without costs. In my own case, I faced trying experiences several times as I endeavored to do so, especially during my days as the leader of US Southern Command in Miami, with responsibility for military operations south of the United States; and running Deep Blue, the innovative think tank put in place by the chief of naval operations in the terrible days immediately after 9/11, when the Navy needed to make the shift to a significant role in the Global War on Terror. One worked out well, the other not so much.

Let's start with Deep Blue. Before 9/11, the Navy was focused primarily on traditional global naval missions—sea control (ensuring we had maritime superiority on the deep ocean), power projection ashore (the ability to launch missile and aircraft strikes at targets on land), strategic deterrence (our ballistic missile submarines), and global sealift (moving supplies, US Marines, and other military cargo). We had no idea how to apply maritime power to the post-9/11 world. Chief of Naval Operations Vern Clark grasped this immediately and created a small cell called Deep Blue (a play both on the ocean and on the IBM chess-playing computer) that could think coherently about the new role the Navy needed to undertake. I was chosen to head Deep Blue because throughout my career, my reputation as an innovator, a challenger of orthodoxy, and a publisher of controversial articles was well known. I often consider that if 9/11 had not demanded that kind of thinking, I might have retired as a one-star officer. I was lucky that my overriding character trait—a hunger to innovate—met a situation that demanded it.

Clark allowed me to handpick a dozen of the smartest thinkers, writers, and briefers in the Navy. I grabbed the top people from each of the warfare communities and committed to briefing the chief of naval operations with at least two or three innovative ideas weekly. We worked unbelievable hours, tapped into the entire Navy's intellectual backbone via the War College, Naval Academy, and various training commands, and created a suite of new ideas. Some were terrific and are in place today; others fizzled. Such is the nature of innovation. What I discovered is that when there is a shared sense of mission, a modest application of high-quality resources (especially people), strong leadership at the top (we reported directly to the CNO), and a determination to take risk, mountains can move. The methods of implementing innovation that I experienced and learned at Deep Blue are the fundamental tools that I used for the final ten years of my career, and that I use today as well.

But when the character traits of innovation and creativity collide with established ideas, it doesn't always work out well. A few years after Deep Blue, I was selected to a fourth star and headed to US Southern Command with a particular vision for the command that had evolved from a series of conversations I had had with then secretary of defense Don Rumsfeld and former Speaker of the House Newt Gingrich. Both felt that the old paradigm for a combatant command—a massive, cumbersome organization organized strictly to conduct combat operations—was lacking in relevance in the twenty-first century. Both believed that for both Latin America and Africa, it was highly unlikely that we would be engaged in state-on-state combat operations. So the idea was to push the two combatant commands responsible for those regions to try to adapt with a vision that included combat readiness but with a very heavy dose of "soft power" capability—humanitarian operations, medical diplomacy, rule of law, personnel exchanges, counternarcotics, strategic communications, interagency cooperation, and so forth.

Given this mandate, I plunged in with enthusiasm—perhaps too much enthusiasm. I underestimated the strong desire of many within the massive command to continue on its current, traditional war-fighting trajectory. When I completely reorganized the staff, getting rid of the Napoleonic traditional military staff system, it created real confusion and resentment. While most of the team went along, cooperation was grudging and halfhearted in many cases. While I continue to believe we had outlined the right mission for the command, I pushed too hard, creating antibodies, and the project crumbled after my departure—effectively negating three years of demanding work. The lesson I took away is that innovation matters deeply, but even if you have the right answer, you must be capable of bringing along the nonbelievers.

So this is a tale of two expressions of the innovation character trait, with the same innovator driving them—one to success and the other a failure. I continue to believe that character drives innovation and, given the right circumstances, it can lead to the most positive and powerful outcomes.

A second vital character quality is *resilience*. It is insufficient to be capable and good when things are going well, because sooner or later they will go badly. We see this in the cases of every one of the admirals, perhaps most vividly (and painfully) for the young Zheng He, undergoing castration as a young boy; or in the case of Nelson, who faced the most difficult of wounds in losing his right arm and an eye. While, thankfully, I've not faced those kinds of physical or medical challenges, I have known my share of career defeats, including at the most senior level. As I mentioned briefly in the previous chapter, I went through a very difficult inspector general investigation from 2011 to 2012 while Supreme Allied Commander at NATO—it fundamentally reshaped my career and life. But I learned from the experience, set new goals, achieved many of them, and sailed on. Generals Allen, McChrystal, and Petraeus—superbly talented leaders all—similarly suffered career reversals but have all rebounded and are leading spectacular second acts. Admiral Michelle Howard faced racial and gender barriers and fought through them, and Admiral Bill McRaven overcame life-threatening leukemia to succeed in command of the nation's special forces. Resilience is a key element in human character, and near the top of the list for success.

Third, we need to find our way to *humility* in the search for good character. Arrogance is a toxic quality in a leader, especially in today's era of total transparency. But even 2,500 years ago, we see the perceived arrogance of Themistocles lead to his humiliation and exile. So often the evil doppelgänger of success is arrogance, and we need to strive against it on the voyage of character. In my own life, I have fallen short many times in this regard.

Perhaps the most vivid example of this occurred in the mid-1990s when I was lucky enough to command a brand-new *Arleigh Burke*–class destroyer, USS *Barry*. I loved that ship, and it had a superstar crew. We won competition after competition on the waterfront in Norfolk, and many of us—especially this young captain—started to believe our own press. Big mistake. We were sent to sea one nice day to conduct a huge and important engineering inspection. All started well enough, and we headed out to sea very confident—arrogant—believing we'd be back in port with another smashing success. Instead, we had a terrible engineering casualty that was so bad we had to stop and lock our propeller shaft and be *towed* back into port. We were towed right down the waterfront past all the other ships. There is nothing more embarrassing for the commanding officer of a warship than to be towed home. We didn't look so hot anymore.

Eventually—with a lot of assistance from other ships, by the way—we fixed our problems and eventually passed the inspection with the lowest passing grade, a "satisfactory," far short of the "excellent" or "outstanding" ratings we were expecting and had routinely delivered previously. My executive officer (second in command), who would go on to be a three-star admiral, called it "the best SATISFACTORY ever." I tried to smile when he said that. What I learned was the importance of humility, of knowing that things will go wrong and that resilience matters. It is a lot easier to be resilient when you are humble to begin with.

A fourth quality is the need to find *balance* in our lives. The ancient Greeks knew this, and carved two aphorisms on the temple at Delphi: "Know Thyself" and "All Things in Moderation." In modern parlance, this can be translated as the need for balance between our natural ambitions and our drive to succeed as opposed to our love of family and time in contemplation. Most of the admirals in this book fail this test, driving themselves relentlessly forward throughout the long sail of their lives. This is certainly an area in which I have failed again and again.

Of all the times I remember the dichotomy between doing what I desperately wanted to in all my ambition and zeal to excel and feeling the need to care for a beautiful family, the most dramatic was in 1998. On August 7 of that year, Al Qaeda blew up US embassies in Tanzania and Kenya, killing 224 people including 12 Americans, and injuring 4,000 others. For most of us it was the first time we had heard of Osama bin Laden. In retaliation, President Clinton approved a series of Tomahawk cruise missile strikes. As the commodore of Destroyer Squadron 21, I was forward deployed under the overall command of the head of the US Central Command, General Tony Zinni (who is one of my idols for his balance and character, by the way).

My mission, executed on August 20, included launching missiles from four destroyers and one submarine under my command. I spent much of the day in the Tomahawk launch center, a long, long day of planning, spinning up the missiles, directing the launches, and evaluating the results. It was exhilarating and exhausting. When the day ended, I went to my small cabin in the carrier *Lincoln* and lay down on my bed. Something was nagging at me. Then it hit me: it was my daughter Christina's twelfth birthday. I had spent it firing missiles. I looked at her picture, and my wife Laura's, and thought to myself, *What the hell am I doing with my life?* I vowed to be a better husband and father—and came back to the Pentagon, made rear admiral, and promptly fell again into the trap of failing to balance my life.

On that fateful date in August, we just missed killing bin Laden. He had departed just before our missiles landed in the training camp in Afghanistan we attacked. The missiles I ordered launched nearly killed him—and in an odd twist of fate, several years later, on September 11, 2001, he almost killed me. I was in the Pentagon on the side of the building hit by American Airlines Flight 77, perhaps 150 feet off the point of impact. I wonder what bin Laden was doing that day. I suspect neither of us were very good at finding balance in our lives, but I'm still here and trying. And let's be honest—it is ambition that so often drives this lack of balance. Struggling with it is an act of character for us all.

Fifth, a crucial element in the development of character is *honesty*—being truthful, no matter the cost. You learn that early at Annapolis, where the honor code of "a midshipman does not lie, cheat, or steal" is driven into the young eighteen-year-olds who show up on the Severn River campus every summer. We see failures in this regard repeatedly in our society at large, especially in the political realm, where lying seems to be an art form at times.

As I mentioned earlier, on the wall in my office hangs an oil painting of USS *Maine*, the US Navy warship that exploded and sank in the harbor of Havana in mid-February 1898. Without knowing exactly what caused the explosion, the Navy seized on the idea that it was the result of "terrorists" under the command of Spain, which at the time was the colonial ruler of Cuba. Whipped to a frenzy by the yellow press—the fake news of the day—of William Randolph Hearst and others, we launched into a "splendid little war," as a young Theodore Roosevelt called the Spanish-American War. He would earn the Medal of Honor at San Juan Hill, many people on both sides would die, and the United States entered the modern era and became a colonial power for the first time.

One lesson of the *Maine* for me is that of resilience, as we discussed earlier. As a person of character, you simply must accept that your metaphorical ship could blow up at any moment, and be ready with a Plan B. Disbelief, whining, and weakness are unacceptable. Men and women of character display resilience in adversity. But there is another meaning to the painting for me, and it goes to the quality of honesty and respect for the truth.

How does truth enter into it? When the Navy salvaged the ship decades later, we discovered that the explosion almost certainly was *internal* in character. There had been no mine attached to the hull by Spanish "terrorists." Yet we launched heedlessly into a war and changed world history when the United States took over both Cuba and the Philippines. Even at the time, there was no real sense of certainty about what had caused the explosion, so both the government and the media filled in the blank space. It was a war built on a lie, and the result was bitter indeed. Truth matters for us all, but especially for leaders whose decisions shape the world. Character that is built around a respect, really a veneration, for the truth is the sort of character to have.

And of course, we all fall short in this regard, in things both large and small. But truth becomes a habit, and it is a good one to cultivate.

Sixth, *empathy* is a fundamental and powerful attribute of character. Most of us are terribly self-centered. The world wires us that way, and nothing that ever happens to us occurs without our presence at the center of the little drama of our lives. The best depiction of that trait of self-centeredness I know is in the brilliant and memorable graduation speech at Kenyon College by David Foster Wallace, "This Is Water." He exhorts the young graduates to fight against the tendency to see everything in a deeply personal and self-important way, and to begin to develop a lifelong habit of trying to put themselves in the shoes of the other.

At heart, this is a matter of character. A virtuous person begins every encounter with the world not from their own perspective alone, but rather by trying to understand the situation, mindset, and challenges that others are facing. There are both moral and pragmatic reasons for doing so. I learned this best toward the very end of my career when I became the Supreme Allied Commander of the NATO alliance. It was a job that demanded a deep well of appreciation for each of the other twenty-seven nations. I thought one of my predecessors, General Wes Clark, summed this up nicely when he was criticized by the then secretary of defense for not paying sufficient attention to the needs of the United States—his own nation. General Clark said, "Mr. Secretary, I am intently listening to you with one twentieth of my mind" (there being at that point twenty nations in the alliance). What he meant was that as the overall commander of NATO, he had to represent the interests of every one of the nations in the alliance.

Commanding NATO and realizing that to do so effectively I had to empathize with not only Americans but Bulgarians, Romanians, Germans, Brits, and every other nation, I had to wake up every morning and think, *How does this come across in Paris/Madrid/ London/Berlin/Rome and every other capital in the alliance?* NATO service is a proving ground for empathy, something many very successful people are not always capable of expressing. Building up wellsprings of empathy is the work of a lifetime. For me, NATO was a crystallizing experience in that regard, but you don't need to be in such rarefied air. Reading the speech "This Is Water" also helped me understand the need for empathy in the most mundane moments of our life, from standing in line at the supermarket to raising our children.

Seventh, believing that a sense of *justice* matters is a powerful part of character. John F. Kennedy famously said that life is unfair. All the character in the world will not undo much of the massive injustice and inequality in the world. But as the Russians have it in a proverb, it is better to light a single candle than to howl like a dog at the darkness. I focused on this even more deeply after I left the military. In military service, it is instinctive to want to create just outcomes. We send our troops to war to protect our nation, deter our enemies, protect the weak, and stop abuses. In the long twilight of the Cold War, I never doubted (nor do I today) that our values are the right ones—democracy, liberty, freedom of speech, gender equality, racial equality. We execute them imperfectly, but they are the right values. And the many times I was involved in combat operations—in the Balkans, the Middle East in Iraq and Kuwait, Afghanistan, Libya, counterpiracy—it was to protect either people or values.

But after I got out of the military and became a civilian for essentially the first time in my adult life, I began to think more coherently and frequently about justice and see the shortfalls all around me. Over the past five years, after leaving the Navy, I have questioned the fabric of our American society in this regard, as do many. I try to empathize with different groups in our nation in a way I never did through the buffer zone of military service. Today I think about poverty in a completely different way and wonder how families in the rust belt survive without jobs or, in many cases, hope. I see the injustice in that and try to help energize discussions that can address it. Likewise, I try to think about what it must be like to be a young black man in poverty, with a very limited set of choices, under constant suspicion by law enforcement. How do we address that? I wonder why some communities are blessed with good schools, clean water, professional police protection—and others are not.

This is not to say we are fatally or even deeply flawed. I'm with Winston Churchill, who famously said that "Democracy is the worst form of government . . . except for all the others." We have tools and ideas for using them that can help us move forward. But it all begins with a desire to seek more just outcomes. Indeed, I have no pat answers for these situations, but I will observe, in the context of character, that the more of us who will at least admit to the injustice in these and other challenges and try to think about practical and meaningful solutions, the better the chances of moving the needle toward a just society. Character can help create that critical mass.

And let's face it, part of operating with a sense of justice is exercising self-control. This was a virtue highly prized by the ancient Greeks, and in particular, is part of the approach to life extolled by the ancient Greek stoics. In today's turbulent, fast-paced world, leaders far too often fail to exercise a sense of justice, and their self-control fails them. When that occurs, they are failing not only to control themselves, but to exercise a judicious sense of character.

An eighth quality that blends across the admittedly fine line between leadership and character is *decisiveness*. While good leaders are generally decisive, I have worked for some fine people who took a long, long time to make final decisions. One of them was a lawyer, and simply could not stop balancing the arguments on both sides of the equation. I was in a support role to him when I was a captain, and he could be exasperating in a kind of lovable way as he pondered, brought in more focus groups to share opinions, encouraged everyone in the room to speak up, and simply refused to decide. This collided with the military's approach, which is to make decisions quickly, move out, and then adjust as necessary. When I became more senior, I worked for President Obama (not directly but through the secretary of defense), and again saw the lawyerly approach. While I commend the idea that we can always get more information before making a decision, I think there are often times when a decisive approach allows a decision maker to seize the initiative.

One story that haunts me to this day was my own inability to act decisively while captain of USS *Barry* sailing through the Suez Canal. We started on the northern approach, and the Canal Authority sent us a pilot as was required. He did not inspire a great deal of confidence and seemed more interested in demanding cartons of cigarettes from our sea store than in safely ensuring the passage of the ship through the shallow and poorly marked waters of the canal. Frustrated with the lack of cigarettes (we had offered him a ship's ball cap, which did not impress him much), he staged a kind of mini-strike and pouted on a folding chair on one side of the bridge.

Halfway through the Suez Canal is the Great Bitter Lake. In this part of the canal, ships traveling southbound are required to pull over and anchor while the northbound convoy passes through. By the time we reached the Great Bitter Lake, I had been awake for about twenty-four hours and was dizzy and slightly dehydrated, the result of guzzling coffee to stay awake. As we turned out of the channel in the canal and motored slowly across the Great Bitter Lake, the pilot suddenly came alive and shouted for us to steer a certain course. Despite my misgivings about him, I felt he was after all the certified pilot for the canal and a former Egyptian naval officer, so I told the conning officer to come around to the recommended course.

Suddenly, from behind me at the navigation table, the young lieutenant shouted, "Captain, the ship is standing into danger on that course." I was stunned, and torn—indecisively—between my own officer, who did not have much experience frankly, and the vastly senior Egyptian pilot. I vacillated, and the ship sailed on at five to seven knots. The navigator shouted again, "Sir, we are headed toward a shoal, we must stop and reverse course." The pilot said, "Your assigned anchorage is just ahead of us, Captain." Other ships were coming behind us headed to their designated moorings, and the risk of a collision was increasing. But I was too addled and exhausted to act decisively. Fortunately for me, my twenty-six-year-old navigator, just a couple of years out of Annapolis, was very decisive. He simply said, "This is the navigator, I have the conn, all back two thirds." The Egyptian pilot exploded, I suddenly woke from my reverie and had the ship's boatswain escort the pilot to the bridge wing and keep him there, and I directed the anchoring procedure.

After we dropped the hook (and were almost hit by an approaching tanker), we lowered a boat into the way and sent it over to the designated anchorage with lead lines to cast into the water and definitively establish the depth. My navigator was right—it was a foot too shallow for us, and we would have gone softly aground in the silt and mud of the Great Bitter Lake. My career would have terminated at that moment, despite the excuse that I was simply following the advice of the pilot. That navigator went on to a brilliant career that continues today, and my money is on him to wear an admiral's stars before too much longer. He was the decisive actor needed at that moment, and I learned several valuable lessons, not only about him, but about character and how exhaustion can degrade your most important qualities.

A ninth quality of character that emerges from these sea stories is *determination*. Each of these admirals demonstrated deep levels of determination in the face of true adversity. Think of the overwhelming odds against Themistocles at Salamis; the massive Spanish Armada facing Drake; the entrenched bureaucracy that Fisher had to overcome; the lack of vision facing Rickover—on and on, we see the value of determination. The ever quotable (and often misquoted) Winston Churchill said it quite simply in October 1941, as his nation reeled from German advances in the early days of World War II: "Never give in, never give in, never, never, never, never—in nothing, great or small, large or petty—never give in except to convictions of honor and good sense."

Sound advice—and we need to understand that determination is a quality of character that needs to be handled carefully. For me, a time of testing was during my leadership of NATO in the Afghan war. By 2009, when I became Supreme Allied Commander, we had more than 150,000 troops in the country and a war-fighting budget of billions. We were throwing lives and money at a problem that seemed intractable. My job was to evaluate our efforts to date and make recommendations to the president. After conferring with General Stan McChrystal, who was the four-star general on the ground as the tactical commander, we ended up proposing a significant troop surge. We were deeply determined to win. That is what combat leaders are supposed to deliver.

Yet in retrospect, I wonder if our determination led us down a wrong path. Perhaps a better strategy would have been a lighter footprint, more special forces, a more aggressive political rapprochement with the Taliban, perhaps spheres of influence within the country. There are fierce counterarguments to all these ideas, and in the end we went with the surge. That resulted in progress on the battlefield, and improvement in the situation that ultimately led to withdrawing 90 percent of the US and NATO/allied troops. We turned the fight over to the Afghans in 2014, and they are maintaining a tenuous hold on much of the urban terrain in Afghanistan today. But these days I often wonder if this was in fact a situation in which Churchill's exception of "good sense" applied, and that perhaps our sense of determination influenced the calculus of our advice. We'll never know, and I remain cautiously optimistic that a peace accord can be delivered in Afghanistan—if so, the surge and the turnover to the Afghans may turn out to have been the right strategy. I offer this as an anecdote to illustrate something Churchill knew—determination is a strength, but not when it overturns good sense.

Tenth and finally, in our voyage of character, we need to

understand that in the end we are but sailing in a tiny ship on a boundless sea. This is the quality of *perspective*, which leads to a sense of humor and the gift of not taking ourselves too seriously. When we look at the oceans, and the great deep waves, we must understand that eternity is rolling out there in front of us, and our time is brief. I used to keep a sign on my desk in USS *Barry*, my first and much-beloved command at sea, that said, "NOTHING IMPORTANT EVER HAPPENS HERE."

It was, of course, written with my tongue firmly in my cheek—certainly the national security missions of the ship were necessary, our Tomahawk missiles could wreak death across 1,500 miles, the lives of my sailors all mattered deeply to me—but in the long run, I would remind myself, the voyage of the USS *Barry* was nothing but a cosmic flicker on a trackless sea. By maintaining that perspective, it became far easier to take the good and bad in stride, to keep my temper in check, to reduce my ambitions, and to laugh when things went wrong, so often well beyond our control. As mentioned earlier, the tombstone of the Greek writer Nikos Kazantzakis says simply: "I hope for nothing. I fear nothing. I am free." In the end, we will all be freed in the most ultimate sense. Remembering that allows us the perspective we need to sail each day through challenging waters. That is the gift of character.

Every afternoon on the ship, after I walked the decks and greeted my crew at the conclusion of the workday, I would go up to the bridge wing and spend some quiet time just contemplating the ocean and the sky. They meet at a distant point and whenever I see that horizon at sea, I tell myself that I am looking at something simple and powerful: eternity. Character is knowing that we are decidedly *not* eternal, and that we should live our lives in the best way we can.

A final thought that can help illuminate character as you understand it: who are your heroes? Ideally they are people you deeply admire for reasons that stem not from their accomplishments—what David Brooks in *The Road to Character* has called "résumé virtues"—but rather from their character values—which he calls "eulogy virtues," as in the things people will (hopefully) say about you at your funeral. Our résumé virtues are the schools we attend, the grades we get, the prizes we win, the salaries we earn, the houses we buy, the books we write; our eulogy virtues are the qualities we embody—and in the case of the principal ones discussed in this book, they include honesty, justice, humor, creativity, balance, empathy, humility, and resilience.

A good exercise as you sail on the longest voyage you will ever take is to actually write down the names of your heroes on a piece of paper. Select them from wherever you want in your experience—family, friends, people chosen from history, current leaders. Then alongside each name, attribute a characteristic that you find compelling about them.

All that is not terribly hard—it merely requires you to stop and think consciously about the people you deeply admire. For me, the list would include my parents (for the unbounded love I was offered as a child); General George Marshall (for his steadiness under pressure as a secretary of state, secretary of defense, and wartime chief of staff of the US Army); Simón Bolívar (for the audacity of his vision to liberate all the Spanish colonies of South America); Condoleezza Rice (for her discipline); and Juan Manuel Santos, former president of Colombia (for his political courage in pursuing a peace agreement despite countless doubters). Your list will be different, but the idea is the same—pick a handful of people you truly admire.

Now comes the hard part—in the column next to the qualities you esteem, indicate how *you* are doing. I ask myself constantly: Am I as good a parent to my daughters as my mom and dad were to me? Do I have the steadiness of a George Marshall? Is my vision as bold as that of Bolívar? Am I as disciplined in my pursuits as Condi Rice? And am I as courageous as a Juan Manuel Santos? I do better in some categories than others, of course, but the point of the exercise is above all to *know yourself*. The unexamined life is not worth living, said Socrates at his trial (on charges of corrupting youth, by the way). This constant process of self-examination is at the heart of improving our character, which is indeed the work of a lifetime for us all.

None of us is perfect, but some are farther along in the voyage of knowing themselves fearlessly and honestly and working hard to improve. That is the voyage upon which I hope you are well and truly embarked, and I wish you Godspeed and open water in all the days of your life.

Acknowledgments

First, I offer my sincere thanks to the team at Penguin Press, notably my superb editor and friend, Scott Moyers. He conceived the idea of my previous book *Sea Power*, and guided the book to a wonderful launch in 2017, ensuring that it continues to help make people around the world aware of the vital importance of the geopolitics and history of the world's oceans. Scott enthusiastically embraced the idea of *Sailing True North* as an important way to draw life lessons from those who have plied the world's oceans.

I am also immensely grateful to Captain Bill Harlow, a former spokesman at both the White House and the Central Intelligence Agency. He has offered me the gold standard of professional advice, editorial assistance, and deeply valued friendship for decades.

My two research assistants on this project are also brilliant graduates of the Fletcher School of Law and Diplomacy of Tufts University, where I served as dean over the two years that went into writing this book: Colin Steele and Matt Merighi. Both are gifted academics and vital shipmates on this voyage, providing solid and accurate research throughout the project.

I am very lucky to be represented in the literary world by my agent, Andrew Wylie, who is also a keen reader and critic. His work helped make this a better book, and I look forward to being part of his team in the future.

Finally, my deepest love and thanks to my wife, Laura, and my daughters, Christina and Julia. They are the heart of my sea story, and always will be.

Selected Bibliography and Further Reading

Chapter I. The Power of Persuasion: Themistocles

Hale, John R. *Lords of the Sea: The Epic Story of the Athenian Navy and the Birth of Democracy*. New York: Penguin, 2009. This is a well-written and highly readable journey through the history of the ancient Athenian navy. It includes good details about Themistocles's life and his role in founding the navy.

Herodotus. *The Histories*. New York: Penguin, 2003. The great historical tome written by the affectionately named "Father of History." Covering the Persian Wars and the prime of Themistocles's life, Herodotus is the go-to source for the period.

Thucydides. *History of the Peloponnesian War*. Indianapolis: Hackett Publishing Company, Inc., 1998. Any student who has gone through an international relations program or a military war college year knows Thucydides, the opinionated but highly incisive commentator on the Peloponnesian War. His work contains information on Themistocles's later life and ultimate fall from grace after the Persian Wars (he fell in with the Persians). His sympathetic portrayal of Themistocles is entirely at odds with Herodotus's contempt, providing an interesting insight into Themistocles's polarizing character.

Chapter II. A Sailor of the Middle Kingdom: Admiral Zheng He

Levathes, Louise. *When China Ruled the Seas: The Treasure Fleet of the Dragon Throne, 1405–1433*. New York: Oxford University Press, 1994. One of the seminal works about Zheng He's life, his voyages, and what happened after his career was over. It weaves in Chinese language and history to help Western audiences understand the context of Zheng He's life in greater detail.

Viviano, Frank. "China's Great Armada." *National Geographic*, July 2005. This is a visually stunning and historically excellent overview of his life and voyages, including high-resolution maps and pictures.

Chapter III. A Pirate and a Patriot: Sir Francis Drake

Corbett, Julian. *Sir Francis Drake*. New York: AMS Press, 1890. This is a glowing account of Drake and his life from Sir Julian Corbett, one of the great thinkers in the British navy in the nineteenth century.

Kelsey, Harry. *Sir Francis Drake: The Queen's Pirate*. New Haven, CT: Yale University Press, 1998. Kelsey provides a scathing take on Sir Francis's life and exploits. It sometimes gets too personal and judges the rogue on modern morals rather than "grading on a curve" reflecting the period in which Drake sailed. It does, however, do an excellent job of providing many small but fascinating details of his actions—many of which do not make it into the mythology of Drake. This is the best overview of a complicated and controversial life.

Wilson, Derek. *The World Encompassed: Drake's Great Voyage 1577–1580*. New York: Harper & Row, 1977. This provides a sweeping operational account of Drake's circumnavigation with a great amount of nautical detail. It features illustrations of how various ship's crews operated in the age of sail, giving a lay audience greater context for the perils of the voyage, and an appreciation for the immense challenges Drake faced in simply getting from point A to point B.

Chapter IV. The Band of Brothers: Vice Admiral Lord Viscount Horatio Nelson

Callo, Joseph F. *Nelson Speaks: Admiral Lord Nelson in His Own Words*. Annapolis, MD: US Naval Institute Press, 2001. Not an overly verbose man, Admiral Nelson had a voice that is well captured in this slim volume. It serves as a highly effective and well-organized version of the very thorough collection of Nelson's writing put together by Sir Nicholas Nichols in the nineteenth century.

Forester, C. S. *Lord Nelson*. Indianapolis: The Bobbs-Merrill Company, 1929. A very readable version of the admiral's life by the author of the Horatio Hornblower series of novels about a character very loosely based on Nelson.

Hibbert, Christopher. *Nelson: A Personal History*. London: Viking, 1994.

Howarth, David. *Trafalgar: The Nelson Touch*. New York: Atheneum, 1969. A highly readable deep dive into the battle that ultimately cemented Nelson's "immortal memory."

Mahan, Alfred Thayer. *The Life of Nelson: The Embodiment of the Sea Power of Great Britain*. Boston: Little, Brown, 1899. An examination of the strategic impact of sea power as channeled through a national hero, by America's greatest maritime thinker and writer.

Nichols, Sir Nicholas Harris. *The Dispatches and Letters of Vice Admiral Lord Viscount Nelson*. London: Henry Colburn, 1846. An in-depth, classic collection of the writings of the admiral. The man himself in significant detail.

Oman, Carola. *Nelson*. London: Hodder & Stoughton Limited, 1947. The standard mid-twentieth-century assessment.

Sontag, Susan. *The Volcano Lover.* New York: Farrar, Straus and Giroux, 1992. A moody and atmospheric but gorgeously written novel about the ill-fated love triangle of Lord Nelson, Emma Hamilton, and her husband Sir William Hamilton, a scholar of volcanoes.

Southey, Robert. *The Life of Horatio Lord Viscount Nelson.* London: John Murray, 1813. A hero-worshipping contemporary portrait, but useful to understand the sociological sources of the reverence in which the admiral is held.

Sugden, John. *Nelson: The Sword of Albion.* London: Henry Holt, 2013; and *Nelson: A Dream of Glory: 1758–1797.* London: Henry Holt, 2012. An extensive and deeply researched two-volume work regarded by contemporary naval historians as a classic in its balance and depth.

Tracy, Nicholas. *Nelson's Battles: The Art of Victory in the Age of Sail.* Annapolis, MD: US Naval Institute Press, 1996. A focus on the tactical and operational acumen of the admiral.

Chapter V. The Influencer: Rear Admiral Alfred Thayer Mahan

Armstrong, Benjamin, editor. *21st Century Mahan: Sound Military Conclusions for the Modern Era.* Annapolis, MD: Naval Institute Press, 2013. This book has three attributes rarely ascribed to Mahan anymore: it is brief, readable, and relevant. By presenting an edited selection of Mahan's shorter writings with well-wrought contextual introductions, this slim volume makes the skeleton of Mahan's thought accessible to any reader.

Lehman, John. *On Seas of Glory: Heroic Men, Great Ships, and Epic Battles of the American Navy.* New York: Free Press, 2001. Written by a dynamic former secretary of the Navy who himself served in the Naval Reserve, this book provides a strong historical overview of the US Navy from its beginnings through the twentieth century—told, as the subtitle implies, through historical vignettes of key people, ships, and events. In addition to Mahan, this book contains brief biographies of Admirals Nimitz, Rickover, and Hopper, as well as some of their most important actions.

Mahan, Alfred Thayer. *The Influence of Sea Power upon History, 1660–1783.* Mineola, NY: Dover, 1987. While nonexperts need not read Mahan's magnum opus in its entirety, it is worth picking up a copy at a local library or finding an excerpt online to get a feel for Mahan's own writing.

Seager, Robert II. *Alfred Thayer Mahan: The Man and His Letters.* Annapolis, MD: Naval Institute Press, 1977. Published in a single paperback volume in 2017, this is probably the single best treatment of Mahan's life and work. Working—and quoting—extensively from Mahan's voluminous writings, this book combines biography and primary sources for a comprehensive understanding of the great naval strategist and writer.

Wimmel, Kenneth. *Theodore Roosevelt and the Great White Fleet: American Sea Power Comes of Age.* Dulles, VA: Brassey's, 1998. A short, readable resource on one of the practical outcomes of Mahan's writings, the "Great White Fleet" built during Theodore Roosevelt's administration.

Chapter VI. Rum, Buggery, and the Lash: Admiral Lord John Arbuthnot Fisher

Fisher, John Arbuthnot, Admiral of the Fleet. *Records.* London: Hodder & Stoughton. Written by Fisher himself, this is an idiosyncratic "autobiography" to say the least. In places rambling, in others sharply realized, but always entertaining. And in the voice of the admiral himself, with all its charm, exuberance, and occasional childishness.

Gough, Barry. *Churchill and Fisher: Titans at the Admiralty.* London: Seaforth Publishing, 2017. This book is focused on a sliver of time, but beautifully illuminates the complex relationship of these two very complicated men.

Massie, Robert K. *Dreadnought: Britain, Germany, and the Coming of the Great War.* New York: Ballantine Books, 1991. Massie is a master of narrative history, and his earlier works on the Russian Empire are classics. In this volume he weaves together history, personality, and geopolitics into a seamless story with a highly accurate sense of the admiral.

Morris, Jan. *Fisher's Face: Or, Getting to Know the Admiral.* New York: Random House, 1995. This short and atmospheric biography captures Fisher's exotic personality and odd physicality well. Its anecdotes are sharply realized, and Jan Morris gives us a brief but clever portrait of Admiral Fisher.

Chapter VII. The Admiral's Admiral: Fleet Admiral Chester W. Nimitz

Borneman, Walter R. *The Admirals: Nimitz, Halsey, Leahy, and King—The 5-Star Admirals Who Won the War at Sea.* Boston: Back Bay Books, 2013. A massive composite biography of the only fleet admirals in US history, this contemporary treatment works from familiar sources on Nimitz but provides essential detail on his working relationship with his peers.

Hornfischer, James D. *The Fleet at Flood Tide: America at Total War in the Pacific, 1944–1945.* New York: Bantam, 2016. A fast-paced, easily read history of the climactic year of the central Pacific campaign. An excellent resource for understanding the integration of the US military services' operations into truly "joint" warfare, as well as the different command styles of Halsey and Spruance at sea. Both campaign integration and the Halsey-Spruance dynamic illustrate Nimitz's role in managing the war.

Potter, E. B. *Nimitz.* Annapolis, MD: Naval Institute Press, 1976. The definitive, authorized biography of America's greatest naval hero. Potter, a longtime Naval Academy professor, draws on the admiral's papers and many hours of interviews with the Nimitz family to construct this comprehensive (though surely somewhat sanitized) view of the admiral.

Spector, Ronald H. *Eagle Against the Sun: The American War with Japan.* New York: Vintage, 1985. A key resource for understanding the US Navy's prewar planning, as well as the strategic and operational conduct of the war in the Pacific.

Chapter VIII. The Master of Anger: Admiral Hyman Rickover

Duncan, Francis. *Rickover: The Struggle for Excellence*. Annapolis, MD: US Naval Institute Press, 2011. Balanced and concise, this biography picks up the thread of the Rickover legacy twenty-five years after his death.

Lehman, John E., Jr. *Command of the Seas*. New York: Charles Scribner's Sons, 1988. The introduction and first chapter, "Rickover and the Navy Soul," is a short masterpiece on the difficult, stubborn, clever character of Hyman Rickover.

Oliver, Dave, Rear Admiral, US Navy (Ret.). *Against the Tide: Rickover's Leadership Principles and the Rise of the Nuclear Navy*. Annapolis, MD: US Naval Institute Press, 2014. This very laudatory study of Rickover's leadership and management principles is written by a high-ranked and well-regarded naval officer who served directly under Admiral Rickover.

Polmar, Norman, and Thomas B. Allen. *Rickover: Controversy and Genius: A Biography*. New York: Simon & Schuster, 1982. This is a balanced, in-depth effort by two serious naval historians, and includes priceless anecdotes throughout (including those about the infamous interviews to join the nuclear program). Completed as Rickover finished his more than six decades of naval service, this stands as the definitive early work on his legacy and life.

Chapter IX. The Angel of Change: Admiral
Elmo R. "Bud" Zumwalt Jr.

Berman, Larry. *Zumwalt: The Life and Times of Elmo Russell "Bud" Zumwalt, Jr.* New York: Harper, 2012. A well-written, easy-to-read, comprehensive biography written about a decade after the admiral's death. Somewhat lauda-tory but gives strong chronology and context of Zumwalt's career.

Zumwalt, Elmo R., Jr. *On Watch*. New York: Quadrangle, 1976. Zumwalt's autobiography, penned around his run for the Senate just a couple of years after he left the Navy. Very much a first-person perspective, and of a piece with the modern trend of tell-all books by just-retired officials, it is neverthe-less invaluable for understanding how Zumwalt saw himself and his own ca-reer. The book is also interesting for its many excerpts of letters, memos, and other original documents from Zumwalt's life.

Chapter X. Don't Go Near the Water:
Rear Admiral Grace Hopper

Beyer, Kurt W. *Grace Hopper and the Invention of the Information Age*. Cam-bridge, MA: MIT Press, 2010. Written by a fellow naval officer who was in-spired to serve in the Navy by Grace Hopper, this book traces the early decades of the computer industry by following Grace Hopper's journey through it. It rises above the clichés of "Amazing Grace" to give a fuller por-trait.

Gilbert, Lynn, with Gaylen Moore. *Grace Murray Hopper: Women of Wis-dom*. Self-published, 1981. Essentially an excerpt from a longer work by the author that puts the broad story of Grace Hopper into her own words.

Pelleschi, Andrea. *Mathematician and Computer Scientist Grace Hopper*. Min-neapolis: Lerner Publications, 2016. A well-written children's version of the story of Grace Hopper.

Williams, Kathleen Broome. *Grace Hopper: Admiral of the Cyber Sea*. An-napolis, MD: US Naval Institute Press, 2012. A traditional telling of the story of Grace Hopper, replete with anecdotes from her surviving family members, with a very personal feel to the writing.

Chapter XI. Resilience and the Modern Admiral

"Admiral William H. McRaven, USN: The Art of Warfare." American Achievement Academy. www.achievement.org/achiever/admiral-william-h-mcraven/.

Fenn, Donna. "5 Tough Leadership Lessons from the Navy's Top Female Commander." *Fortune.* May 25, 2015.

Graves, Lucia. "For Michelle Howard, Saving Captain Phillips Is Her Least Impressive Accomplishment." *The Atlantic.* May 15, 2015.

Mazzetti, Mark, et al. "SEAL Team 6: A Secret History of Quiet Killings and Blurred Lines." *The New York Times.* June 6, 2015.

Whitlock, Craig. "Adm. William McRaven: The Terrorist Hunter on Whose Shoulders Osama bin Laden Raid Rested." *The Washington Post.* May 4, 2011.

Index

INDEX